A. E. King
4 Jan 1992

Marion D. Hanks

Bread Upon the Waters

BOOKCRAFT
Salt Lake City, Utah

*This is not an official Church publication.
The author alone is responsible for
the views it expresses.*

Library of Congress Catalog Card Number: 91–075911
ISBN 0–88494–808–0

First Printing, 1991

Printed in the United States of America

Contents

I

Love

CHAPTER 1

The Great Commandments

If you were asked the question, Which element of Christ's life or attribute of His character or part of His ministry best represents to you His majesty and personal relationship with us, what would your answer be? I am going to talk specifically about one potential response. It is the answer I have been thinking about for some time; it would likely be my reply to the question.

Let me lay a foundation by presenting to you a few ideas to consider. I hope they will evoke appropriate inspiration. I have been thinking about speaking on this subject at this school for a long time because I have had very strong feelings about it—and, of course, for this school and you who attend it. But I have not done so—intimidated, perhaps, by the supposition that so important a theme has already been sufficiently treated or that it surely should and would be by those more qualified to address it.

I have also had the recurrent remembrance of a college experience to deal with, and I confess that worries me even now. I had carefully prepared and presented quite well, I thought, a briefing of a consequential law case in an important course, and I then awaited the response of the learned professor and

Fireside address given at Brigham Young University 7 August 1988.

several students previously assigned to critique my efforts. I had the feeling that all were poised somewhat in the fashion of runners straining at the blocks waiting for the starter's gun.

But it was not of the students that I was most apprehensive. The dean of the school, who was teaching that class, had earned a reputation as a crusty and vigorous defender of the law against ignorant and callow students. His brief comment came soon enough to my anxious ear: "Thank you, Mr. Hanks," he said, "for that thoroughly unnecessary delineation of the obvious." The class then undertook to consider the deeper meaning of the matter at hand.

So basic is this subject I wish to deal with today, and so widely discussed and written of and so generally thought to be believed and understood already, that there may be those present, less charitable than others, who may be tempted to murmur when I am through, "That was an unnecessary delineation of the obvious."

Nonetheless I cheerfully undertake the challenge of speaking about the "great commandments" and, specifically, though to me they are inseparable, about the second great commandment. The Apostle James called it the "royal law" (James 2:8). Paul told the Galatians that "*all the law* is fulfilled in one word, even this; Thou shalt love thy neighbour as thyself" (Galatians 5:14; italics added).

Love the Lord and Your Neighbor

There are fundamentals of our faith so essential to the enjoyment of our ultimate creative opportunities, possibilities, and associations that we call them first principles and ordinances. Perhaps not all of us are inclined to consider loving and serving and giving to our fellowmen as being among them. Yet the Savior of mankind thought of them as critical, as manifested in His totally unselfish life and in His teachings.

When Christ was asked by a contentious lawyer, "Which is the great commandment in the law?" (Matthew 22:36)—or, as another Gospel writer reported it, "What shall I do to inherit eternal life?" (Luke 10:25)—He answered, as Matthew recorded it: "Thou shalt love the Lord thy God with all thy heart, and with all thy soul, and with all thy mind. This is the first and great commandment. And the second is like unto it, Thou shalt love thy neighbour as thyself." (Matthew 22:37–39.)

In Luke's version, Jesus first asked the questioner what the old law said that would answer his own question. Quoting from the books of Deuteronomy and Leviticus, the man responded just as Jesus did in Matthew's Gospel. From Deuteronomy 6:5: "And thou shalt love the Lord thy God with all thine heart, and with all thy soul, and with all thy might." From Leviticus 19:18: "Thou shalt love thy neighbour as thyself." In Matthew's account the Savior adds these words: "On these two commandments hang all the law and the prophets" (Matthew 22:40).

Luke's Gospel then provides the setting for Christ's sobering parable of the Good Samaritan by quoting the lawyer asking Christ, "And who is my neighbour?" (Luke 10:29). Out of this powerful story known to all of you—this story of a traveler from Jerusalem to Jericho who was set upon, robbed, wounded, and left at the wayside by thieves—comes a basis for understanding who is the neighbor we are commanded to love and what our own status is as a neighbor to those in need.

You will remember that involved in the story were a priest (one who officiated in sacrifices at the altar in the temple) and a Levite (one assigned to supportive temple service). Both of them "passed by on the other side," neither stopping to help (see Luke 10:31–32). Both were preoccupied or too busy with important assignments; or both were too unimpressed, perhaps, with the "weightier matters" of which Christ spoke. Christ joined mercy with just judgment and faith as the "weightier matters" with which we should be concerned (see Matthew 23:23), and in this parable he defined mercy for us as the care and concern shown by the Samaritan who did not pass by on the other side but stopped to give immediate and sustained assistance.

Having given the parable and taught the lesson, Jesus said to the questioner and to us, "Go, and do thou likewise" (Luke 10:37). Loving neighbor, mercy, giving, service, caring, sacrifice—all are brought together in one compelling, understandable, and personally applicable example.

I hope we all know by memory what many people outside the Church who are committed to strong religious conviction can repeat: "For God so *loved* the world, that *he gave* his only begotten Son, that whosoever believeth in him should not perish, but have everlasting life" (John 3:16, italics added). It is written again that Christ "so *loved* that *he gave* his own life" (D&C 34:3, italics added) that we might become His spiritual sons and daughters. And it is again written: "Give, and it shall be given unto you; good measure, pressed down, and shaken together, and running over, shall men give into your bosom. For with the same measure that ye mete withal it shall be measured to you again." (Luke 6:38.)

And again: "Ye are to be taught from on high," said the Lord in the latter times. "Sanctify yourselves and ye shall be endowed with power, that ye *may give* even as I have spoken" (D&C 43:16, italics added).

Obedience to the Principles

God loved and gave. Christ loved and gave. We are here to learn how to love enough to get our minds off ourselves, at least sometimes. As a commitment to Christ and as an element of our religious faith, we must look for and respond to the needs of those about us. As children of God, loving Him, we have all His other children as our neighbors and we have received the commandment to love them. We are neighbors to them; we are to show mercy. This royal law—this one word in which all the law is fulfilled, this law on which, in company with love of God, all the law and the prophets depend—is indispensable as a solid base upon which our eternal opportunities rest.

Now, these fundamental laws we speak of, upon obedience to which all blessings are predicated, are in nature really opportunities—gifts—since they open the way toward that spiritual maturity possessed in its fulness by our Father and our Lord and which they desire us to develop. These laws are not designed to limit us. They are the laws the scripture says "also maketh you free" (D&C 98:8)—coupled with the *truth*, which "shall make you free" (John 8:32).

These laws are more inclusionary than exclusionary. The spirit of entitlement is in them as well as commandment. Gifts they are, bestowed to support as a foundation, pointing us toward the ultimate development of our eternal potential.

But, you ask, is giving help, across the wide spectrum the scriptures teach us, really as important as those other first principles? Yes! And that I believe is the burden of my message and conviction. Yes, it is as important, as a principle! For all of these fundamentals relate to and include each other indivisibly, inseparably. Jesus so lived and so declared, and so the scriptures teach.

We do not need an extensive rehearsal of what these first principles and ordinances are—only a line or two about each: "Without faith it is impossible to please [God] for he that cometh to God must believe that he is, and that he is a rewarder of them that diligently seek him" (Hebrews 11:6).

Justice will have its place, but mercy claimeth the penitent, and "none but the truly penitent are saved" (Alma 42:24).

"Except a man be born again, he cannot see the kingdom of God," and "Except a man be born of water and of the Spirit, he [she] cannot enter into the kingdom of God." (John 3:3, 5.)

Paul taught us (and our experience corroborates it fully) that the things of God can only be taught and only be understood through the Spirit of God (see 1 Corinthians 2:11–14). We have learned that affliction and tribulation are part of living mortally, and that "whosoever shall put their trust in God shall be supported in their trials, and their troubles, and their afflictions, and shall be lifted up at the last day" (Alma 36:3).

We know that there are other essential sacred ordinances available in sacred places for those who desire them. We know that nothing unclean can be received into the kingdom of God. Affirming these and other commandments, the principle we are thinking about announces that our salvation and our happiness depends as much upon how we treat other human beings and help them meet their needs as they do upon the other great fundamentals. Indeed, this is the test of our understanding and internalizing of the other fundamentals. If through this prin-

ciple of loving concern for others we do not become more
Christlike, we have not felt the efficacy and power of those sacred principles and ordinances.

This principle is as important as missionary work and
temple work and, indeed, is of the same spirit and same significance—inseparable, I repeat, from the heart of that work. One
signal verse of scripture gives promise to those who worthily experience the ordinances of the temple: "And that they may
grow up in thee, and receive a fulness of the Holy Ghost, and
be organized according to thy laws, and be prepared to obtain
every needful thing" (D&C 109:15).

What remarkable consequences flow from obedience to the
principles and ordinances of the gospel! All of them lead us to
Christ and our Father in Heaven.

When Christ commanded His disciples to go into the world
to teach and baptize, what else did He say? He told them to go
out to all nations, "teaching them to observe all things whatsoever I have commanded you" (Matthew 28:2). And what would
this include?

In His last three great summational parables recorded in
chapter 25 of Matthew, Christ taught about the wise virgins
who prepared themselves and the foolish virgins who did not.
And then He taught about talents and their bestowal and their
enjoyment and their application—or lack of it—and the consequences of our choices. Then in the third, one of the best
known of His parables (verses 31–36), He taught about a time
when the King will return and separate the sheep on His right
hand from the goats on His left. To those on His right the King
will say:

> Come, ye blessed of my Father, inherit the kingdom prepared for
> you from the foundation of the world: For I was an hungred, and
> ye gave me meat.

You know the rest of that special parable:

> I was thirsty, and ye gave me drink: I was a stranger, and ye took
> me in: naked, and ye clothed me: I was sick, and ye visited me: I
> was in prison, and ye came unto me.

The modest people on the King's right hand will say—because they are honest, or they would not be there—"Lord, when saw we thee an hungred, and fed thee?" They want more than anything to enjoy the blessing He is holding out to them, but they don't really feel worthy. They don't remember ever finding Him hungry and feeding Him, or thirsty and giving Him drink, or naked and clothing Him, or a stranger and taking Him into their homes, or sick or in prison and visiting Him.

I pray that all of you know the answer, and you should know it verbatim: "And the King shall . . . say unto them, . . . Inasmuch as ye have done it unto one of the least of these my brethren, ye have done it unto me."

But that isn't the end of the story. In the rest of the parable the King says some harsh things to those on His left hand: "Depart from me . . . into everlasting fire . . . for I was an hungred, and ye gave me no meat." And then He goes through the whole litany. His listeners are indignant: "Why are we here? Why aren't we on your right hand? When saw we thee an hungred? Why, Lord, we would have crawled from here to wherever to give you our last morsel, had we known it was you!"

Do you remember how He finished?

> Verily I say unto you, Inasmuch as ye did it not to one of the least of these, ye did it not to me. And these shall go away into everlasting punishment: but the righteous into life eternal.

These, the book says, did not "minister" to those to whom they were neighbors. They did not *minister* to those who were their neighbors!

Does this sound like an option to you, this second law interpreted in terms of our relationship with others, with the way we *treat* others, the way we look upon them, the way we regard them, interpreted as Jesus did, in the parable of the Good Samaritan (see Luke 10:30–37)?

Readiness to Meet the Lord

Out of the Book of Mormon, that strong source of so much that is so good, I read from Alma where he establishes a series of questions as the standard by which we may judge our own readiness to meet the Lord. "If ye have experienced a change of heart [if you have ever felt it in your viscera, your eyes, or your backbone; if you have ever tasted it, sensed it, felt it, responded to it; if you have *ever* had this], I would ask, can ye feel so now? Have ye walked, keeping yourselves blameless before God? . . . [Have you] been sufficiently humble? . . . Are ye stripped of pride? . . . If ye are not ye are not prepared to meet God." (See Alma 5:26–28.) "Is there one among you who is not stripped of envy? . . . Such an one is not prepared; . . . And . . . is there one among you that doth make a mock of his brother, or that heapeth upon him persecutions? Wo unto such an one, for he is not prepared, and the time is at hand that he must repent or he cannot be saved!" (Alma 5:29–31.)

The specific and significant prophetic instructions in the teachings of the Lord on our responsibility to each other are so numerous and clear that it would seem beyond misunderstanding. And yet I wonder if in our own minds we have elevated to its true holy significance this relationship established by that invitation and command: Love God, and love your neighbor as yourself.

I have earnestly sought to understand what the scriptures teach about this matter. I believe and attest and testify that the way we treat each other and our fellowmen is as significant a criterion of our character and the quality of our faith and our future as any other principle or ordinance of the gospel. Repeatedly and unequivocally the Lord ties our eternal future specifically to our response to those who are poor, needy, afflicted, hungry, thirsty, naked, homeless, sick, and imprisoned, and also to those who have other needs.

In the days of serious struggle in the fledgling Church in June 1831, a conference was held in Kirtland, Ohio, at which significant priesthood matters were announced. By revelation, missionary emphasis was given and assignments were made, sending out the men two by two. "And let them journey from thence preaching the word by the way, saying none other things than that which the prophets and apostles have written, and that which is taught them by the Comforter through the prayer of faith. Let them go two by two, and thus let them preach by the way in every congregation, baptizing by water, and the laying on of the hands by the water's side." (D&C 52:9–10.)

This is a plain statement of fundamental first principle and ordinance. Note what is subsequently said in this same section. The place of ordinances is discussed. We often hear the greatest of emphasis given to *ordinances,* and so we should, but note the pairing of ordinances and personal preparation: "Wherefore he that prayeth, whose spirit is contrite, the same is accepted of me if he obey mine ordinances. He that speaketh, whose spirit is contrite, whose language is meek and edifieth, the same is of God if he obey mine ordinances." (D&C 52:15–16.)

There is no question here about the significance of the ordinances. Then this plain and unequivocal declaration is given: "Let the residue of the elders watch over the churches, and declare the word in the regions round about them; and let them labor with their own hands. . . . And remember in all things the *poor* and the *needy,* the *sick* and the *afflicted,* for he that doeth not these things, *the same is not my disciple.*" (D&C 52:39–40, italics added.)

The charity taught in the scriptures is defined as the pure love of Christ (see Moroni 7:47). It is very broad in its meaning, but to me it seems never better expressed than when we share with others in the spirit of His unselfish life—doing what good we can, giving, serving, sharing, listening, lifting the burden. "Bear ye one another's burdens," wrote the Apostle Paul, "and so fulfil the law of Christ" (Galatians 6:2).

Out of a multitude that might be read, there is one magnificent summation that I want to share with you to express my understanding of the spiritual maturity the Lord represents and wants us to attain. It came in the words of a solemn and stirring witness by Amulek as he testified of Christ's atoning gift— the last great sacrifice, infinite and eternal. He referred to the great question in the people's minds—whether or not Christ was indeed the Son of God. Then he said, "And now behold, my beloved brethren, I say unto you, do not suppose that this is all" (Alma 34:28).

Amulek talked about the fundamentals, about exercising

their "faith unto repentance," about prayer and all that it implies. Do you remember that long list of remarkable, repetitious, and yet fresh invitations? This is how it finishes. Surely every missionary would have this marked in his mind and his book:

> And now behold, my beloved brethren [and sisters], I say unto you, do not suppose that this is all; for after ye have done all these things, if ye turn away the needy, and the naked, and visit not the sick and afflicted, and impart of your substance, if ye have, to those who stand in need—I say unto you, if ye do not any of these things, behold, *your prayer* is *vain*, and *availeth you nothing,* and ye are as hypocrites who do deny the faith.
>
> Therefore, if ye do not remember to be *charitable*, ye are as dross, which the refiners do cast out, (it being of no worth) and is trodden under foot of men. (Alma 34:28–29, italics added.)

Time does not permit me to share much more of the wealth of the scriptures now, but I urge you to be interested as you read for understanding. Think what the Lord has to say about our response to the needs of each other. His words are sobering, to say the least: "If any man shall take of the abundance which I have made, and impart not his portion, according to the law of my gospel, unto the *poor* and the *needy,* he shall, with the wicked, lift up his eyes in hell, being in torment" (D&C 104:18, italics added).

I presume that means whoever he is and whatever else he has done. "Behold, they have not learned to be obedient to the things which I required at their hands," the Lord said to a group of His people who had a great commission and had not succeeded in it, "but [they] are full of all manner of evil and do not impart of their substance, as becometh saints, to the poor and afflicted among them; and are not united . . . and Zion cannot be built up unless it is by the principles of the law of the celestial kingdom" (D&C 105:3–5).

Obviously those laws include the very matters of which we speak.

In an important passage in King Benjamin's great sermon there is a remarkable line about one who turns aside a beggar: "O man, whosoever doeth this [taking the attitude that he has had his chance, he won't work, his problems are his own fault], the same hath great cause to repent; and except he repenteth of that which he hath done he perisheth forever, and hath no interest in the kingdom of God" (Mosiah 4:18).

That doesn't sound very optional, does it? After we have done, with as much sincerity as we have to commit to the cause, all the good things we have been called to do, if we do not take a lively interest in those who have special needs, then we do not meet the conditions.

We have mentioned only those fundamentals in the Savior's initial declaration which early in these few remarks I pointed to as the heart of what I wanted to say. Christ talked of the hungry, thirsty, naked, homeless, sick, afflicted. There are many who have other needs. Look around you with your minds for a moment. Are there those who have need of a kind word or a gentle arm? Is there someone who could prosper from a personal note that says something sincere and generous and encouraging?

You Have Much to Give

I will open very slightly the door to my modest closet of remembered personal experiences of this kind and tell you about a time when I was a missionary standing on a street corner in a major city in the United States with my companion, without a cent in our pockets. We had laughed about that; our money hadn't come. It was scarce anyway; we had little, but we had always had sufficient for our needs. This day we only had carfare to go to and return from an area where we were teaching some people—we had transfers for the streetcar in our pockets. We were quite a way from our apartment.

I looked out of the corner of my eye and saw a man standing by a light pole. He seemed to start toward me hesitantly, and I quickly turned away. I just had an intuition he was going to ask me for help. My first thought was that I could not help him, and I panicked a bit at that. I looked again and he had quickly retreated. He had seen my turning away. I felt sick as I saw his embarrassment. I went to him and said: "I sense that you need help, and I have to tell you that we are missionaries and that we have no money."

He was immediately apologetic, backing away and saying: "I didn't know that. I wouldn't ask missionaries for anything. Please forgive me."

I said, "Tell me about your problem."

"I'm from Hamilton," he said (a town fifty miles away). "I lost my job recently. I came here this morning trying to find a job but didn't get here in time. I have no way to get home. I have not eaten, I haven't money to telephone my family, and I know my wife and children will be worrying and afraid."

I said: "We're not far from where we live. I have a transfer for the streetcar. Please use it and get on with my companion. I won't be much longer than you getting there."

He said, "Oh no, no."

I said, "Yes, yes, please. I have already had a heartbreak in turning away because I sensed your need and had no money to give you. We cannot leave you here."

It wasn't a big speech. It was a young man's guileless expression of what I had learned all my life in a widow's home. He finally agreed. He was discouraged and afraid. And so I ran fast and hard and got there a little ahead of them. We had good food in the apartment and I prepared some. The landlady was a gentle person who had a room where our new friend could stay. We called Hamilton, Ohio, and he talked to his family.

I said: "Please tell them you will stay here tonight. Maybe tomorrow there is something we can do to help."

The next morning I called the branch president, a wonderful, gracious, Christlike man who built and rebuilt and refurbished and brought homes up to date. I told him the story. He said, "He can have a job starting this morning." President Gilliam provided a place for him to stay and, soon, a place for his family, and he was on his way up. And I have nurtured in my heart for more than forty-five years a blessing I would have missed had we not helped this man.

I honestly believe this sense of concern was motivated both by the Spirit and by a home where helping an elderly Scandinavian lady who lived a block away from our house was normal and expected. Sister Olsen needed help and had no helping family, so Mother regularly saw that she had food and that her little room was cleaned, and we children tagged along. It was not particularly palatable for a little boy. I used to hold my nose, and I'm ashamed of that. But we would go in and clean the rooms where she lived.

I think often of my mother, to whom so many people came for help when she had heavy burdens of her own—including taking care of her little children by herself after our father died. She had the disposition to help others, and she seemed to find the time and resources necessary to meet the needs.

Look around you. Maybe, just maybe, limited as you are, and perhaps pressed financially yourself, there is someone to whom your outreach can mean much. There are so many who have needs that we may be able to help.

I desire to mention another special personal experience. I was teaching a class at the institute—a class too large to permit much participation—and one night, facing maybe several hundred people, I looked down and saw a face I had known before. I said, "Bishop, do you have something you would like to share with us on the subject we are discussing?" This startled him for a moment, and then he said, "Yes, I think I do, Brother Hanks."

He came to the front and spoke about a wonderful older couple who had lived in his ward, with whom he had formed a strong mutual affection. They had no relatives and few close friends. When they moved from the bigger city to a small town some distance away, they kept in touch by an occasional telephone call.

One night as he traveled to an early meeting of his bishopric, there came into the bishop's mind an impression of a long, narrow room with a casket at one end and a lady standing alone by it. He and his wife had learned of the husband's death and that a public viewing was to be held that evening. Because of the pressures of business and meetings they felt that they could not go.

The impression that had come to him changed his mind, and he rushed to the meeting and told his counselors that he had made a mistake, that he should be someplace else, and asked them to carry on the meeting without him. He then drove as fast as he could to the small town with its small mortuary and went inside. There was a long, narrow room, a casket at one end, and a single, solitary little soul standing by the casket of her beloved, her husband of many years. He went to her and held out his arms. She said, "Oh, bishop, I knew you would come."

Well, we ended the class with a testimony and an expression of gratitude. I knew what the Lord had wanted us to learn that night.

I pray that some of the same sweet spirit from these scriptures we have read tonight will cause you to understand that you have much to give.

I want to add that one time I had wisdom enough to pick up a pen and paper and write a letter to a football coach in our state. He had dismissed almost his entire offensive and defensive starting team because they had conspired to break training rules. They thought he would not dare cut them off prior to their very big, publicized game, but they had clearly broken the rules under plain understanding of the promised sanctions. The few that remained did valiantly, but their team was beaten badly that weekend by the lower-ranked school.

I had never met the coach and have not yet, but I said in my note to him: "I have one son, and it probably won't happen, but if the good Lord were willing and that boy could play under your leadership, I would do anything I could to get him to you. I honor you. I commend you. I am grateful to live on earth where there is somebody like you, because I love kids, and you have just done something important."

He wrote back: "You would be interested, Mr. Hanks, to know what has happened to me since that day when I cut those boys off the team. I have had the ugliest threatening letters and warnings, been hanged in effigy, had a cross burned in my lawn, and been told to get out of town or else, had parents who would like to beat me up. I have had all kinds of letters from the other side, and two—yours and the college president's— that commended me. Because of those two letters I have stayed."

This note didn't come until more than a year later—when he had met the same opposing team with a team he now had that understood him and kept the rules. He was a great coach.

They won the game, but that isn't really important. It isn't the publicity or the fame; it is the deed that counts. He had that kind of backbone. I had no such grand ideas when I penned that note. I was just honestly telling him how I felt as a human being.

You and I need to look around, reach out, assess our own capacities, and see those who are lonely, disaffected, and feeling unloved. Those people are no whit less valuable in God's eyes than the sweetest and handsomest and most talented of you. I am not suggesting that you run about foolishly, but I am suggesting that you open your eyes.

This principle is sacred in the eyes of God Almighty and His holy Son. We are not justified if we "pass by on the other side," hurrying to our priesthood meetings or to the temple or to do visiting teaching or anything else if there is something at hand we should do that the Lord wants done. I don't think we should or need to choose between serving God and serving our fellowmen. We cannot run faster than we have strength, and it is true also that there are seasons in our lives when we can do more than at other times. But all of us can do something, and most of us more than we are doing. I honestly think you won't be overwhelmed with competition if you begin quietly to look!

Let it not be said of us: "For behold, ye do love money, and your substance, and your fine apparel, and the adorning of your churches, more than ye love the poor and the needy, the sick and the afflicted. . . . Why do you adorn yourselves with that which hath no life, and yet suffer the hungry, and the needy, and the naked, and the sick and the afflicted to pass by you, and notice them not?" (Mormon 8:37, 39.)

> I have wept in the night
> For the shortness of sight
> That to somebody's need made me blind.
> But I never have yet
> Had a twinge of regret
> For being a little too kind.

May God bless you. I testify that there is the sweetest joy in this world that I know of in the small and seemingly unimportant things we do, not for the fame or glory or so we can talk about them but because we see a need and we act. I pray that we may have a sweet sense of relationship with our Savior that comes about because what He did we are trying to do, too, in our own small patterns. God bless you. In the name of Jesus Christ. Amen.

CHAPTER 2

He Means Me

At a family gathering a few nights ago we discussed the fact that today is the anniversary of my mother's birth.

I thought that night how much the generations owe each other, how much we learn from each other, how we should love and appreciate each other. One of Mother's grandsons said he had watched with wonderment as his tiny daughter paged through her storybook, moistening her first finger to turn the pages as she had seen her daddy do as he read his books. Actually, she was moistening the finger on her left hand and turning the pages with the finger on her right hand! But that only served to emphasize both the power of example and the fact that she, like all the rest of us, is yet learning.

As I observed two of our lovely grown daughters that night an incident from the past came to mind that forms the burden of my brief message. I still think of it with a tendency to tears. Another little girl had joined our family and was of course much loved. Occasionally I had called her older sister "Princess," but had thought about that, and, since the second young lady was equally deserving of royal treatment, had concluded that it would be well for her to share the title, if it were used at all.

Address given at general conference April 1979.

So one day I called to her: "Come on, Princess. Let's go to the store for Mother."

She seemed not to hear. "Honey," her mother said, "Daddy is calling you."

"Oh," she answered, with a quiet sadness that hurt my heart, "he doesn't mean me."

In memory I can still see the resignation on her innocent child face and hear it in her voice, when she thought that her father didn't mean her.

I am one who believes that God loves and will never cease to love all of His children, and that He will not cease to hope for us or reach for us or wait for us. In Isaiah it is written: "And therefore will the Lord wait, that he may be gracious unto you, and therefore will he be exalted, that he may have mercy upon you" (Isaiah 30:18).

God Really Means Us

And yet over the earth across the years I have met some of God's choicest children who find it very difficult to believe in their hearts that He really means them. They know that He is the source of comfort and pardon and peace and that they must seek Him and open the door for Him and accept His love, and yet even in their extremity they find it difficult to believe that His promised blessings are for them. Some have offended God and their own consciences and are earnestly repentant, but they find the way back blocked by their unwillingness to forgive themselves or to believe that God will forgive them, or sometimes by a strange reluctance in some of us to *really* forgive, to *really* forget, and to *really* rejoice.

The plan of the Lord and His promises are clear in the teachings of the scriptures. The heart of that plan, as I understand it, is announced in these verses of scripture: "For God so loved the world, that he gave his only begotten Son, that whosoever believeth in him should not perish, but have everlasting life. For God sent not his Son into the world to condemn the world; but that the world through him might be saved." (John 3:16–17.)

The Plan of Mercy

Christ came to save us. His plan was called, by a prophet who understood it very well, a "plan of redemption," a "plan of mercy," a "plan of happiness" (Alma 42:13, 15–16). The Lord taught the letter-bound Pharisees the parables of the lost sheep, the lost coin, and the prodigal son to impress the worth of all of God's children, to emphasize, as He said, the "joy [that] shall be in heaven over one sinner that repenteth"; and to teach us the nature of a father who, when his son came to himself and made his way home, had compassion and ran to meet his boy (see Luke 15:3–31). In this and many others of His teachings, He manifested the intensity of His love and of His expectations of us in our treatment of each other and in our responsibility to Him.

Reverently I remind you of the incident of the woman who, in the home of the Pharisee, Simon, washed the feet of the Lord with her tears and dried them with her hair, and anointed them with ointment (see Luke 7:37–39). The Savior taught the critical Simon the story of the creditor and the two debtors: "The one owed five hundred pence, and the other fifty. And when they had nothing to pay, he frankly forgave them both. Tell me therefore, which of them will love him most? Simon answered and said, I suppose that he, to whom he forgave most. And he said unto him, Thou has rightly judged." (Luke 7:41–43.)

Then, speaking of the woman, He said: "Her sins, which are many, are forgiven; for she loved much: but to whom little is forgiven, the same loveth little. And he said unto her, Thy sins are forgiven. . . . Thy faith hath saved thee; go in peace." (Luke 7:41–43, 47–48, 50.)

There is here, of course, no encouragement or condoning of sin. She had been converted by the Lord and sorely repented, and would obey His commandments and accept His forgiveness. And there would be rejoicing in heaven and should be on earth.

The story of Alma the Younger, the Book of Mormon prophet, is well known. He taught these principles with courage and compassion perhaps never excelled. Himself the son of the prophet, he and other youthful companions were guilty of serious sins. Through angelic intervention they were turned to a better way; and Alma, repentant and restored, became a strong leader for the Lord. "Wickedness never was happiness," he declared, and gratefully testified also of the "plan of mercy" that brings forgiveness to the truly penitent (Alma 41:10; 42:15). As the leader of his people he was uncompromising in defense of righteousness, and warm and compassionate with those who had repented and turned from unrighteousness. With his own children, including one son who had been guilty of serious moral error, he shared the anguish that follows transgression and the unspeakable joy that accompanies repentance and forgiveness: "Yea, I say unto you, my son, that there could be nothing so exquisite and so bitter as were my pains. Yea, and again I say unto you, my son, that on the other hand, there can be nothing so exquisite and sweet as was my joy." (Alma 36:21.)

This man of great integrity and no pretense became the first chief judge of the people and the high priest over the Church. He who had cried out unto the Lord Jesus Christ for mercy "in the most bitter pain and anguish of soul . . . did find peace to [his] soul" (Alma 38:8) and thereafter taught the people with such power and love that multitudes of them turned to the Lord, obeyed His commandments, and received that "mercy [which] claimeth the penitent" (Alma 42:23).

The message is consistent through the scripture. The noble young prophet-leader Nephi wrote the sweet psalm of contrition and faith that is so encouraging and edifying and can be read in the fourth chapter of the second book of Nephi: "Notwithstanding the great goodness of the Lord, in showing me his great and marvelous works, my heart exclaimeth: O wretched man that I am! Yea, my heart sorroweth because of my flesh; my soul grieveth because of mine iniquities. I am encompassed about, because of the temptations and the sins which do so easily beset me. And when I desire to rejoice, my heart groaneth because of my sins; nevertheless, I know in whom I have trusted." (2 Nephi 4:17–19.)

Nephi understood that true remorse is a gift of God; not a curse, but a blessing. True remorse involves sorrow and suffering; but the sorrow is purposeful, constructive, cleansing, the "godly sorrow" that "worketh repentance to salvation," and not the "sorrow of the world" (2 Corinthians 7:10).

Through the prophet Ezekiel the Lord taught us that He has no "pleasure at all" in the suffering of His children through sin. His joy comes when the sinner "turneth away from all his transgressions," for such a person shall "save his soul" (Ezekiel 18:23, 27–28).

The Apostle Paul, disappointed with certain behavior on the part of the Corinthian Saints, wrote them a letter chastising them. They repented; and when he learned of it he wrote them again, saying that he was comforted in their comfort: "I rejoice, not that ye were made sorry, but that ye sorrowed to repentance" (2 Corinthians 7:9).

Alma summed it all up in magnificent instruction given his wayward son Corianton. He concluded that powerful lesson with these significant words—they can be saving words for some: "And now, my son, I desire that ye should let these things trouble you no more, and only let your sins trouble you, with that trouble which shall bring you down unto repentance" (Alma 42:29).

Almighty God has promised to forgive, forget, and never mention the sins of which we have truly repented. But He has given us the gift of remorse to help *us* remember them constructively, thankfully, and humbly: "Do not endeavor to excuse yourself in the least point because of your sins, by denying the justice of God; but do you let the justice of God, and his mercy, and his long-suffering have full sway in your heart; and let it bring you down to the dust in humility" (Alma 42:30).

Corianton was sent to preach the word.

As leaders, we deal with the most sacred and sensitive creation of God—His children. We need to consider this as we carry out our duty to keep the Church free from iniquity.

It is good to remember what Joseph Smith wrote a long time ago to the Saints scattered abroad:

Let everyone labor to prepare himself for the vineyard, sparing a little time to comfort the mourners; to bind up the broken-hearted; to reclaim the backslider; to bring back the wanderer; to reinvite into the kingdom such as have been cut off, by encouraging them to lay to while the day lasts, and work righteousness, and, with one heart and one mind, prepare to help to redeem Zion, that goodly land of promise, where the willing and obedient shall be blessed. Souls are as precious in the sight of God as they ever were; and the Elders were never called to drive any down to hell, but to persuade and invite all men everywhere to repent, that they may become the heirs of salvation. (*History of the Church* 2:229.)

My child at first did not understand that my invitation was meant for her. She thought it was for someone else. "He didn't mean me." If any who read these words need assurance that God's call to repentance and His invitation to mercy and forgiveness and love are for them, I bear you that solemn witness. In the name of Jesus Christ. Amen.

CHAPTER 3

Failing Never

The coming of Jesus Christ in the meridian of time was God's supreme effort to make His love known and effectual among His children. The Father had always acted out of love, but the plan of things required a Savior whose life would be the highest expression of God's love and whose sacrifice would represent a greater love for His Father and brothers and sisters than could be equalled. He made the sacrifice and finished His mission. He left an equally great lesson when He forgave His executioners. Not the least of His gifts was a legacy of example of what a Christian's relationship should be with himself, his family and fellowmen, and his God.

It was said of Jesus by one who knew and loved Him that He went about doing good (see Acts 10:38). From the beginning the shadow of the cross was upon Him in all the acts and teachings of His life, yet He spent His time doing kind things—teaching, comforting and restoring, making people well, taking little thought for His own comfort and convenience or His own concerns. He radiated the deep inner assurances that came with knowing who He was and why He was here and what His mission would mean. His disciples received from Him not only the sense of His eternal power and godhood but also clear di-

Ensign article September 1975.

rection about how a child of God should live. The disciple-writers of the epistles of the New Testament reflect this intense focus. Paul and the others had special reasons for writing as they did: they had something to say, and a commission—and a compulsion—to say it.

"I greatly desire to see you," wrote Paul in his touching letter to Timothy shortly before his martyrdom. "Please try to come before winter. Bring my cloke . . . and the books, but especially the parchments." He was cold and alone, he wanted his coat and his friends, he missed his beloved books, but he especially wanted the parchments! There was something he had to say, and since the time was at hand when he was "ready to be offered . . . the time of departure," he had to put it in writing for his people and for us. (See 2 Timothy 1:4; 4:6–8, 13, 21.)

We have at least some of the letters he wrote, and some written by other inspired disciples. What is the message? What is there for us in the books?

The Message of the Apostles

With fervency and at highest cost the writers of the epistles testified of the eternal truths associated with Christ's mission: of God's gracious love; the Lord's atoning sacrifice; the divine plan through which the Father's children may accept that glorious gift, the resurrection; and the everlasting nature of life and love. They explained the relationship of the Church, God's instrument, to both Christ and Christians. And they demonstrated, each in turn, that they had learned from the Lord and through the Spirit the central importance of love and service in God's plan.

The sacred strains of Christ's parables of judgment sound throughout the New Testament writings. Sins of commission are not even mentioned in that great story of the sheep and the goats, the time when "the Son of man shall come in his glory . . . and he shall set the sheep on his right hand, but the goats on the left" (Matthew 25:31–33). Those on the right hand of the King shall be invited to inherit the kingdom prepared for them from the foundation of the world. Who will they be? Those who have met the simple, charitable tests—who have fed the hungry and given drink to the thirsty, cared for the stranger, clothed the naked, visited the sick, and gone to those who were in prison.

They who have not done these things will be rejected from the kingdom and will go to their own place to suffer the consequences of their failures.

This was the message in the day of Paul and Peter and James and John. It is likewise the message in our time. Those who understand it and give it life are true Christians. Christianity is not a religion of abstraction nor of unfeeling legalisms. "For the kingdom of God is not meat and drink; but righteousness, and peace, and joy in the Holy Ghost" (Romans 14:17).

Christianity does not contemplate the production, by declaration, of a perfect person or a perfect world. Rather it provides the objective, the plan, the motivation, and the power to produce persons who make a difference. Repeatedly the New Testament epistles talk about newness—the new creature who emerges from an honest confrontation with Christ. "Therefore if any man be in Christ, he is a new creature: old things are passed away; behold, all things are become new" (2 Corinthians 5:17). This new creature, serving "in newness of spirit, and not in the oldness of the letter" (Romans 7:6), is what is to happen; this is what the disciples learned, and this is what they wanted all Christians to learn, then and now.

The Pure Love of Christ

We usually sum up the Apostle Paul as a preacher and teacher of uncompromising commitment. We do not customarily think of him—or at least I have not—in terms of loving compassion and consideration and concern for others. We may have noticed a growing tenderness and ripening of love in him as he selflessly served the cause of Christ, but it has not seemed to be his chief message. Yet as one reads the epistles carefully and repeatedly, the witness comes through strongly: he knew and gave love.

Paul's heavenly vision and subsequent revelations turned him completely around from the hostility of the persecutor to the fervor of the disciple. His beautiful and brilliant testimony of Christ, his exposition of Christian theology, and his determined opposition to legalistic teachers who sought to Judaize the Christian converts constitute much of his writing, but woven strongly throughout are his undeviating declarations of the love, quality, and service which must characterize Christians. His "noble eulogy" to the Corinthian Saints on the value and power and enduring quality of love was spoken to us as well. Without love, he declares, eloquence, prophecy, mysteries, knowledge, and even faith are nothing, nor are charitable works or martyrdom. With love these have meaning. With love we can endure all things. Love never fails.

When Paul wrote to the Ephesians, he told them that he prayed to God that they might be "strengthened with might by his Spirit in the inner man," that they might have Christ in their hearts and be "rooted and grounded in love . . . and . . . know the love of Christ, which passeth knowledge, that [they] might be filled with all the fulness of God" (Ephesians 3:16–19).

In Paul's teaching the pure love of Christ is more than compassionate condescension, more than sharing goods. The "charity" which is Christ's love is more understandable in the light, again, of the Lord's personal identification with the hungry, the thirsty, the naked, the stranger, the sick, and the imprisoned (see Matthew 25:40).

Some years ago in a civic setting I proudly listened to two young men; one, born in Mexico, who had started ninth grade at the age of nineteen while still a migrant farm worker, the other, part Indian, born in a small village near the reservation where many of his relatives lived.

Both of the young men were handsome and articulate, exuding strength, sincerity, and a sense of urgency. One had filled a mission for the Church—the other was about to go—and each was en route to advanced university training, preparing to serve the special needs of those with whom he shared proud heritage.

A civic committee sought their help in understanding the problems of their people and offering possible solutions. Each answered searching questions knowledgeably, effectively, earnestly. When asked what could be done to help, each responded repeatedly and firmly that what his people needed was not handouts but opportunities, equal *opportunities* so that through their own efforts they could reach the goal—they would do the rest themselves.

Both pointed to faith in God and a religious commitment as basic needs of their people, and each explained that active involvement in The Church of Jesus Christ of Latter-day Saints was the key to his own development. How had this blessing come about?

It came to the young Mexican-American through a school administrator in a small Latter-day Saint community in Nevada, where the verbal answers concerning salvation and redemption through Christ had been personalized into the *experience* of kindness and concern and contagious love. There the young man had found not only the answers which gave meaning to life but also direction and inspiration and purpose in living it. The love he found came not chiefly from books or lessons but from *persons* who were able and willing to give it.

For the Indian, it had been a next-door neighbor, a Latter-day Saint bishop, whose interest and kindness had opened his heart and his home to this youngster. The little boy was not prepared to understand theological answers; loving concern he could readily comprehend. Through the life of a good man he learned to care about and to know Christ.

For these two choice young men, Christ's love, shining through others, brought newness of life.

Like Paul, the Apostle Peter knew the importance of faith. He knew also that enjoying this great gift—in whatever measure—is the *beginning* of our life in Christ, not the end. Thus, declaring that through knowledge of God and our Savior we "might be partakers of the divine nature," he said we must "add to [our] faith virtue; and to virtue knowledge; and to knowledge temperance; and to temperance patience; and to patience godliness"; and in that remarkable construction of qualities and gifts, the Apostle continued the crescendo: "and to godliness brotherly kindness; and to brotherly kindness charity" (2 Peter 1:4–7)—the pure love of Christ! Like his brother Paul, with whom he sometimes had controversy, in this central matter Peter had no question: to all the sacred attributes named, a

Christian must add love. Without love the others, singly and together, were not enough.

Peter taught the believers that though there were those who were disobedient, who had "disallowed"—rejected—the "chief corner stone," Jesus Christ, yet the true followers of the Lord were "a chosen generation, a royal priesthood, an holy nation, a peculiar people" whose duty it was to "shew forth the praise of him who hath called you out of darkness into his marvellous light." (1 Peter 2:6–7, 9.)

Likewise, the Apostle James warned the early Christians that in fulfilling "the royal law according to the scripture, Thou shalt love thy neighbor as thyself" (James 2:8) they would do well, but not if they showed partiality to the rich. The message was not a slogan but the guiding theme of life, the directing goal, and the power by which they were to govern their conduct toward themselves, others, and the Almighty.

Love in Family and Society

If there is a key for resolving the many great social problems of our time it must be in developing homes that are training places for Christian qualities, families in which the relationships between individuals teach the responsibility to be good citizens in the home, in the neighborhood where the influence can be vitally effectual, and also in the community and the country. The instructions of the epistles demonstrate that the Apostles taught with conviction this approach to solving the problems of their ancient world. Christians were expected to have sound marriages and strong families, to be good wives and good husbands, good parents and good children. Paul to the Ephesians and Colossians, and Peter and John in their writings, taught the same truths: wives and husbands must love each other and fill their major responsibilities in the home. Children must obey their parents and honor them. To fathers comes an especially significant invitation: "Provoke not your children to wrath: but bring them up in the nurture and admonition of the Lord" (Ephesians 6:4).

Wrath, Paul adds perceptively to the Colossians, will leave

the children "discouraged" (Colossians 3:21). Peter saluted the strength of the woman to influence her husband through deep intuitive faith—that "quiet spirit, which is in the sight of God of great price" (1 Peter 3:4). Husbands were enjoined to give honor unto their wives "as being heirs together of the grace of life" (1 Peter 3:7).

How significant these instructions are for family love and interdependence was emphasized for me recently. When a convert to the Church and his twelve-year-old son arrived early for a stake conference session, they saw water spilling over a basin and into the hall. They stopped the water, obtained cleaning equipment, and taking off their shoes and stockings and rolling up their trousers, waded in and cleaned up the problem. Learning of this and feeling that I wanted the privilege of knowing such people, I talked with the man and his boy, and in the course of our conversation learned that the family had suffered a tragedy just a week before. While the father was attending a meeting he was notified of the death of his beautiful little girl, whose hospital room he had just left with the assurance that she was going to be well.

Distraught, the family struggled through the necessary arrangements of the next day or so with broken hearts. After the funeral service they gathered for a family home evening. I will never forget the joy shining through the anguish as this wonderful father talked of the feeling for each other as they met that night, and of the resolve they had made. "We looked at each other and our children and they at us for perhaps the first time as *individuals*, as *persons* with strengths and needs and beauty and a precious place in our circle. In the terrible agony of losing our little one we gained a new vision of each other. Words of love and of kindness were spoken, testimonies borne, thanks given, and prayer offered as we knelt together. I don't anticipate any problem in holding family home evening from now on," he said. "We have learned in a very hard way how much we mean to each other and how important it is to be together to enjoy each other and share with each other and express our love."

So the message of love and family unity is vital still. The ancient writings so teach and ring with personal meaning in the instructions of the Apostles and prophets. The major social problems of our time existed also in their day. Opportunities for the Christian to exercise the wonderful gifts of the Spirit were available then and are all about us now. "The fruit of the Spirit is love, joy, peace, longsuffering, gentleness, goodness, faith, meekness, temperance" (Galatians 5:22–23).

In business the Saints were instructed to avoid sloth, to be honest, to produce with their hands, to provide for their own.

The affluent learned that the love of God cannot be thought to dwell in one who "hath this world's good, and seeth his brother have need, and shutteth up his bowels of compassion from him. . . . My little children, let us not love in word, neither in tongue; but in deed and in truth. And hereby we know that we are of the truth, and shall assure our hearts before him." (1 John 3:17–19.)

The Apostle James laid the responsibility of being considerate and concerned for others not on the affluent alone but on all who follow after Christ: "But whoso looketh into the perfect law of liberty, and continueth therein, he being not a forgetful hearer, but a doer of the work, this man shall be blessed in his deed. . . . Pure religion and undefiled before God and the Father is this, To visit the fatherless and widows in their affliction, and to keep himself unspotted from the world." (James 1:25, 27.)

Has someone been overtaken in a fault? The message of the prophets is that such a one should be "restored" in the spirit of meekness. "Bear ye one another's burdens, and so fulfill the law of Christ" (Galatians 6:2).

The Way of the Christian

There is another principle of living that the Apostles and prophets knew well. They were men, sometimes rather ordinary men, charged with an extraordinary mission and the responsibility to grow into capacity to fill it. There were extraordinary demands upon them. Having come from different backgrounds, they did not always function out of the same base of experience, and it was necessary for them to listen and learn. To them and all who should hear and follow them came the message to the Hebrews: "Follow peace with all men, and holiness, without which no man shall see the Lord: looking diligently lest any man fail of the grace of God; lest any root of bitterness springing up trouble you, and thereby many be defiled" (Hebrews 12:14–15).

There would be wrongs done and some mistakes made. Peter knew this special trial well, and we understand when he says: "For this is thankworthy, if a man for conscience toward God endure grief, suffering wrongfully. For what glory is it, if, when ye be buffeted for your faults, ye shall take it patiently? but if, when ye do well, and suffer for it, ye take it patiently, this is acceptable with God." (1 Peter 2:19–20.)

In the beginning of Paul's letter to the Ephesians he said that he had heard of their "faith in the Lord Jesus, and love unto all the saints" (Ephesians 1:15), and commended them. Much was expected of them now that Christ had "broken down the middle wall of partition" (Ephesians 2:14) between who and what they had been and who and what they had become. Until Christ they were Gentiles, "aliens from the commonwealth of Israel, and strangers from the covenants of promise, having no hope, and without God in the world," "far off" and walking "according to the course of this world." (Ephesians 2:12, 13, 2.) God had brought them "nigh by the blood of Christ" (Ephesians 2:13). They were no more "strangers and foreigners," but had become "fellowcitizens with the saints, and of the household of God . . . built upon the foundation of the apostles and prophets, Jesus Christ himself being the chief corner stone" (Ephesians 2:19–20).

There was no more Jew and Gentile; all who had through the rich mercy and great love of God been brought to Christ were now Christians.

Something had happened! It was to be different now! They were to "walk not as other Gentiles walk, in the vanity of their mind" (Ephesians 4:17), but would henceforth be expected to put away corrupt communication, lying, anger, stealing, bitterness, wrath, clamour, evil speaking, malice. They would tell the truth, labor with their own hands to earn their own way, and to share, speak that which is edifying, and be "kind one to another, tenderhearted, forgiving one another, even as God for Christ's sake" had forgiven them. (See Ephesians 4:25–32.)

As "children of light" they were to walk in "goodness and righteousness and truth," being good husbands, wives, parents, and children (see Ephesians 5:8–9, 22–25; 6:1–4).

A perusal of the Christian's passageway seems almost too much. How can ordinary mortals walk it? If we are to regard our religion as a "packet of beliefs and practices" to be borne, it will indeed be too much. But this cannot be for the Christian. Our religion is "not weight; it is wings." It can carry us through the dark times, the bitter cup. It will be with us in the fiery furnace and deep pit. It will accompany us to the hospital room and to the graveside. It can assure us of the presence of a captain on the rough voyage. It is, in short, not the path to easy disposition of problems but the comforting assurance of the eternal light by which we may see and the eternal warmth that we may feel. All of this comes to us through the love of Christ. "He that saith he abideth in him ought himself also so to walk, even as he walked" (1 John 2:6).

CHAPTER 4

My Specialty Is Mercy

My theme is mercy. Shakespeare wrote that mercy is "twice blest; / It bless[es] him that gives, and him that takes," and added, "And earthly power doth then show likest God's / When mercy seasons justice." (*The Merchant of Venice*.)

I am sure that everyone who reads these words is in favor of mercy. But mercy merely as a principle, impersonal mercy, is no more useful or virtuous than impersonal faith or impersonal repentance or impersonal love.

Justice and Mercy

As a new mission president years ago I visited, by somewhat imperious invitation, the home of a good and strongly opinionated man who wanted to discuss with me an error of judgment made by a young missionary. The harmless action involved was the result of a misunderstanding for which the young man had sincerely apologized. I was fully satisfied with the resolution. My friend was not. He insisted on some form of punishment, public punishment, that assured humiliation. The young man must pay, and I must see to it.

Address given at general conference October 1981.

We reasoned together. His position was that justice demands payment and that mercy cannot rob justice. I agreed and reminded him that the words he had quoted came from a Book of Mormon incident wherein a choice servant of God, who early in his life had desperately needed mercy and had received it, was now teaching an unrepentant son who was seeking to justify his own serious sin. Alma, the father, taught Corianton the meaning and consequences of the Atonement, in the course of which, acknowledging the place of justice, he three times testified of God's "plan of mercy," brought about through Christ's holy gift.

"Mercy claimeth the penitent," he said.

"Mercy claimeth all which is her own."

There is "a repentance granted; which repentance, mercy claimeth; otherwise, justice claimeth the creature." (Alma 42:22, 23, 24.)

"And thus he shall bring salvation to all those who shall believe on his name; this being the intent of this last sacrifice to bring about the bowels of mercy, which overpowereth justice, and bringeth about means unto men that they may have faith unto repentance" (Alma 34:15).

The sin of Corianton was major, the incident involving the missionary was innocent and minor. I thought our discussion would resolve the issue. It did not.

My host leaned across the table and said to me with intensity, "I want justice!"

Quietly I replied, "I want mercy."

Three times with growing force he repeated his message: "I want justice!"

Each time I responded to his crescendo with diminuendo, saying more quietly, "I want mercy."

We parted with the agreement that it was my responsibility to handle the matter, to give justice its due, and to let mercy claim her own.

He is gone now to his eternal reward. I remember him with respect and affection. I came to know him well and love him and to be aware that he, like all the rest of us, needed the promised mercy of Christ to the penitent.

Many times I have mused on that moment: "I want justice!" "I want mercy!"

Recently, half a world away, I sat with another good man. He had brought light and warmth and good humor into the room with him, and I was listening with deep interest as he told his "before and after" story. The "before" involved his life as a nominal but nonpracticing Christian employed in a stressful occupation with rough associates and with a tendency to follow the crowd in all their bad habits. He was not attentive to his wife and children and was worried about his family, suffered from an unhappy conscience, and had developed a serious physical ailment.

Then two young men came to his door. They represented the Lord, they said, with a message of eternal truth for him and his family: the gospel of Jesus Christ is restored to the earth, the Church of Jesus Christ re-established; every individual and every family are important to God and through His plan can find purpose and meaning; families are meant to be together forever; and there is a way to know for oneself the truth of these things, for the Holy Spirit will confirm the knowledge for those who sincerely seek.

He listened and believed. Immediately he put aside bad habits. His wife and children responded also. Their lives changed. They studied and prayed and worshiped, joined the Church, and lived in the light of the Spirit. His work improved, and soon new opportunities and trust and renewed reputation for dependability resulted. At the conclusion of his story came a ringing declaration of faith, without self-consciousness, without bluster, without guile. "I am like the Lord in one thing," he said; "my specialty is mercy."

My specialty is mercy!

God Specializes in Mercy

One cannot live long with the scriptures without recognizing that God our Father and His holy Son have specialties also.

The specialty of the Father is mercy.

"God . . . is rich in mercy" (Ephesians 2:4).

The Savior spoke to the world those things which He had heard of His Father. "As my Father hath taught me, I speak these things" (John 8:28).

The scriptures teach that He took upon himself the form of man and was "touched with the feeling of our infirmities" (Hebrews 4:15). "Wherefore in all things it behoved him to be made like unto his brethren, that he might be a merciful and faithful high priest" (Hebrews 2:17).

There is one who understands, who sympathizes. He was misunderstood, rejected, knew supreme loneliness, was poor and had not a place to lay His head, suffered anguish, and "though he were a Son, yet learned he obedience by the things which he suffered" (Hebrews 5:8).

He understands.

He can give pardon and bring peace.

The specialty of the Savior is mercy.

And He requires that we be specialists in mercy. "Be ye therefore merciful, as your Father also is merciful" (Luke 6:36).

Through Micah we are taught man's whole duty, which is to walk humbly with God, to do justly among our fellowmen, and to "love mercy" (Micah 6:8).

Our individual need for mercy and its conditions the Savior explained in a parable of two men who went up to the temple to pray. One proudly announced his own perfections and righteousness. The other "would not lift up so much as his eyes unto heaven, but smote upon his breast, saying, God be merciful to me a sinner." Of this honest, unpretentious man the Lord declared that he "went down to his house justified rather than the other." (Luke 18:13–14.)

The meaning of mercy He taught in a parable of a man beaten and left at the roadside and concluded the sweet story of the Samaritan by referring to two men who passed by without helping, and to one who stopped to assist him. Which of these three, the Lord asked, was neighbor to the man? And He received the answer, "He that shewed mercy on him." Then Jesus said, "Go, and do thou likewise." (Luke 10:37.)

Thus the mercy of God must be mirrored in the mercy of

man, and the field is as broad as the needs of the whole human family. The Psalmist cried, "Have mercy upon me, O Lord, for I am in trouble" (Psalm 31:9).

All of us are in trouble. There is no just man on the earth who doeth good and sinneth not (see Ecclesiastes 7:20).

In the most personal of His parables the Savior identified himself fully with the hungry, the thirsty, the naked, the homeless, the sick, and the imprisoned (see Matthew 25:35–36). So many are burdened with earthly care, the stain of sin, poverty, pain, disability, loneliness, bereavement, rejection. The promise of Christ's mercy is sure and certain to those who find Him and trust Him. He who stilled the winds and waves can bring peace to the sinner and to the suffering Saint. And we as His agents are not alone to declare His word but also to represent Him in doing unto the least of His brethren that which He himself would do were He now here.

In a refugee camp in Asia was a young former schoolteacher who with her mother had escaped their country after having watched the brutal murder of others in their family. She had been viciously violated to the point where she had vowed never to speak again in this depraved world. It was her way of protesting against the wickedness imposed upon her and countless others. For more than five years she spoke not a word. Then one day she came into the influence of some of our Church representatives who were performing daily miracles of love in several refugee camps. They had no medical magic, these selfless young ladies representing us there, no professional competence to deal with a tortured mind and spirit. They prayed for her, took her hand, and spoke words of love to her, and she answered! For the first time in five years she spoke, and she has been speaking since. The Spirit of Him who said, "Peace, be still" (Mark 4:39) reached out through faithful instruments, touched the storm center of a troubled soul, stilled the winds and waves of torment, and brought faith and hope again.

For me and mine, and for you, I pray to be worthy to carry the same banner as our beloved brother who found the way to mercy and who exemplifies in his life what I heard him humbly declare—"My specialty is mercy."

"Let us therefore come boldly unto the throne of grace, that we may obtain mercy, and find grace to help in time of need" (Hebrews 4:16).

In the name of Jesus Christ. Amen.

CHAPTER 5

Willing to Receive

In the book of Moses a conversation is recorded that for me is one of the most instructive and tender in all literature. Enoch had "built a city that was called the City of Holiness, even Zion," which "in process of time, was taken up into heaven. . . . And . . . the God of heaven looked upon the residue of the people [that is, upon those who had not been taken up], and he wept." (Moses 7:19, 21, 28.)

Then Enoch said to the Lord: "How is it that the heavens weep, and shed forth their tears as the rain upon the mountains? . . . How is it that thou canst weep, seeing thou art holy, and from all eternity to all eternity?" (Moses 7:28–29.)

Enoch then reminded God of the limitlessness and ongoing nature of His creations, and of His holy perfections and glory and accomplishments, and said:

Naught but peace, justice, and truth is the habitation of thy throne; and mercy shall go before thy face and have no end; *how is it thou canst weep?*

The Lord said unto Enoch: Behold these thy brethren; they are the workmanship of mine own hands, and I gave unto them their knowledge, in the day I created them; and in the Garden of Eden, gave I unto man his agency;

Address given at general conference April 1980.

And unto thy brethren have I said, and also given commandment, that they should *love one another*, and that they should
choose me, their Father; but behold, they are without affection,
and they hate their own blood. . . .

And the whole heavens shall weep over them, even all the
workmanship of mine hands; wherefore should not the heavens
weep, seeing these shall suffer? (Moses 7:31–33, 37, italics
added.)

God, from whom all blessings come, asked of His children
only that they should love each other and choose Him, their
Father. But as in our day, many neither sought the Lord nor
had love for each other, and when God foresaw the suffering
that would inevitably follow this self-willed, rebellious course of
sin, *He wept.* That, He told Enoch, was what He had to cry
about.

The Holy One at the Gate

Long ago I heard an important story which has been helpful
to me. I have not seen it in writing and therefore cannot give
credit as I would like. The story has obviously been deliberately
fashioned to teach in a provocative way principles in which I
believe.

Over a period of time three men, as each of us ultimately
will, passed from mortal life to ongoing immortality. Each, as he
made the transition, at once found himself in the presence of a
gracious person who made him feel comfortable and calmed his
apprehensions.

Each man in turn found himself responding to questions
which somehow formed in the mind and heart, vital above all
other considerations. "What do you think of Christ? What is
your relationship with Him? Do you know Him?"

The first man answered reluctantly, with some chagrin. He
said he had not been one who had participated in organized religious activity. There seemed to be too much formalism, too
much hypocrisy, too little real religion. Neither had he on his
own sought a personal relationship with the Lord. He had been
a good husband and father, an active citizen, a man of integrity,

but it now came to him very clearly that he had missed a central purpose of his life, that he had been distracted from what he should have been seeking. With gratitude, he received entry into a circumstance where he could begin to learn what he needed to know.

The second man had a briefer interview. Quickly perceiving the import of the questions, he quickly answered. He had been a soldier for Christ, he said, a crusader for Him in business, a spokesman for Him in industry. He seemed crestfallen to be ushered after a time into a circumstance where he too could begin to learn what he needed to know.

The third traveler came into the presence of his host with an overwhelming sense of warmth and wonder. Understanding the questions, looking tearfully into the loving eyes of Him who stood at the gate, he fell to his knees at His feet and worshiped Him.

In the scripture it is written: "O . . . my beloved brethren, . . . the way for man is narrow, but it lieth in a straight course before him, and the keeper of the gate is the Holy One of Israel; and he employeth no servant there; and there is none other way save it be by the gate; for he cannot be deceived, for the Lord God is his name." (2 Nephi 9:41.) Salvation and exaltation, I believe, are not matters of heavenly bookkeeping but of the qualifying of the soul that comes with knowing the Lord.

We Will Enjoy What We Are Willing to Receive

It is also written that one who does not abide laws pertaining to the various conditions of eternal opportunity cannot enjoy the blessings of those kingdoms. There are those who will not enjoy the blessings of *any* kingdom of glory, but must function, says the record, in a kingdom *not of glory*. (See D&C 88:22–24.) And of them it is written: "And they who remain shall also be quickened; nevertheless, they shall return again to their own place, to enjoy that which they are willing to receive, because they were not willing to enjoy that which they might have received. For what doth it profit a man if a gift is bestowed upon him, and he receive not the gift? Behold, he rejoices not in that which is given unto him, neither rejoices in him who is the giver of the gift." (D&C 88:32–33.)

Each of us will enjoy all of God's blessings that we are willing to receive!

We Choose Him Through Serving

But how do we manifest that willingness? A prophet answers: "How knoweth a man the master whom he has not served, and who is a stranger unto him, and is far from the thoughts and intents of his heart?" (Mosiah 5:13.)

We know and choose Him and enjoy His blessings through serving Him, through qualifying for His friendship, and by keeping Him always in our hearts and minds. In our afflictions and gropings and forebodings we turn to Him for comfort and support. He is always accessible to those who seek Him.

"Come unto me, all ye that labour and are heavy laden, and I will give you rest" (Matthew 11:28). "Lo, I am with you alway," He said, "even unto the end of the world" (Matthew 28:20). "I will not leave you comfortless" (John 14:18).

He understands our infirmities and pressures and problems. Better than any other, He understands how it is to feel all alone. "My God, my God, why hast thou forsaken me?" (Matthew 27:46.)

But loving Him, reaching out to Him, we have also to live His commandment to love each other. He taught us and showed us the paths we must follow. When He returned to Nazareth and entered the synagogue on the Sabbath day, He opened the book of Isaiah and read what had been written some seven hundred years earlier about His ministry: "The Spirit of the Lord is upon me, because he hath anointed me to preach the gospel to the poor; he hath sent me to heal the broken-hearted, to preach deliverance to the captives, and recovering of sight to the blind, to set at liberty them that are bruised" (Luke 4:28).

In the magnificent story of the return of the King, He taught us unforgettably our responsibility to the hungry, the thirsty, the stranger, the naked, the sick, and those in prison. "Inasmuch as ye have done it unto one of the least of these my brethren, ye have done it unto me" (Matthew 25:40).

Millennia before that time, through Isaiah, God had delineated the course of helpfulness He expected His children to follow: "To loose the bands of wickedness, . . . undo the heavy burdens, . . . let the oppressed go free, . . . deal thy bread to the hungry, . . . bring the poor that are cast out to thy house, . . . when thou seest the naked, . . . cover him, . . . satisfy the afflicted soul." (Isaiah 58:6, 7, 10.)

We know, you and I, that we need the Lord. And He made it plain that He also needs us as instruments of His love to His other children.

A little girl living in a place for homeless children earned displeasure from annoyed attendants by depositing a note in a tree limb which could be reached from outside the institution. The apprehended little rule-breaker was quickly taken to the superintendent, who opened the note. It read, "To whoever finds this, I love you."

God's children need to be loved, and to have someone to love.

But it is written, "Let us not love in word, neither in tongue; but in deed and in truth" (1 John 3:18). "Not with eyeservice, as men-pleasers; but as the servants of Christ, doing the will of God from the heart" (Ephesians 6:6).

In the sermon Amulek preached, encouraging prayer and faith, there was added this invitation: "And now behold, my beloved brethren, I say unto you, do not suppose that this is all; for after ye have done all these things, if ye turn away the needy, and the naked, and visit not the sick and afflicted, and impart of your substance, if ye have, to those who stand in need—I say unto you, if ye do not any of these things, behold, your prayer is vain, and availeth you nothing, and ye are as hypocrites who do deny the faith" (Alma 34:28).

The poet expressed it in another way:

> Love is not all: it is not meat nor drink
> Nor slumber nor a roof against the rain;
> Nor yet a floating spar to men that sink.
> (Edna St. Vincent Millay, "Love Is Not All.")

Obviously, love is an action word.

We speak of the love of Christ that is greater than faith, greater than hope; that expresses itself in sacrifice, in service, in giving.

Some of those who need our love are near at hand, others are far away. A few of the latter are arriving in our communities to remind us that vast numbers of displaced people are now and will be increasingly in need of help across the earth. We have heard a little of the tragedy of the boat people. Yet the problem of the hungry, the homeless, the hopeless, the poor and cast out, is beyond anything most of us can comprehend.

There are others nearer at hand who struggle with problems with which we must also be concerned. Major organized institutional welfare and social service efforts are in process, thank the Lord, but these are to augment our individual concern for the strangers who are among us, resident or passing through, for the wayward, the elderly, and the ill.

The widowed and divorced suffer devastating displacement, also, often alone and often in need of encouragement and help. Brokenhearted parents who have really tried, but whose progeny have chosen another path, are heartsick and often find little comfort in sermons or in the success of others. The numbers of single parent families burgeon, each one representing special needs not fully understood by those who have not experienced them.

We have the testimony of scripture that the Lord God weeps when we do not choose Him or truly love each other. The saddest circumstance any of us can envision, indeed the only evil that ultimately can really harm us, is in not choosing Him and thus to be separated from Him. But the companion tragedy—one that also brings suffering that makes Him weep— is to fail in our affection for each other, affection expressed in unselfish efforts to give Christian service—Christian service to the hungry, the naked, the oppressed, those who are cast out, the widow, the orphan, the afflicted, the brokenhearted, the bruised, the abandoned, the elderly, the sick, and the imprisoned.

We have two great challenges, you and I, and the challenge never ends as long as breath lasts: to choose Him and to love each other. Then we may be sure we will know Him in this world and at last in that kingdom which is not of this world. It is there that "God is with men, and he will dwell with them, and they shall be his people, and God himself shall be with them, and be their God. And God shall wipe away all tears from their eyes; and there shall be no more death, neither sorrow, nor crying, neither shall there be any more pain; for the former things are passed away." (Revelation 21:3–4.)

God bless us that we may meet the test. In the name of Jesus Christ. Amen.

II

Values

CHAPTER 6

Be and Not Seem

I have been thinking about the story of a person who was imposed upon by a bully after a traffic accident. When the police found the victim he was in pretty rough condition. They asked him, "Can you describe the man who hit you?" He replied, "That's what I was doing when he hit me."

While I will not attempt to describe the situation I now find myself in, I want to congratulate you on *your* situation, on the special privilege you have of attending this great university. I am anxious this morning that my visit—an opportunity I always treasure—may be helpful to you. I am particularly prayerful that of the many thoughts that have crossed my mind I may be directed to those that may be helpful to you, and that we may be in tune with the Spirit so you may hear and feel what is expressed. Listening can be critical. One of my notes reminds me of a single-line message inscribed on a tombstone in England—it really is—that reads, "I told you I was sick." We do not always listen wisely or well.

The Seemers

Things are not always what they seem, and neither are

Address given at Brigham Young University devotional 23 January 1979.

people. In that context I invite you to listen carefully as I read some lines from Matthew chapter 23 that will establish my theme. Listen to this scripture as it is reported from the teachings of the Lord. Let each hear it as if we personally were being addressed. Hear the word of the Lord:

> Then spake Jesus to the multitude, and to his disciples,
> Saying, The scribes and the Pharisees sit in Moses' seat:
> All therefore whatsoever they bid you observe, that observe and do; but do not ye after their works: for they say, and do not.
> For [he is going to give some examples] they bind heavy burdens and grievous to be borne, and lay them on men's shoulders; but they themselves will not move them with one of their fingers.
> But all their works they do for to be seen of men: they make broad their phylacteries, and enlarge the borders of their garments,
> And love the uppermost rooms at feasts, and the chief seats in the synagogues,
> And greetings in the markets, and to be called of men, Rabbi, Rabbi. . . .
> [Then He counsels that no one is to be called master save He.]
> But he that is greatest among you shall be your servant.
> And whosoever shall exalt himself shall be abased; and he that shall humble himself shall be exalted.
> But woe unto you, scribes and Pharisees, hypocrites! for ye shut up the kingdom of heaven against men: for ye neither go in yourselves, neither suffer ye them that are entering to go in.
> Woe unto you, scribes and Pharisees, hypocrites! for ye devour widows' houses, and for a pretence make long prayer: therefore ye shall receive the greater damnation.
> Woe unto you, scribes and Pharisees, hypocrites! for ye compass sea and land to make one proselyte, and when he is made, ye make him twofold more the child of hell than yourselves. . . .
> Woe unto you, scribes and Pharisees, hypocrites! for ye pay tithe of mint and anise and cummin, and have omitted the weightier matters of the law, judgment, mercy, and faith: these ought ye to have done, and not to leave the other undone.
> Ye blind guides, which strain at a gnat, and swallow a camel.
> Woe unto you, scribes and Pharisees, hypocrites! for ye make clean the outside of the cup and of the platter, but within they are full of extortion and excess.
> Thou blind Pharisee, cleanse first that which is within the cup

and platter, that the outside of them may be clean also.

[Finally,] Woe unto you, scribes and Pharisees, hypocrites! for ye are like unto whited sepulchres, which indeed appear beautiful outward, but are within full of dead men's bones, and of all uncleanness.

Even so ye also outwardly appear righteous unto men, but within ye are full of hypocrisy and iniquity. (Matthew 23:1-7, 11-15, 23-28.)

That terrible indictment against the Pharisees came because they were addicted to the policy of *seeming* instead of *being*. In contrast, it is said of one of the magnificent leaders in olden times that he acted always in every circumstance with grace and graciousness and goodness. Early in his young manhood he had adopted a motto, a guiding principle that was inscribed inside his shield. In acts of combat or kindness he looked to it for direction. It read: "To be and not to seem."

The Pharisees, fastidious and meticulous in their adherence to the letter of the law, were "seemers." "Pretence," "ye say and do not"—these were words the Lord used to describe them; and He used on them that terrible word which makes all of us cringe: *hypocrite*.

Pretence Is Vanity and Foolishness

Many who have understood what the Lord meant have given us additional counsel in consequence of what He said; and of them all I choose one that has been of special meaning to me for many years. Thomas à Kempis was born nearly six hundred years ago. He wrote these powerful words:

The doctrine of Christ exceedeth all the doctrines of holy men; and he that hath the Spirit, will find therein an hidden manna.

But it falleth out, that many who often hear the Gospel of Christ, are yet but little affected, because they are void of the Spirit of Christ.

But whosoever would fully and feelingly understand the words of Christ, must endeavour to conform his life wholly to the life of Christ.

What will it avail thee to dispute profoundly of the Trinity, if thou be void of humility, and art thereby displeasing to the Trinity?

Surely high words do not make a man holy and just; but a virtuous life maketh him dear to God.

I had rather feel compunction, than understand the definition thereof.

If thou didst know the whole Bible by heart, and the sayings of all the philosophers, what would all that profit thee without the love of God and without grace?

Listen to part of the next paragraph also:

Vanity therefore is to seek after perishing riches, and to trust in them.

It is also vanity to hunt after honours, and to climb to high degree.

It is vanity to follow the desires of the flesh, and to labour for that for which thou must afterwards suffer grievous punishment.

Vanity it is, to wish to live long, and to be careless to live well.

(Thomas à Kempis, *Of the Imitation of Christ*, chapter 1.)

Vanity it is, I add, and foolishness indeed, to pretend, to say and not to do, to seem and not to be.

In its worst form, that is hypocrisy. In its best form, I suppose, it might be thought of as pursuing the "as if" principle— that is, to say to oneself: "I will behave as if I were honest, decent, moral, courteous, gracious, sensitive, and courageous; and in so behaving establish the habits and acquire the capacities that will help me become all those things."

I suspect that most of us fall somewhere in between. We do not savor, and in fact sicken at, the thought that we are hypocrites, and yet we seem to do so much to be seen of men. We sometimes say that which will tickle their ears. We pretend, knowing that we are not really what we seem.

The Savior's Life

This is not to suggest that only the perfect may act with

credibility in matters of important principles. All of us fall short and are inevitably visited with the pangs and pains of our own failures; there is a universal understanding of that, since none of us is exempt from it. But to deliberately pretend, to put on a show, to give long prayers when we have devoured the widow's house, to do less than we can and should yet pretend to do, to go through motions—not as honest efforts to do better, but simply because we are falsely trying to fit somebody's conception of what we are—all of this is vanity and foolishness indeed.

Christ's life, His instruction, and His testimony centered in being what one ought to be. And there is great room in His holy heart to forgive when we fall short while genuinely trying to be what we ought to be.

Early this morning, under the heading "Be and not seem," I thought of Him and an example or two of His genuineness and consistency. Let me share an expression so profoundly admirable and beautiful and worthy of emulation.

Think of His acute awareness of and sensitivity to the lives and needs of others, to the point that when the woman in the crowd who touched the hem of His garment found immediate response He felt her timid touch, and she felt the power of His integrity. When Jesus inquired who had touched Him, His disciples, seeing the thronging multitudes, wondered how He could ask such a question. Who had touched Him? Many were touching Him. But one touched Him with a special need and a heart ready for the response, and He knew it. (See Mark 5:25–34; Luke 8:43–48.)

Another characteristic of the Lord was His acceptance of others as they were, without the intention to leave them as they were. He could heal the body, bless the mind, and help change the soul of one who was willing—the prodigal, Zacchaeus, Mary Magdalene. Remember also that moment on the cross when He expressed forgiveness. Most of all, I am touched by that tender scriptural occasion when a father who loved his ailing son, and who had sought help from the disciples and had not received it, presented himself to the Lord pleading for help. To him the Lord said, "If thou canst believe, all things are possible to him that believeth." Do you remember his courageous, wonderful reply? "Lord, I believe; help thou mine unbelief." He did not have perfect faith, he didn't understand everything, but he knew to whom he spoke, and he trusted in Him. (See Mark 9:17–27.)

The Lord's courage was consistent, clean, strong, noble, and godly. He spoke the truth and He acted in conformity with it. He also had great humility. He made full use of His powers to serve, heal, help, and teach, always making it clear that He relied on His Father and the Spirit. Knowing always who He was and what powers He might have invoked, He did all His wondrous works in the spirit of "the least among us."

Perhaps we should not have favorite scriptural stories at the expense of many others that another time, another day, more prayers, more tears, and more living might make favorites, but over many years I have come to love this one.

> And he spake this parable unto certain which trusted in themselves that they were righteous, and despised others:
>
> Two men went up into the temple to pray; the one a Pharisee, and the other a publican.
>
> The Pharisee stood and prayed thus with himself, God, I thank thee, that I am not as other men are, extortioners, unjust, adulterers, or even as this publican.
>
> I fast twice in the week, I give tithes of all that I possess.
>
> And the publican, standing afar off, would not lift up so much as his eyes unto heaven, but smote upon his breast, saying, God be merciful to me a sinner.
>
> I tell you, this man went down to his house justified rather than the other: for every one that exalteth himself shall be abased; and he that humbleth himself shall be exalted. (Luke 18:9–14.)

Christ possessed the love that was greater than faith and greater than hope, the love that never faileth, that expresses itself in service, in sacrifice, in giving—the love that opened to mankind the door to all that is good here and all that is creative, progressive, challenging, exciting, satisfying, and sweet hereafter. This love was not just encouragement or testimony but was also specific instruction. In what to me may have been the high point of His teachings about love, He said that there are those who are hungry and thirsty, who lack sufficient clothing, who are strangers or feel such, who are sick, who are in prison.

Love means doing something for them. And when you do something for even the least of them, it is counted as if you had done it for Him. (See Matthew 25:31–40.) This is not a catalog of His virtues but a testimony of His great heart.

We who do not want merely to seem but would really like to *be* will find that the path He laid out in His instruction, in His example, in His testimony—in His life—is one not beyond our capacity to follow. There are those who need to feel a response of acceptance, affection, and mercy. There are those who are hungry, who may still feel strange in this great institution and who need to be remembered and nourished and helped. There are people in hospitals and prisons who are generally not over-burdened with others who care and who are not really out of our reach if we will be sensitive to their need, to their reaching.

In Being We Can Give

In trying to make plain what my heart is yearning to share, let me set before you two examples of giving that are modest but real and recent and understandable. They could be examples from the lives of many of us.

First let me share a recent report from a Latter-day Saint leader serving in important Church responsibilities and also serving in our military. I listened as this modest, gentle, manly father told of his work among other officers in the prosecution arm of the United States Army, men who were not like him, who were not living the kind of life he was living. They had not been very much interested in the fact that he was a Mormon leader, or that he had a strong sense of loyalty to his wife and children and to God, or that he had control of his tongue and had a way of speaking that was different from their own. None of that impressed them very much. He and his wife found themselves leaving required social events early quite frequently because the activities of the evening were not wholesome. As such an evening progressed, other guests would occasionally become ugly as they imbibed additional spirits, lost their normal restraints, and sometimes acted less like men and women than like animals. He was not one to judge lightly or readily, and he was not expressing harsh judgments against them; he was simply presenting a setting for an incident that I shall not forget.

He said that they went to a Christmas party, more happily this time because the host family was a fine family with little children of the same general age as their own. The children came in their pajamas by invitation and, joining the host family children, played together in another room while the adults ate their dinner. Periodically the children came out and interrupted proceedings with childish playing or questioning, until finally the Mormon father, his sense of humor tried a little bit, said, "Now, look—you kids go on in the other room and stay there and don't come out again, *or else!*"

They sat at dinner in peace for a time; then the bedroom door opened and a little line of children filed out, the two-year-old in the vanguard. (They were sure Daddy would not do too much violence to him.) The older brother had him by the shoulders and was egging him on. The two-year-old said, "Daddy, you and Mamma forgot family prayer."

Instead of expressing embarrassment, the mother said, "Honey, we did forget." She pushed her chair back, he rose from his, and they excused themselves and quietly took their children and the other children into the bedroom, where they performed that simple act of family unity and faith. Then they quietly came back to the table, seated themselves, and went on with dinner.

"It was a different night," he said to me, "and there has been a different feeling. That party didn't end like all the rest. And at the office things are different now."

To be and not to seem brings great blessings.

To conclude, here is my own recent experience. There sits a man on this stand today whom I admire very much. He has a brother who is a physician and a medical researcher. I had the honor to visit that brother and his family and others in a stake presidency. The visit was pleasant and productive. We met the families of the stake and ward leaders, had a chance to talk with them and came quickly to know and love them, and left the stake feeling like brothers to these choice people.

After some months had passed I met the physician on the street in Salt Lake City, and we stopped to chat for a little while. He seemed pleased that I would remember him, and I got the feeling that there was something he would like to tell me; but both of us had to hurry, so we just put our arms around each other and parted. A few days later a letter came. I shall read it to you just as it is written. If I had any inkling that you would misunderstand it or the purpose I have in reading it, I would not share it. I plead with you, let your hearts tune in for just a moment.

Dear Brother Hanks:

Meeting you on the street the other afternoon was a very pleasant surprise for me and I'm sorry we were in such a hurry because I wanted to share an experience with you that's been very dear to me. Thus, I thought I'd take the opportunity to write you this note and tell you.

Perhaps you remember that when you visited our stake, the lunch was served by my wife and my young daughter. You asked my daughter her name and she replied, "Mary." You told her that was a most beautiful name for many reasons. You told her that you also had a daughter named Mary and told her about your Mary.

That episode changed Mary's attitude about her name. Up to that point, she had not liked her name very well because she thought it so plain. Thereafter, she thought of her name in a very different light. I don't know exactly what you told her or what message she received from you, but I must tell you that it changed her life.

My wife and I have reflected on that experience a great deal during these past few months and it has brought back such pleasant and very choice memories. We will be forever grateful to you for that brief encounter and for what it did for Mary. I'm sure that you had no way of knowing that Mary passed away a short time after that. Her death was very sudden and was due to medical reasons that are not yet explained. I wanted you to know how you touched her life and thank you for it.

We have nothing to give? We are so weak and so simple? You and I? Our consciousness of our personal failings and inadequacies disqualifies us from helping others? We really cannot expect anybody to care very much or respond to us? Oh, God help us to *be* and not to *seem,* to give, to love, to be humble. If we cannot lift up even our eyes unto heaven, then God help us to have sense enough to cry, "God be merciful to me, a sinner." But you have so much to give.

Let this simple incident say what I could not if I had tried for an hour, and tell you that I know this is God's work and that we are really neighbors, brothers, sisters—His children. There is in the least of us—even in the most dependent—that which is better than we understand; shared, it can bring more than we know to those who seek.

In the name of Jesus Christ. Amen.

CHAPTER 7

Appreciate Your Opportunities

I'm here today physically subdued from an interesting afternoon and evening spent in swinging an ax and pushing a saw in the snow at Aspen Grove, but I'm built up to an exultation of spirit and emotion through that great experience. On this note I am reminded of a beautiful observation I recorded long ago from the writings of David Grayson: "It is not the time of the day nor the turn of the season nor yet the way of the wind that matters most to us, but the ardor and glow we ourselves bring to the fragrant earth. It is a sad thing to reflect that, in a world so overflowing with goodness of smell or fine sights and sweet sounds, we pass by hastily and take so little of them. Days pass when we see no beautiful sights, hear no sweet sounds, smell no memorable odor, when we exchange no single word of deeper understanding with a friend. We have lived a day and added nothing to our lives."

I'd like to qualify my being here today. I didn't come for just another meeting, of course. I really like the comment of the Englishman who watched his first game of American football, saw all those huddles, and said: "Seems like an interesting game. I think I could learn to like it, but they hold too many committee meetings." No, I didn't come for just another meeting.

Address given at Brigham Young University devotional 28 October 1975.

Nor did I come to see the local attractions. I was reading the other day about the archbishop of Canterbury who had been warned about the American news media before visiting this country. Upon arrival in New York he met a group of these interesting people, who of course asked him questions. One said, "Archbishop, do you intend to visit the night clubs in New York?"

Warily he answered, "Oh, are there night clubs in New York?"

The next day the newspaper printed the story: "The first question the archbishop of Canterbury asked upon arriving in New York was 'Are there night clubs in New York?' "

Well, I'm not here today to see anything except you, really, though I certainly enjoyed the beauty of the sky and the mountains on my way here.

I didn't come expecting to teach much that's new, either. I came because I like to come, and so I accepted the invitation. I like to get the feel of this place. Someone has written: "New leaves do not come because old leaves are falling. Old leaves fall because new leaves are coming." You are the new leaves. We look with optimism to your coming but bid you remember with Charlie Brown that there is no heavier burden than great potential.

Information and Appreciation

I came to deliver a nosegay of flowers collected along the road, tying together these blossoms with the frail thread of my understanding, acceptance, conviction, and appreciation. I'd like to begin what I have to say with a quotation from a hero of mine whose name is Abraham Heschel. He is gone now but was a great rabbi and teacher. Abraham Heschel said:

> Two things a man needs—information and appreciation. Now when I look at our educational system and many other institutions for civilization, I see a tremendous emphasis upon information, but hardly any cultivation of the sense of appreciation. Mankind

will not die for lack of information. It will perish for lack of appreciation. Unless there is appreciation there is no mankind. The great marvel of being alive is the ability to discover the mystery and wonder of everything. The real dignity of anything that is, is in its relationship to God who created it. Unless we learn how to revere, we will not know how to exist as human beings. (From a radio interview conducted by Ronald Beck, 21 January 1968.)

For what information and appreciation shall we seek? Let me share a story you may have heard. If so, you will appreciate it the more, and if not, it will be a thoughtful experience. An older man and a young man were drifting in a rowboat on a quiet lake, beneath the earthen dam that formed the lake. They had newly become friends. The older man, as they talked, picked up a leaf from the surface of the lake. He said, "Son, do you know very much about biology?"

The young man said, "I'm afraid I don't, sir."

"Well," he said, "you've lost 25 percent of your life."

After they had gone a little farther, the old man took from the bottom of the boat a rock. He held it up, examined it, and said to his companion, "Son, do you know very much about geology?" A little embarrassed, the younger man said, "No, sir, I'm afraid I don't."

"Well, you've lost 50 percent of your life."

As they drifted it became dusk, and the first evening star appeared. The older man asked, "Son, do you know very much about astronomy?"

The other answered, "I'm embarrassed to tell you, sir, that I don't."

The older man responded, with a smile, "You've missed 75 percent of your life."

They drifted a little longer and then, sensing some unusual current in the water beneath them, looked up and saw coming at them a huge wall of water from the dam, which had burst. The young man said, "Sir, do you know how to swim?"

"No, I'm afraid I don't," was the answer.

"Well," said the boy, "you're about to lose all of your life."

A leaf, a rock, a star, swimming, biology, geology, astronomy—all are significant areas of knowledge. It would be wonderful if each of us had a broad enough base in the laws of nature and the basics of science and the facts of history and the principles of philosophy to be interested in and understand in a measure the great advances being made around us. This knowledge contributes richness to life and perhaps helps one to make a living. But more important than any of it, central to all of it, giving it all meaning and coherence, is information about and appreciation of man himself; of his relationships with others and with God; of his understanding of his origins and heritage, his possibilities and responsibilities, and his everlasting future. Let us look at two or three matters of appreciation selected out of a multitude I've been turning over in my mind in the past few hours.

Appreciation for Life

Appreciate life. Grayson's comment about ardor is complemented for me by something I heard a long time ago from two perceptive psychologists, a husband-and-wife team, who were teaching a group of adults. Out of all that they said, much of which I remember, one thought is foremost in my mind: "Nor heaven nor hell can him surprise, who loves his home, and loves the rain, and looks on life with quiet eyes."

You may have heard the last interview recorded with Dr. Tom Dooley before he died of leukemia. This conversation was replayed on the day he died. He had given the young years of his medical career, when he could have been making a lot of money, to the people of Indochina. These two or three sentences constituted the valedictory, of sorts, of Tom Dooley.

Said the questioner, "Dr. Dooley, you are living on borrowed time, yet your contributions to humanity seem to take no account of the trials you personally are called to bear."

"Yes," Dr. Dooley said, "I am living on borrowed time. So are you; so is every man who walks this earth. I may live to be as old as you are now; I may not live to see my next birthday. This does not matter. What really counts is what I do in *terms of human good* with the days, the weeks, the months, or the years allotted to me by my creator."

Appreciate life.

Appreciation for Others

Appreciate others and be respectful of their values. I was called upon to pray at a public gathering a few days ago and found myself without premeditation thanking God for the qualities of gentility and civility and caring which permit people of diverse points of view and diverse ways of living to be together in an atmosphere of courtesy and graciousness. I've thought about that since. I think the Lord blessed me to say that. It certainly was consonant with how I feel and what I would like my life to represent.

I think of the words of the great Apostle who encouraged all of us in this respect: "Honor all men. Love the brotherhood. Fear God. Honor the king" (1 Peter 2:17). We also read of the Prophet Joseph Smith, under the inspiration of God, preceding the marvelous words "let virtue garnish thy thoughts unceasingly" with the admonition that we be filled with love toward all men, and to the household of faith (see D&C 121:45). This message is repeated again and again. I wonder if we are always sensitive to it.

Do you know the story of Mike Gold? I didn't until a year or so ago.

In the 1920s, the philosopher of American Communism was a Jew named Mike Gold. After communism fell into general disrepute in this country, Mike Gold became a man of oblivion. In this oblivion he wrote a book, *A Jew Without Knowing It*. In describing his childhood in New York City, he tells of his mother's instructions never to wander beyond four certain streets. She could not tell him that it was a Jewish ghetto. She could not tell him that he had the wrong kind of blood in his veins. . . .

In his narration, Mike Gold tells of the day that curiosity lured him beyond the four streets, outside of his ghetto, and of how he was accosted by a group of older boys who asked him a puzzling question: "Hey, kid, are you a *kike?*" "I don't know." He had never heard the question. "Are you a Christ-killer?" Again, the small boy responded, "I don't know." He had never heard that word either. So the older boys asked him where he lived, and, trained like most small boys to recite their address in the case of being lost, Mike Gold told them where he lived. "So you are a kike; you are a Christ-killer. Well, you're in Christian territory and we are Christians. We're going to teach you to stay where you belong!" And so they beat the little boy, bloodied his face and tore his clothes and sent him home to the jeering litany: "We are Christians and you killed Christ! Stay where you belong! We are Christians, and you killed Christ. . . ."

When he arrived home, Mike Gold was asked by his frightened mother: "What happened to you, Mike?" He could answer only: "I don't know." "Who did this to you, Mike?" Again he answered: "I don't know." And so the mother washed the blood from the face of her little boy and put him into fresh clothes and took him into her lap as she sat in a rocker, and tried to soothe him. Mike Gold recalled so much later in life that he raised his small battered lips to the ear of his mother and asked: "Mama, who is Christ?" (John Powell, *Why Am I Afraid to Love?* [Valencia, California: Tabor Publishing, 1982], pp. 112–13, 116.)

I read from the Book of Mormon:

> And now, my brethren, I have spoken unto you concerning pride; and those of you which have afflicted your neighbor, and persecuted him because ye were proud in your hearts, of the things which God hath given you, what say ye of it?
>
> Do ye not suppose that such things are abominable unto him who created all flesh? And the one being is as precious in his sight as the other. And all flesh is of the dust; and for the selfsame end hath he created them, that they should keep his commandments and glorify him forever. (Jacob 2:20–21.)

Do you remember Shaw's *Pygmalion?* One of the lines from this play is, "The difference between a flower girl and a lady is not how she behaves but how she is treated." When I think of

Mike Gold and of Jacob 2, from which I have just read, I think of another sentence from Abraham Heschel. "Holocausts," he said, "are caused not only by atomic explosions, holocausts are caused whenever a person is put to shame."

Appreciation for Yourself

Appreciate your own special spiritual heritage and value. I read in a fine Christian-Protestant magazine a little while ago a somewhat strange, and to me sorrowful, statement: "Like all other institutions of liberal Protestantism, this magazine is suffering from an erosion of self-confidence. There is a pervasive feeling that we no longer have anything particularly distinctive to offer by way of religious insight." In this world, where the Lord needs every strong heart and devoted hand and tongue He can find, I think that's very sad indeed.

What I'm saying to you is that we need to appreciate the special heritage and values that have come to us. Think for a moment what particularly distinctive insight the kingdom of God offers you in these matters: God, Christ, mankind, life, sex, marriage, family, resurrection, eternity. Special instruction has been given to us concerning conservation, pollution, liberation, population, elections, freedom, abortion, government, Christ. In these and many other very important principles, programs, doctrines, and matters, there are distinctive, special insights we have to share. But just knowing that to be so or hearing it doesn't really suffice, does it? We must learn to understand these insights, become really converted to them, and act on them.

I wish it were appropriate to tell you all the details of a conversation I once had with a young lady, a lovely person, who was professionally qualified in an important field. I would not want you to know those details, so I simply share a headline. She was about to make a decision that would influence her and her generations. She came into my office reluctantly, but she came because both she and I loved her parents. She was not really interested in anything I had to say and acknowledged it openly when

I asked her. I said to her, "When did you last do any serious reading about the Church?"

"Oh," she said a bit blithely, "in the ninth grade. We were reading the Book of Mormon. I quit, though."

I said, "Did you also quit praying and going to church?"

"Yes," she said.

"And pretty soon you stopped living the life of the Church?"

"Yes."

I said, "I really just have one other question to ask you. The new Church Office Building is about ready to be completed— all those many stories. Your specialty will be involved in its completion. I'd like to do what I could to get you the job to work on that great big building. Would you like that?"

Looking a little dubious, she said, "Well, sure!"

I said, "All right, I think I can do it on one condition. You agree to perform your professional specialty on that building on the basis of what you knew about it in the ninth grade."

She looked a long time at the floor before the teardrops came, then she said: "Oh, Brother Hanks, I'm in terrible trouble. Can you help me?"

I said, "Yes, I think I can now."

To learn and then to act. I know a man who as a bishop won an award for his great skills and success in training teachers who work among underprivileged people. Some of his fellow teachers who knew him and knew the quality of his record and the nature of his life and his attitude toward his fellowmen said: "We just don't get it. How can you, being a Mormon, do the kind of work you do?"

He said, "You really don't get it, do you? I do the kind of work I do precisely because I am a Mormon."

Appreciate your own particular, distinctive heritage and the religious insights which it offers.

I stood under an awning one day, low in spirit, soaked by the rain. I had some law books under my arm, and they had been soaked also. There were a lot of other problems on my shoulders, problems concerning people I loved very much, other demands made on me, and many Church assignments. I hardly knew where to turn, and I was depressed. There were two others under the awning whom I did not at first even notice in my preoccupation with my own problems, but I couldn't keep from hearing them speaking to each other. One of them, a beautiful person very near the birth of a child, said to her friend, "How are things going with you?"

"Just fine," was the reply, "but we can't find an apartment. Have you found one yet, with the baby coming?"

"Oh, yes," said the pregnant girl, "we found one."

"You did? How could you? We've looked and looked."

"Oh," she said, "we did, too. Bob and I looked till we were exhausted, and then, having tried as hard as we could, we fasted and prayed for a couple of days and he went out and found a nice place."

"Oh," said the other without any hint of surprise. And I stood feeling ashamed, considering some things I hadn't even thought of for a while.

Appreciation for Humility

Appreciate the importance of being humble. Do you remember the poignant words of an anguished father recorded in the scripture? "Lord, I believe; help thou mine unbelief" (Mark 9:24)? Do you remember the Savior's strong statement about matters of great consequence—"weightier matters," He called them—judgment, mercy, and faith? (See Matthew 23:23.) Do you remember the wise scribe who knew how to treat his neighbor, who knew how to love God and his fellowman though he wasn't a member of the kingdom? The Savior said to him, "Thou art not far from the kingdom of God" (Mark 12:34). There was something more he had to do, but he had the spirit and the meaning. And do you remember the Pharisee and the publican, the one so self-congratulatory over his religious rigidities, and the other who "would not lift up so much as his eyes unto heaven, but smote upon his breast, saying, God be merciful to me a sinner" (Luke 18:13)?

Appreciation for Responsibility

Two other suggestions and I'm through. Appreciate the responsibility of being an individual in an organized society, a person and a social being with responsibility to others. Avoid, I pray you, that lone-eagle complex that makes some people say: "It's my life and I'm going to live it. I'm going to do what I want to do in spite of what it does to anybody else, what effect it has on anyone else."

Remember Niemoller's interesting bequeathment—he who got along for a time with the Nazis and finally was imprisoned. "They came after the Jews, and I was not a Jew so I did not object. Then they came after the Catholics, and I was not a Catholic so I did not object. Then they came after the trade unionists. I was not a trade unionist so I did not object. Then they came after me, and there was nobody left to object."

Christ asked, at the end of a story well known to all of us, "Which now of these three, thinkest thou, was neighbor unto him that fell among the thieves?" (Luke 10:30). Six hundred or more years before that, Jeremiah had asked, "Is it nothing to you, all ye that pass by?" (Lamentations 1:12.)

Appreciation for Covenants

Appreciate, please, the need we all have to keep the pledges we have made. When Sister Hanks and I visited the tomb of Gandhi in India, we read there a few words that I have treasured since—words about pledges, words that I have found mirrored within the standard works and my own covenants and the memory of them reflected in the little piece of bread and the cup of water we take on the Sabbath. Gandhi said: "Even for life itself we may not do certain things. There is only one course open to me, to die but never to break my pledge. . . . How can I control others if I cannot control myself?" I remind you to be grateful for your pledges, and to keep them.

I exemplify my pledges in an experience I once had. In a small town I had a talk with a lovely young woman about her going on a mission, an opportunity she desired and now felt ready for. We were talking about her qualifications. She was candid and humble and gentle and forthright, anxious for her great opportunity. As we finished, I said to her, "Does anyone else know about the problem that makes this conversation necessary?"

She said, "My bishop and my stake president and my parents."

I said (and I have more often felt blessed by the Spirit to ask a question than in answering one), "What was the reaction of your parents when you told them?"

She said: "My father put his arms around me and wept. He said, 'Ah, sweetheart, how could you carry this heavy burden alone without us to help?' "

I said: "Was that his first response? Was that his reaction?"

She said, "Yes."

I said: "Do you know how blessed you are? Could I have the honor of meeting your father before we leave here?"

The arrangement was made. I said to him as we shook hands, "If I can express in my own life the maturity of Christian understanding of the gospel and the wisdom and compassion that you have, I will be very grateful."

I bid you remember that, please. It is important to have that quality of character, that kind of mature understanding of what life is really all about, and that kind of love. I see that as an appreciation of what God really expects us to grow to and is pulling for us to accomplish.

This is a good place to stop, save one, and that one is a scripture:

> And now I, Moroni, bid farewell unto the Gentiles, yea, and also unto my brethren whom I love, until we shall meet before the judgment-seat of Christ. . . .
>
> And then shall ye know that I have seen Jesus, and that he hath talked with me face to face, and that he told me in plain humility, even as a man telleth another in mine own language, concerning these things. (Ether 12:38–39.)

And I join Moroni in this invitation:

And now, I would commend you to seek this Jesus of whom the prophets and apostles have written, that the grace of God the Father, and also the Lord Jesus Christ, and the Holy Ghost, which beareth record of them, may be and abide in you forever. (Ether 12:41.)

This is His work. I think to learn of it and appreciate it is the main undertaking and highest blessing of us all. In the name of Jesus Christ. Amen.

Highest and Holiest Realities

I love to be near university campuses, and particularly this one at this time of the year. The season's mix of apprehension, anticipation, anxiety, rejoicing, rush, and wait blends into an excitement that charges me. For more than twenty years I stood behind a teacher's table by a chalkboard and had my joy. God gave me in pleasant measure the gift of appreciating present delight, so I loved it then, demanding as it was. But the years away from it have intensified within me the assurance that there is no greater or more rewarding work than to teach. I think and am reminded of it often as I meet some of those (and their families) with whom I had the blessing of sharing in a classroom.

T. S. Eliot gave us some lines that have special meaning and application here as a new school year begins, a new chance for us as individuals. These are the lines:

> We shall not cease from exploration
> And the end of all our exploring
> Will be to arrive where we started
> And know the place for the first time.

Address given at Brigham Young University annual university conference 26 August 1976.

That engaging thought is literally true for some of you who began your college work here and now have come to serve. It was true of Ernest Wilkinson and of Dallin Oaks when each returned to lead. It can be true of each and all of us as we undertake another beginning—trustees, administration, staff, students. Some of us who have never physically removed from here may have departed, in some measure, in terms of love, loyalty, or labor. We have been exploring. This new time is the time to come home, replant roots, restudy priorities, make refreshed commitments, begin to give our fullest measure of contribution. This is a great place to be. This is a great business to be in. This is a unique and choice institution.

A Thing of Spirit

Like a person, like a home, this university is a thing of spirit as well as body. It has a soul. Yes, it has a beautiful campus that is part of its corpus, and it has staff and teachers and administration, but it is also a thing of spirit—intangible, incorporeal—real spirit, a kind of immaterial scepter that symbolizes what it is and what it stands for. That spirit influences how people feel (maybe more than what they think) about the place when its name is mentioned.

Among the glorious promises made in Doctrine and Covenants 121 to those who qualify as being "full of charity towards all men, and to the household of faith," and having their thoughts unceasingly garnished with virtue, recall that promise full of meaning and little mentioned: "Thy scepter shall be an unchanging scepter of righteousness and truth." To me there are no greater covenants made by God or man than those of which this one is a part. Do you remember the others? Confidence that will "wax strong in the presence of God"; the "doctrine of the priesthood" distilled upon the worthy soul "as the dews from heaven"; the Holy Ghost as "constant companion"; an "everlasting dominion." Can any blessings be more glorious than these (and the contemplation of our realizing them in the presence of beloved family and friends)?

What does it mean to have an "unchanging scepter of righteousness and truth"? A scepter is a symbol, an emblem. For me, with whatever else it may mean about the permanency and purity of priesthood calling truly magnified and thus honored, this promise pertains to the perceptions others have of one so blessed. I think of it when I think of a selected few—a sainted mother, a brother, a sister, a prophet; in my grateful heart their scepters are unchanging scepters of righteousness and truth.

So it is with Brigham Young University. This institution has a soul, a spirit, a scepter. Central in establishing and maintaining that spirit are the individuals who, moving under the sweet influence of the Lord, have served here and do now serve here. Not surprisingly, people are the major element in establishing the spirit of an institution. Our academic ancestors were worthy instruments in getting things started. In my view their places are now held by others equally worthy. It would be well if all of us were; God grant that we may move to become so if we are not. This is the time to begin.

I think of this institution and its magnificent campus and structures, its great staff, administration, and faculty, and its fortunate students when I hear in my mind again the words of Emerson, written long ago. He talked of a time when there were wooden chalices and golden priests. But now, he said, perhaps looking to another day than his own, there are golden chalices and wooden priests. The history of this institution is well known to most of us, and when it started it certainly didn't have golden chalices. But it had golden priests. By any standard of measurement it now has golden chalices. The finest compliment I can pay you is to say what I believe, that it also has priests—that is, leaders—worthy of and equal to its great physical blessings.

Everyone Associated Is Important

I have said that teachers are of prime importance to the university. Are others also? An individual's perception of the institution may come from so narrow a base as the way he was treated in a registration line, or a dean's office, or a parking lot, or by a gardener as the person crossed a lawn. It is important that everyone connected with the university, from the maintenance crew to the president's office, accept that—really believe it—because it is true.

I face this situation regularly in a public institution with which I have some responsibility; unconcern or lack of civility or gentility on the part of an assistant manager or a maintenance man or a masseur makes the whole program look bad— "worse than I have seen it in years," said a recent complaining letter, notwithstanding the fact that new facilities have been added at large costs, and repairs, painting, and refurbishment accomplished throughout. Having seen that institution from its infancy, I know the place is in better condition than it has been for years. Yet a bad experience with one individual who works there, then a seeming unconcern on the part of others when the incident was reported, rendered the whole institution "worse than it has ever been" in the eyes of the man who had the bad experience.

Let me give you another example, even closer to home. Our sixteen-year-old son, our only boy, has been working for some months in a theater-restaurant, hustling food to the steam tables, washing dishes, cleaning up the kitchen at night. He has generously shared, almost daily, an account of what has gone on. There have been days of delight, hours of despair, times of triumph, occasions of defeat. There have been spilled food, new bosses to please and educate, misunderstood instructions, unfair judgment, appreciation, commendation. I have listened, and smiled, and encouraged, and been pleased.

Recently the time came for him to resign; school is just ahead. His superiors were complimentary, strong recommendations for future employment were given, he was invited back. Rich felt good. After his last night he confided to me in sincerity and guilelessness that he wasn't at all sure the place would be able to run without him! The boy he'd trained hadn't responded seriously or energetically enough. Food wasn't reaching the tables hot enough or soon enough. The place wasn't clean. Well, so far as I know, the enterprise is still operating, though Richard reported the other day, not without satisfaction, that two boys were now employed to do what he used to do.

The principle is, of course, that every individual is important in an institution. In ancient Damascus, the "pearl of the desert," was the famed Street of the Swordmakers. It is recorded that here, in one corner of the oldest inhabited city in the world, lived a guild of artificers, and here they produced the famous blades of Damascus. These blades were incredibly sharp and wonderfully elastic—they would bend almost double then spring back straight. Death by strangling, the most shameful punishment of the time, was the sentence passed on any member of the craft found guilty of producing and selling an inferior product, because by placing on it the proofmark of this honored craft they had brought discredit upon all the master swordmakers of Damascus. It was as if each sword bore the fingerprints of its creator, a projection of his personality.

So it is at this institution, but in terms of something finer than Damascus steel. For while we care about the perceptions of those who may pass casually by or learn a little about us, there is one group upon whom this institution and all who have anything to do with it seek to make a proofmark of high, enduring quality. That group, of course, is the students. For them and their eternal well-being this institution exists.

Education in Appreciation

What do they need? What should they take when they leave here? What can we help them discover? What are our responsibilities?

The student comes here to be educated. Education includes information; skill in the processes by which it is discovered, tested, understood, applied; and love for the search. But education means also the cultivation of the sense of appreciation and the development of character.

Long ago, at a place that came to be called Bethel, a young man of promise on an important mission had an experience that profoundly affected and shaped the attitude of mind that carried him to a historic destiny. Jacob was starting a journey to find a wife, an enterprise which would affect his whole future and that of many others. En route he stopped overnight at the roadside, fashioned a pillow from some stones, went to sleep, and dreamed. In the dream a ladder reached from earth to heaven, with angels ascending and descending on it and the Lord standing above it. "And Jacob awaked out of his sleep, and he said, Surely the Lord is in this place; and I knew it not. . . . This is none other but the house of God, and this is the gate of heaven." (Genesis 28:16–17.)

At Brigham Young University and at few other places a student can be helped to a sense of reverence, of appreciation for God, helped to know that wherever we are—in our homes, the hills, our centers of enterprise, places of recreation—we can, according to our desires, our will, and our humility, qualify for that spiritual presence and power which will surely bring us the strength we need and the joy we desire. This requires that we appreciate that we are a little more than human, that we are related to Him who is much more than human; it requires that we remain open to an increasing sense of wonder and worship before His eternal holiness.

Life can be and is meant to be rich in its endless opportunities for doing the holy and the good. To live that life we need to have faith, an appreciation of God our Father and Jesus Christ our Savior which can make even the wayside a part of the path to the gate of heaven, to the house of God.

Education at this school should, above all else, be education in appreciation, appreciation which will make the highest good not the capacity to repeat the insights of philosophers, poets, or even prophets, but to be a personal witness of the Lord Jesus Christ in thought, speech, behavior, and spirit.

Following the Lord's remarkable statement recorded in section 88 of the Doctrine and Covenants as to the magnitude of the appropriate fields of inquiry and instruction which He commands us to pursue and teach to one another, is this declaration of purpose for us all: "That ye may be prepared in all things when I shall send you again to magnify the calling whereunto I have called you, and the mission with which I have commissioned you. Behold I sent you out to testify and warn the people, and it becometh every man who hath been warned to warn his neighbor." (D&C 88:80–81.)

Without denigration to the sacred text I have sometimes

wished that verb were spelled w-a-r-*m*, because that's how we interpret it and try to apply it. Having been *warmed* by the sweet spirit of concern and commitment and conscience, and the sense of unity and closeness and the love of the Lord, we would wish to *warm* others.

A century ago the brilliant Negro orator Frederick Douglass was mournfully declaring to a large audience an utterly pessimistic appraisal of his then despairing people. Suddenly out of the balcony a shrill voice cried: "Frederick, Frederick, is God dead?" It was the voice of Sojourner Truth, faithful, noble leader of her people. The message electrified the moment.

Central Truths

God lives. Christ lives. The kingdom is restored. The priesthood is bestowed from heaven and is powerfully present among mankind. The commandments of old in all their strength presently pertain to contemporary circumstances and important truths. The path leading to the gate of heaven and the house of God is marked. The Holy One of Israel stands at the gate and assures us that He employeth no servant there. None but the penitent may enter. Christian joy is available, a joy broader than but inclusive of those wholesome pleasures of our time, a joy reaching to the very meaning of the Creation and the purposes and aims of life.

These truths are to me the highest and holiest of realities, and contributing to a student's appreciation of them, I earnestly believe, is the major meaning and prime purpose of this institution and all who serve here or sustain it. Understood, made flesh, and given life among us, these truths lead to character, the true aim of education. They will help to produce qualified scholars and practitioners in all the avenues of man's learning. They will also, as President David O. McKay said, "produce honest men . . . with virtue, temperance, and brotherly love— men and women who prize truth, justice, wisdom, benevolence, and self-control as the choicest acquisitions of a successful life" (*Gospel Ideals* [Salt Lake City: Improvement Era, 1953], p. 441).

Knowing these truths can lead individuals to behave as they do not now behave. Helping students to know them is our employment at this school, and it is a demanding task. "It is," said Ruskin, "a painful, continual and difficult work, to be done by kindness, by watching, by warning, by precept, and by praise; but above all else by example."

Other Principles to Be Taught

There are many other principles of truth that both lead to and flow from the central ones mentioned; these also students should be exposed to at this special place of learning. Discipline, obedience, faith, a sense of belonging, good work habits, unselfish service, forbearance, slow judgment, modesty, mercy, compassion, long-suffering, loving-kindness, civility, gentility, a good self-image—all of these should be learned or better defined after association with you and others in these rooms and halls and on these walks. Students should come here from their homes with a good foundation in them, yes, but whether they do or do not they should depart from here having heard, seen, and experienced these virtues and values in a way they cannot misunderstand and will not forget. No classroom in any field of inquiry can avoid offering some lessons in these principles, either favorable or unfavorable, nor can life in any dorm or apartment, nor relationships in any branch or stake. A good experience here may in many ways counteract, balance, or mitigate the damage done by a poor home, or by friends, or by previous unconstructive conduct. Those who deal with youth are responsible for the total effect of their influence. Nothing says it better for me than that.

These principles, or the absence of them, are reflected in several special experiences I have had in the last few days and which have come to mind as I have thought of this moment. I am thinking of a marriage performed in the Salt Lake Temple just before we came here tonight, and of others involving my own children; of a funeral for a choice twenty-seven-year-old father who left a beautiful little family; of a missionary run over and killed on his bicycle; of a boy who had taken his own life. I am thinking of conversations with a convert who was seeking understanding of his recent temple experience, and with others seeking comfort and counsel. All are realities with which we come in touch, about which we must have some serious views, and to which we should come with understanding and something to share.

With my friend who was perhaps not adequately prepared for the solemn covenants and the complexity of the temple experience I rehearsed the moving story of Naaman, captain of the Syrian host, who contracted leprosy. You may remember the events that brought him to Elisha's door seeking help for his terrible malady.

Perhaps because there was a seeming sense of imperious demand in Naaman's summons, the prophet would not come out to see him, but sent a message saying, "Go and wash in Jordan seven times, and thy flesh shall come again to thee, and thou shalt be clean." How would that direction go with certain skeptical persons these days? Naaman thought it an imposition on his intelligence and "was wroth." He had expected the prophet to cure him in some exciting, dramatic way. In effect his response was that if he were going to wash himself in a river like a little child, at least he would do so in the clean rivers of Damascus rather than in the Jordan. It is written in the record that "he turned and went away in a rage"—went away to the tragic future of a leper.

Naaman is described in the Bible as a "great" and "honorable" man. Beneath his pride and arrogance he must have also been a very good man, because when he haughtily started to ride away to destruction his humble servants pleaded with him to do what the prophet bade him: "If the prophet had bid thee do some great thing, wouldest thou not have done it?"

It is not recorded what then went on in Naaman's head and heart, but we are well enough acquainted with pride ourselves to understand in a measure. The great man won the battle with himself, turned his entourage around, and went back to the Jordan. There he got off his high horse literally and figuratively and "dipped himself seven times in Jordan, according to the saying of the man of God: and his flesh came again like unto the flesh of a little child, and he was clean." (See 2 Kings 5.)

Why did this happen? Was it that the Jordan had curative capacities? No. But obedience to Almighty God's commandments through His prophets, even though we may not at the moment understand all about them, is indeed salutary, even healing.

The application of that great lesson should be clear to all of us who, sometime along life's way, must learn to bow our heads and obey. There are those in the room tonight whose spiritual lives will be saved through learning that truth. What of those who come within range of your spirit on campus or in class? Will they in the moment of crisis be led to humble themselves, overcome pride, obey? Or will they turn and go away in a rage?

What of the lonely and the fearful? Will they gain a sense of belonging? Will there be one person they can call friend? I hope so. Recent Boy Scout surveys revealed that there are many young people in this broad, beautiful, bountiful land who say that they do not have one friend in the world. Why are there so many youth suicides and so much despair? There is no simple answer, but we know some elements of the answer. Is it possible that any young person could move through this campus and feel that he or she had not one friend? I earnestly hope not.

The Energies of Love

An hour or two ago in the Salt Lake Temple I shared with two wonderful young people preparing to kneel at the altar an experience that helped me build upon the high vision of courtship, marriage, family, and eternal creative relationships that I gained in my parents' humble home. This experience had taken place in the apartment of President and Sister David O. McKay as they prepared to celebrate their last wedding and anniversary together—married nearly a score of years more than fifty. I was there on other business and was privileged to remain while a photographer took a picture of them. They were in their nineties—he soon to leave mortality and she only a little time thereafter—and each was brought into the room in a wheelchair. As they were seated together on a small divan they laughed and joked about their physical infirmities, about

Huntsville nearly seventy years before, about their family; he spoke of his beautiful bride. The tiny frail hand was completely encased in the big still-strong one. At the precise moment when the photographer prepared to snap the picture, the tiny frail hand lifted the big strong one to her lips and kissed it. It was a spontaneous, beautiful expression of her love, the product of more than threescore years of cherished courtesies and kindness, of repentance and forgiveness, of graciousness and giving and receiving. He wept, and so did we. You see, we knew at that moment, nothing doubting, that these eternal relationships, these everlasting commitments, this boundless love are much more than pleasant possibilities the Mormons hope for and believe in. They are the true, natural consequence of two persons' accepting and living God's law of marriage, of living together in love. They are the inevitable, blessed future for those who have learned how to love.

I share with you—somewhat shyly, I acknowledge—a very personal family experience of my own. It has been my privilege to perform the wedding ceremony for our four daughters, two of them this past summer. The experience I speak of has been about the same with each daughter, so I mention the last as the example. The night before the temple ceremony we sat in our home together, we seven who have formed the Hanks family circle since Rich was born sixteen years ago. It was our last family home evening before Ann moved on to her own special adventure on the morrow. We sang and prayed and looked at some old films and photographs and laughed and cried and talked and testified and listened to each other. Three sisters and a brother in their turn spoke to Ann of their love and appreciation. Mom and I had our chance, and Ann responded through her tears. We knelt together and visited with the Lord, and then Ann sat in a chair with her family around her while I had the special privilege of giving her a father's blessing.

I am not sure that I can in any degree convey to you what this occasion meant to me. When I think of the good fathers, in and out of the Church, who are not enjoying the blessings they could have I am sad for them. Not everyone can perform a wedding in the temple, but every father could have the experience I have mentioned, and I testify that it is a sweet and choice one. It represents a body of blessings that I believe can be prepared for at this university.

Perhaps I should not mention without time and proper occasion to discuss it fully the sobering experience of sitting with the family and speaking at the services of the boy who took his own life. But I am impressed to share with you the strong assurance that came and was expressed: he is in the loving care of the Holy One of Israel, who stands at the gate and "employeth no servant there"—that Holy One who took not upon himself "the nature of angels; but . . . the seed of Abraham" in order that He might have "the feeling of our infirmities." He has "descended below" the fiercest of our sufferings. Better than anyone else in all of history, He understands what it means to feel all alone. It was He who on the cross cried out, "My God, my God, why hast thou forsaken me?"

I know some of the theological implications of that moment of aloneness, but I confess that since I was a boy I have harbored a special and private feeling of my own about it. Perhaps it came from my never having known my own father, from wondering about him, from responding to tender accounts from Mother about the humility and gentleness of his loving heart. Thinking about my father, it seemed to me that likely the Father of us all had to turn away from that awful scene for a moment to wipe away a tear. Our Heavenly Father understands. The Lord Jesus Christ understands. "Wherefore in all things it behoved him to be made like unto his brethren, that he might be a merciful and faithful high priest in things pertaining to God, to make reconciliation for the sins of the people" (Hebrews 2:17).

I pray that on this campus there may be a spirit of true Christian compassion, of forbearance and kindness. Obedience and discipline must be learned, else life will teach them to us in harsher ways. There must be fair rules, understood by all and impartially applied, with sanctions when they are broken. But for each other there needs be compassion.

I love a statement of Brigham Young that may surprise some:

Every man, and more particularly my immediate associates who are with me daily, know how I regret the ignorance of this people—how it floods my heart with sorrow to see so many Elders of Israel who wish everybody to come to their standard and be measured by their measure. Every man must be just so long, to fit their iron bedstead, or be cut off to the right length: if too short, he must be stretched, to fill the requirement.

If they see an erring brother or sister, whose course does not comport with their particular ideas of things, they conclude at once that he or she cannot be a Saint, and withdraw their fellowship, concluding that, if they are in the path of truth, others must have precisely their weight and dimension.

The ignorance I see, in this particular, among this great people is lamentable. Let us not narrow ourselves up; for the world, with all its variety of useful information . . . is before us; and eternity, with all its sparkling intelligence . . . is before us, and ready to aid us. (*Journal of Discourses* 8:8–9.)

Pierre de Chardin is reported to have said: "The day will come when after harnessing the ether, the winds, the tides, gravitation, we shall harness for God the energies of love, and on that day for the second time in the history of the world man will have discovered fire."

I believe, beloved friends, that we can harness that energy and discover that fire in this choice and compact environment if we do all we can, all we should, to help our younger brothers and sisters prepare for living lives of contribution and genuine concern. We shall fail of that grand achievement, though, if through pride or sloth or selfishness or fear or incompetence or small vision we do not do what we here have the blessing to be privileged to do.

I leave you with a certain sense of unfulfillment, yet I must say that I have said what I do feel and I pray God to sanctify it, that out of it may come some sense of the important individual responsibility each has to make this school what it can be for those who come to it. In the name of Jesus Christ. Amen.

CHAPTER 9

No Watch, No Medal

Georgia Young had taught every one of my five brothers and sisters at Salt Lake City's West High School. As the youngest, I had enjoyed the generosity and unselfishness and labors of all the others. But Miss Young taught me a valuable lesson about doing my very best.

Coupled with a reasonable scholastic record and some extracurricular activity, my high school sports participation qualified me as one of those who could be considered to receive a special award upon graduation. My brother had won the award before me, and I hoped for this same recognition.

As the final month of school concluded and various award and scholarship winners were being considered, my name surfaced as one of the finalists for the award, with its accompanying medal and watch. I was not confident that I would win, but I was hopeful, and I went through the final report card day collecting the grades that could make a vital difference in my chances.

From each class through that morning came the coveted *A* that would enhance my prospects for the award. Only Miss Young's fifth-period English class remained, and I went there

Ensign article June 1989.

quite confident that my marks and other qualifications would combine to make me a serious candidate. I was sure I would get an *A* from Miss Young, since my performance through the year had supported that grade each month preceding this final one. The sixth and last period was athletics, and I knew I would get an *A* there, which would make my report card perfect for that month and my year's record worthy of consideration for the award.

The report cards were passed to the front in our English class and handed to the teacher in the customary fashion. While we waited for our grades, we read books and talked.

From hand to hand my card came back down the aisle, eliciting a certain amount of attention from students sitting ahead of me who caught a glimpse of what was written there. A wave of apprehension passed over me, but it was quickly dissipated by my confidence that there would be an *A* on the card that reached me.

When I finally received the card, I stared at it unbelievingly. In the space alongside the English literature class was an *E*, a failing mark. Georgia Young had signed her name across from that mark.

The True Comparison

I was stunned and deeply surprised and hurt and angry. Others looked at me with curiosity as they passed from the room. I waited until they were gone and then went to Miss Young's desk. She was looking at her attendance book and didn't raise her eyes when I laid my card in front of her and said: "This is my card. You have made a mistake."

She looked up, her face white and grim, looked at the card, and said, "You are right, I have made a mistake." She took the card, superimposed a large *C* over the *E* and handed it back to me. "You don't deserve an *E*," she said. "That might keep you from graduating. So I will give you a *C*."

"Miss Young," I pleaded, "how can you do this to me? I have scored high on every test, and I am sure that in comparison with the other students I deserve an *A*."

"Yes," she replied, "you have done well on the tests. You have done well in the class. You came here pretty well equipped to sail through this class, the product in part, no doubt, of your wonderful mother's love of literature. You had already read much of what we have been studying. If I were marking you in comparison with all the other students, I would probably give you an *A*. But I am not marking on that basis this time.

"I think you have not been fair with me," she continued. "Many times you have been absent from this class to prepare for ball games of various kinds, and you have excused yourself because you thought the ball game was more important and the coaches would support you. I have watched with great anxiety what you have done. I love your mother. I have enjoyed and loved every one of your brothers and sisters. I have watched you through your years at this school, and you have done well. But you have not been conscientious in your responsibilities in this class. So for this month, I am not grading you in comparison with all the other students. I am grading you on the basis of what you have done compared with what you could have done and should have done. You get a *C*."

Sobered and ashamed, I said, "Miss Young, do you understand what this will do to me?" I had in mind the award. She replied, her face pained but determined: "Yes, I know what this will do to you. I would like you to know that I love you and have great hopes for your future, and that I have been up all night thinking about this and making the decision. You get a *C*."

"Thank you, Miss Young," I said quietly, and I went my way. I did not receive the award.

God Too Requires Our Best

But I lived long enough to stand as a General Authority of the Church before a group of retired schoolteachers in the Lion House in Salt Lake City and recall this incident. I had been invited by the president of the retired teachers organization to speak to this group. Sitting there among them was Georgia Young.

I told our story, and I said at the end: "I am glad I lived long enough to face Georgia Young and tell her, in the presence of her respectful peers, that the most important lesson I ever learned in school was the one she taught me that spring day. In the eyes of God and wise men, none of us will be judged in comparison with what others do with their time and talents and opportunities; we will find our judgment on that scale that reports what we did compared with what we could have done and should have done."

As a teacher myself who has for many years been blessed with the possibility of influencing for good the lives of others, I have never had far from my mind and heart that incident in fifth-period English literature at West High School. I see clearly in my mind's eye that doughty little soul agonizing through the night making her decision with an eye to the future of a student she loved and cared about too much not to require his best.

CHAPTER 10

His Light in My Life

In a prominent place in my office, where I can always see it, is a small, very old lantern which once lighted the binnacle on the H.M.S. *Clarion,* an old sailing ship registered out of Bournemouth, England. Not many people these days know what a binnacle is. Yet it is the forerunner for very important equipment on any ship.

A binnacle is a stand for a ship's compass, usually placed before the steering wheel. The binnacle holds the compass by which the mariner steers his ship. And because ships travel at night, there must be a light over the compass.

The lamp that lighted the binnacle of the H.M.S. *Clarion* is important to me because it was given me by a friend who had retrieved it from the old ship, now far from home and long out of service, and because that friend had inscribed on the front of it, to me, these words: "Your light in my life made the difference."

This tribute may be undeserved in my case, but I think everyone recognizes what a great privilege it would be to truly be a light in the life of another. Like the lantern over the binnacle, such a light may help point the way.

New Era article November 1984.

A good man shed some light on a bright path for me in earlier years, and I would like to share his story with you.

The Anticipated Adventure

I was twelve years old and a Tenderfoot Scout when I experienced my first overnight excursion away from home. I was excited, and I was frightened; we all were.

The group of boys who lined up with their gear on the lawn of the old Nineteenth Ward building in Salt Lake Stake were variously equipped for the planned adventure to Lake Blanche in the high mountains to the south and east of us. Some had elaborate and expensive sleeping bags and pack frames, and some had bedrolls attached to old army knapsacks. I was in between, having the use of a homemade bag fashioned by my brother-in-law, together with the pack frame he had built on which the bag and contents would be lashed.

All of us had been told to lay out our equipment for inspection by the man in charge, and we each fearfully waited by our stuff as the examiner approached. No marine trainee facing his drill instructor could have been more apprehensive.

The man passed down the line rather quickly, commenting on this item or that boy's pack, directing the abandonment of this extra baggage, sending one boy home to his mother with the three clean sheets she had sent along for his big trip.

I was last in line and thus nearest home, since our little house lay just alongside the old Relief Society building that separated us from the chapel. There was a narrow alley between the chapel and that building, and at the end of it a wall which formed the east border of our yard.

Being closest to home might have been an indicator of my frame of mind, because I was not altogether sold on this adventure and I was a bit apprehensive about the equipment I had borrowed, having been admonished carefully to keep it very clean and in absolute good repair.

By the time the inspector reached me, many foolish questions had been asked and answered, with increasing impatience on his part, I suspect, so that the man as he faced me had become a bit short on goodwill. He was, in fact, quite a dynamic person of whom I was somewhat afraid, though he had always been appropriately dignified in his calling and never had been anything but kind to me.

The Leader's Mistake

This day, under the circumstances and with the provocation of so much juvenile incompetency, he reached the end of his rope. Observing the number of items I was carrying which seemed to him superfluous for the high mountains and which he felt should not be carried in my pack, he sternly directed me to remove them and take them home to my mother. He seemed to dwell a bit sarcastically upon the pronunciation of my first name, about which my life on the west side of town by the railroad tracks had made me a bit touchy, if not defensive.

The Boy's Protest

When he seemed to be making fun of me, the other boys up the line, having had their turn, snickered or broke into open laughter. Everybody but I thought it was funny. When he had left me and returned up the line to begin to herd the crowd onto the trucks which were to transport us, I made my gesture of protest. Not having anything else to do that I could think of, I just bent over, picked up the pack frame in one hand and the two ends of the sleeping bag on which my gear was resting in the other, and walked up the alley, dragging it all behind me. When I reached the wall I dropped over, retrieved the equipment, and dragged it all behind the coal shed which was separated by a few feet from our house. Then I sat down on the ground under the basketball hoop on the back of the coal shed and suffered the pains and anguish of the damned—that is, those who have through willfulness and stubbornness painted themselves into an impossible position. I was twelve years old and in trouble.

I could not retreat and keep my self-respect; this man of authority had made a fool of me in front of others and had, to me quite unjustifiably, subjected me to ridicule. I was resentful and hopelessly frustrated. I could not see a way out of my dilemma, and I was deeply distressed.

The Long Walk

After a long time—no doubt it seemed much longer than it actually was, but it was a long time—I heard footsteps coming up our pathway from the front street, heard the pause and a murmured conversation at our back door, and then felt and heard him resume his pace toward me. Mother had told him where I was.

He came down the little passageway between our house and the coal shed, around the corner, and sat down beside me on the dirt. He said nothing for a time, but joined me as I nervously flipped little rocks and clods of dirt with a stick between my feet. I didn't look at him. After a time he spoke.

"Do you ever get up on Kotter's garage?" "Does Brother Kotter care?" "Do walnuts from the Perkinses' tree fall in your backyard?" "If you take ten shots at this hoop from the line over there, how many can you make?"

I gave brief answers to all questions, and again there was silence.

Then a large, strong hand reached over to my knee and grasped it warmly.

"Son," he said, "I made a mistake and I'm sorry."

"That's all right, Bishop," I said.

"Are you ready to go now?" he said. "The others are waiting."

"Okay," I said.

"We'd better get your pack ready."

He helped me roll the gear into the sleeping bag, secure it to the pack frame, and lift it to my back. We then walked out past our back door to the street and onto the truck where the others were waiting. I later learned that after I had left he called all of them together and explained that he had made a mistake and had been unkind to me and that my reaction had been understandable. He apologized to them in my behalf, prepared them to receive me without clamor when I arrived, got them all ready in the truck, and then made the long walk back to find me.

I do not dramatize what might have happened if a good man who was also a great man and a generous man had not made that long walk, if he had not been mature enough and humble enough and capable of acknowledging and correcting a mistake. I know I was wounded and frustrated by the impossibility of my circumstance. I know that he was the bishop we prayed for by name at our house every day. And I know that my wonderful mother, who did not intrude on my dilemma, must have helped pray him up the path.

I also know that boys and girls, even stubborn and rebellious ones, or hurt ones or bewildered ones, are worth something to our Heavenly Father and should be worth something to all the rest of His children. I do know that I myself have taken a few long walks when my own sense of pride or impatience might have prevailed, whispering to me: "Ah, let him go. Let him sit there and see how he likes it. Why should I be bothered?"

To this hour I remain grateful that my wonderful bishop overcame any such thoughts, if he had them, and made that long walk.

His light in my life has made a difference.

CHAPTER 11

Diversities of Authority

I am grateful to be in this the fourth temple I
have been in during the last twenty-four hours; this temple of
learning, appropriately thought of. I was in the Salt Lake
Temple this morning, where nine new temple presidents and
their wives were being greeted and a lovely seminar was begun.
Yesterday I had the great blessing of being in my home—there
is no more sacred place to me—and I also had the blessing of
using a saw and an axe for a time outdoors under the shadow
of the Wasatch Mountains, in that great temple of God's beautiful world. I also used a rake and a shovel and, as part of my
outdoor experience, spent some time trying to separate a
honeysuckle vine from an Oregon grape bush. (And I can report to you that for most of that time I was patient and pleasant!)

In all those places I sat thinking or stood thinking or swung
thinking. One strange set of thoughts came. Regarding my visit
to this temple of learning, I recalled some newspaper items that
over the years have segregated themselves from tens of thousands in memory. One of them is strictly relevant to this place.
I read not the original article but a letter to the editor about an
article in an Arizona newspaper. Apparently a public official,

Address given at Brigham Young University annual university conference 23 August
1988.

perhaps the governor, was under obligation to release a number of workers because of budgetary constraints. The newspaper had printed the story with a headline that said, "Whom Shall Be Fired First?" The letter to the editor said: "I read your article and your headline 'Whom Shall Be Fired First?' My answer is this: Whom wrote the headline? *Him* shall be fired first."

Brigham Young University Objectives

This is a university, and presumably one of the things expected of a university is that its personnel know when to use *who* and when *whom*. But of course there are a lot more important things a university ought to represent, and in these days and months and years of your association I am sure you have been reminded of some of them, because they have been clearly declared, generally understood, and often stated. As a kind of foundation, I would like to repeat three of them as I understand them.

First, BYU is a university that has as the broad basis of its educational goals scholastic success for its students *and* their spiritual/religious/moral development. This spiritual objective applies also to all who are connected with the school in any way, in any assignment or relationship. For this it was founded, organized, funded, staffed, nurtured, and built into a great, growing university. Of course, there is nothing in this objective that in any way vitiates or compromises the university's high scholastic aim and the effort to achieve it; rather, it serves to *define* and *support* those particular scholastic objectives. This school is meant to be a bastion of decency in a coarsening world where there is continual corrosion of moral and spiritual sensibilities.

Second, BYU retains a commitment to the principle, as I understand it, of "in loco parentis," *in the place of a parent.* In an educational climate in which that principle is largely abandoned now, BYU cares, as a true parent should, about the whole lives of those who come to study here—their educational preparation, the nature and quality of their life-style, and the enhancement of their sensitivity and the quality of spirit that relates to the inner world of each individual. *BYU cares what kind of people they are.* And that, after all, is what matters—not slogans, not even high and holy objectives. BYU stands in the place of a parent.

Third, those who serve here in any capacity—administration, faculty, staff, all others—represent the school in their various positions, and for this reason undertake a solemn trust. The pipe fitter and professor as well as the policeman represent authority, the attendant as well as the administrator, the carpenter and the controller, the gardener and the geologist. Each is under obligation to honestly support in their service and their lives the purpose, the policies, and the standards that are the reason for this university's existence. And it is about this authority and responsibility and opportunity, which each of you bears, that I would speak a few minutes this evening.

I plead with you to consider thoughtfully what I am about to say, not because I say it but because I believe from a lifetime of observation and consideration that it is true.

Authority Figures

For years on Temple Square, where I had some of my sweetest and holiest and happiest experiences, I observed an interesting phenomenon. I noticed with amusement at first, surprise somewhat, and then with wonder the number of tourists, guests in our city and on our grounds—a few of them every day—who avoided the well-dressed guides and the receptionists with their identifying badges and instead quietly cornered a gardener planting flowers, or a plumber fixing a fountain, to ask their religious or curiosity questions. Somehow they wanted to avoid what they conceived to be a professional person—who is ready to answer and probably will give you a lot more than you want to know—and went to hear what they hoped to hear from the "regular" people how they felt about their religion.

I remember reading as a youngster the story *The Grand Hotel*. A movie made of it was famous for many years. I only remember one thing about it: that when the secret of the Grand

Hotel, the greatest hostelry on earth, became evident it was that every person who worked there—from the custodian, the gardener, through the food services people, to the manager of the hotel—thought his or her job was the most important one in the establishment and that the place could not succeed if he didn't do his job.

Well, let me look at you tonight as authority figures. And, on the premise—actually, to me it is much more than that—on the *experience* and *conviction* that people like to listen to important things or like to get a viewpoint or feeling from those who are not, as it were, professionally involved in the exercise (though that doesn't cut out those who are), I invite you to consider these simple ideas.

Varieties of Authority

Authority is a very important subject among us and very basic in our religion, but I do not wish to talk about it in the conventional sense now. There are several varieties of authority. It is important to understand their diversity and their meaning and the use and effect of each.

First there is the authority of position, the one I suppose we normally think about, of *appointed* power, of leadership and supervision under authorization. This kind of authority may be exercised because one is *there,* empowered to act, and with the force of that position may control or significantly affect others. Such authority has the capacity to invoke consequences if its direction is not followed, if adherence and obedience are not forthcoming. This authority is recognized as having the power to get its way.

Beyond offices of appointment and power there are other forms of authority that do not depend for their efficacy, for their success, on command or the power of position. Although the kind of authority we perhaps generally think of when we allude to the word or the concept is this power of position, I want to talk about some other kinds.

Before I do, though, permit me to say that "position" authority is clearly defined in a scripture verse where a centurion approaching the Savior asks the Lord to help his servant, who suffers from a terrible illness. Christ is agreeable to go with him to the centurion's home. The latter says no, that would be asking too much. "But speak the word only, and my servant shall be healed." In the course of the experience this man describes himself: "For I am a man under authority, having soldiers under me: and I say to this man, Go, and he goeth; and to another, Come, and he cometh; and to my servant, Do this, and he doeth it." (Matthew 8:8–9.)

This authority of position is the kind the old Montenegrin proverb refers to: "The best test of a man is authority." Plutarch elaborates: "There is no stronger test of a man's real character than power and authority, exciting, as they do, every passion, and discovering every latent vice."

Shakespeare sounds the warning:

> Man, proud man,
> Drest in a little brief authority, . . .
> Plays such fantastic tricks before high heaven
> As make the angels weep.
> (*Measure for Measure.*)

And the scriptures—ah, you know where we would turn, don't you? because they give us the wisest and strongest and most sobering counsel concerning this manner of authority and those who bear it in the Church, in the home, and, I believe, with application everywhere else.

> Behold, there are many called, but few are chosen. And why are they not chosen?
>
> Because their hearts are set so much upon the things of this world, and aspire to the honors of men, that they do not learn this one lesson—
>
> That the rights of the priesthood are inseparably connected with the powers of heaven, and that the powers of heaven cannot be controlled nor handled only upon the principles of righteousness.

Then the choice verse:

That they may be conferred upon us, it is true; but when we undertake to cover our sins, or to gratify our pride, our vain ambition, or to exercise control or dominion or compulsion upon the souls of the children of men, in any degree of unrighteousness, behold, the heavens withdraw themselves; the Spirit of the Lord is grieved; and when it is withdrawn, Amen to the priesthood or the authority of that man.

And then a verse that applies to all of us, and certainly there are none holding authority in the kingdom who are not meant to heed its warning voice:

We have learned by sad experience that it is the nature and disposition of almost all men, as soon as they get a little authority, as they suppose, they will immediately begin to exercise unrighteous dominion.

Hence many are called, but few are chosen.

No power or influence can or ought to be maintained by virtue of the priesthood, only by persuasion, by long-suffering, by gentleness and meekness, and by love unfeigned;

By kindness, and pure knowledge, which shall greatly enlarge the soul without hypocrisy, and without guile—

Reproving betimes with sharpness, when moved upon by the Holy Ghost; and then showing forth afterwards an increase of love toward him whom thou hast reproved, lest he [or she] esteem thee to be his enemy.

Do you know the last in that series of beautiful verses?

That he may know that thy faithfulness is stronger than the cords of death. (D&C 121:34–37, 39–44.)

So this kind of authority is the one the prophet, the poet, the philosopher warn against in terms of its misuse. I leave that as a lesson in itself, which you didn't really need to hear, and move on to suggest some other kinds of authority, some varieties more effective and powerful than "You do it because I said so," or "It is so because I say so; I am in charge here." There are diversities of authority more powerful than that. I name three:

The authority of *personality,* centering in one's view of life, of oneself, of one's fellowmen, of God, of eternity.

There is the authority of *competence*, the demonstrated capacity to do what the one in authority is commissioned to lead and help others do.

And there is the authority of *integrity*, of character.

Authority of Personality

The authority of personality is expressed not through position or power or command but in one's view of the meaning of life and the worth of those who live it alongside us.

One who truly values other human beings and their potential and their uniqueness and their individual importance will lead by an authority that *evokes* respect because it *radiates* genuine respect. This kind of authority will be no less stable or even necessarily less demanding than that of position or command, and it will be infinitely more effective because it will inspire confidence and elicit respect and motivate commitment to accomplish the assigned task. It will preserve the dignity of those being led, even when the leader must do something that hurts them. It has to do with being human, being humane. It has to do with feelings and spirit.

The great Goethe issued a simple, profound invitation to all of us: "If you treat an individual as he is, he will remain as he is; but if you treat him as if he were what he ought to be and could be, he will become what he ought to be and could be."

Our perceptions are of great importance. If we perceive others to be intelligent, loyal, trustworthy, and they know it, they will generally seek to justify that perception. They may openly seek to be all those things, or may be all those things without our perceiving it, but they will be supported and sustained and very likely successful in their desires if we, perceiving these good things about them, let them know we do.

There are a lot of brilliant people in positions of authority who are ineffective leaders. Why? Today I picked up a civic bulletin and read these sentences: "Because they never get around to understanding and appreciating the feelings of the other people who are sharing this world with them. . . . Sometimes, usually later in life, these egocentric individuals suffer painful hardships. They understand then, often for the first time, the kind of problems less talented or less fortunate people have suffered all their lives. They suddenly discover a new and important dimension: sensitivity to the feelings, emotions, and experiences of other people." (John Luther, quoted in *The Rotary Bee* 9, no. 7, 16 August 1988, p. 3.)

I have nurtured for nearly a lifetime the story of Martin Luther's boyhood teacher who reportedly refused to wear the then usual pedagogic bonnet as he taught his class. He would wear the robe but would not wear the hat. Why not? Because, he said, "I do not know but that there sits among them one who will change the destiny of mankind. I take off my hat in deference to what they may become." (Quoted in Marion D. Hanks, *The Gift of Self* [Salt Lake City: Bookcraft, 1974], p. 126.) And it happened that a lad named Martin Luther was sitting there when he spoke.

One who was a missionary associate of mine in England twenty-five years ago sent me recently a copy of a talk he had given in church. In it was a single sentence spoken to him personally by President David O. McKay in Wales when that great, saintly man visited his mother's ancestral home. He was apparently touched by an act of courtesy from this fine young missionary. President McKay said to him, "Son, once a gentleman, always a gentleman." H. Perry Driggs has treasured that thought for half his lifetime, and I am sure he has tried to measure up to the invitation. He succeeds.

In the authority of personality we speak not of charisma or charm but of character, the expression of character, the way one treats others. We speak of compassion and concern, of patience and pride and accomplishment.

Authority of Competence

And what of competence as a base for authority? If those coming under the influence of authority figures—and I remind you that every one of us may fill that designation for some others—can do so with admiration for the competence and capacity of the leader, then learning and following become acceptable, right—even easy—without resistance or rebellion.

The authority of personal competence announces, without pomposity and beyond language: "I know what I am talking about. I am doing something I know about. I speak not by authority of position but with the authority of involvement and acquirement and experience. If you are willing I can help you learn to do it. I admire you when you do it well, because I am able to appreciate the strength of your performance and the difficulty of the preparation. I can also appreciate how it is not to know how to do it, and I will be patient and respectful as you develop your capacity in the undertaking."

I went once as a frightened new employee to a Boy Scout summer camp. Royal Stone was its director, a great man. Royal was a kind of remote figure in the camp, though he soon made it otherwise; but I became quickly attached to a man named Don Carlos Kimball as my mentor and leader. Lank and lean, a professional Scout executive, he was spending his summer there. He helped us learn how to be leaders. And the lesson I remember best is that, beginning one morning with an adz and an axe and a tree, he carved out—from sunup to past sundown, without stopping—a two-bladed canoe paddle and then knelt in a canoe with that paddle and beat the old motor boat across the lake.

I saw all of that in one day. He took his adz and his axe, and out of available materials he created an instrument and used it. I will never forget him.

During an early period in my college life I worked two jobs to meet needs at home and to keep alive my dreams of a mission. One of those jobs was at a repair shop for vacuum machines. We worked on motors and chassis and parts, then prettied them up and sent them home. One model then in vogue had a black Bakelite top, a heavy plastic cover, for the motor. It was breakable.

During my first hour on the job the manager of the shop came out from his office in his business suit to reinforce the instruction I had just had from a senior bench man. M. K. Bradford took off his jacket, turned on the powerful buffing wheel, put some compound on it, grasped this black Bakelite top strongly in his big hands, and buffed it into shiny beauty without a word. Then he cautioned me for a moment about catching an edge, a sharp edge, on the wheel, explaining that the wheel was very powerful and that I should wear protective goggles and be cautious.

He went back to his office. I turned to the wheel, applied the compound, forgot the glasses, grasped an unpolished top strongly in my then athletic hands, and put it to the wheel. The wheel accepted it quickly, tore it from my too tenuous grasp, turned it into a flying mass of tiny sharp parts, and spit it back in my face. I went to the sink, washed the blood away from many small cuts, checked my eyesight, clenched my teeth, and headed back to the wheel.

M. K. Bradford came from his office, checked my wounds to assure himself there was no serious damage, gave me no comfort—in fact, said nothing—took off his jacket, put compound on the wheel, picked up another unpolished Bakelite top, grasped it strongly in his big hands, and burnished the top to shiny brilliance. He then picked up his coat and walked back into his office. He said not a word about my first performance, then or ever. I went back and began to buff tops and do the work. In the many months I worked at that shop before my mission I did not lose another Bakelite top.

The great teacher Howard R. Driggs was asked by an admiring grandson how he in his early nineties retained in his mind and could quote almost endlessly the words of philosophers and poets and prophets. "Well, I had to pay the price of long, consistent labor to acquire and memorize the knowledge," he said, "and then I gave it and I gave it and I gave it until it was mine."

Thus the authority of competence.

Authority of Integrity

And then there is the authority of integrity. This announces to others that this person of authority is honest, that he is fair, that he understands, that he is modest, that he doesn't pretend perfection, that he cares. He can be counted on to listen and to consider and to lead with undeviating decency and appropriate example. He will act with authenticity, with wholeness, being at one with himself, with others, and with God. He is not petty, self-centered, judgmental, anxious to put down; he is a man of integrity.

As I think through the stories of many examples of integrity, I desire to share one only, and it is an example that almost capsulizes all that the good minds among you could supply of example and quotation.

Moroni was in the battlefield. He was facing armies of enemies, and for a time, because of Helaman and his success in another sector, he thought they were winning the war. But things changed. Neither of the Nephite armies received any logistical support; no troops were sent, no food. They began to lose, and, indeed, were losing severely when Moroni sent his second epistle to Pahoran, the governor of the land, calling him to task. He "was angry with the government, because of their indifference concerning the freedom of their country" (Alma 59:13).

Thus he wrote to Pahoran and to those working with him who had been chosen by the people to govern, and in the most intemperate of language he threatened that if they didn't do what they were under obligation to do—that is, support these armies in the field—he would leave the battlefront, come home with an army, and clean up the inner vessel, the inward leadership.

The language is interesting. Their people were being slaughtered, he said. He accused the governor of "thoughtless stupor," saying: "Your brethren . . . have fought and bled out their lives because of their great desires which they had for the welfare of this people; yea, and this they have done when they were about to perish with hunger, because of your exceeding great neglect." (Alma 60:7–9.)

He worked up a great anger: "Could ye suppose that ye could sit upon your thrones, and because of the exceeding goodness of God ye could do nothing and he would deliver you? Behold, if ye have supposed this ye have supposed in vain."

And then he said it: "We know not but what ye are also traitors to your country," and he warned them that if they didn't begin to perform he would take military action against them. "Except ye do administer unto our relief, behold, I come unto you, even in the land of Zarahemla, and smite you with the sword, insomuch that ye can have no more power to impede the progress of this people in the cause of our freedom." And then he attributed to *inspiration* his criticisms of Pahoran and his associates. (Alma 60:7–9, 11, 18, 30, 33.)

In the next chapter, Alma 61, Pahoran's answer is recorded. We don't know very much about Pahoran (though we know quite a bit about Moroni). Pahoran responded: "Behold, I say unto you, Moroni, that I do not joy in your great afflictions, yea, it grieves my soul. But behold, there are those who do joy in your afflictions, yea, insomuch that they have risen up in rebellion against me, and also those of my people who are freemen."

He tells then that he and his associates have had to flee "to the land of Gideon, with as many men as it were possible that I could get. And behold, I have sent a proclamation throughout this part of the land [trying to gather an army to come to your support; but we haven't been able to do what we wanted to do because we ourselves have been forced to flee]." He adds that the rebels "have got possession of the land, or the city, of Zarahemla; they have appointed a king," and so forth. And then a verse I have wept over many times because it reflects by contrast, I suppose, the nature of my own limitations. Pahoran somehow, somehow, manages to meet calmly this accusation, this question about his patriotism, even the suggestion that Moroni has been inspired to believe that he and his associates are traitors. This is how Pahoran answers: "And now, in your epistle you have censured me, but it mattereth not; I am not angry, but do rejoice in the greatness of your heart. I, Pahoran, do not seek for power, save only to retain my judgment-seat that I may preserve the rights and the liberty of my people. My soul standeth fast in that liberty in the which God hath made us free."

And then he defends quietly and modestly what he and his associates have tried to do and tells what they will do. He invites Moroni to return and with him and other loyalists to form an army and engage the enemy.

"It mattereth not; I am not angry, but do rejoice in the greatness of your heart." (Alma 61:2–3, 5–6, 8–9.)

I read what Peter, who had learned to know the Lord, said of him who "reviled not" but left judgment in the hands of one who is just. "Christ [left] us an example, that [we] should follow his steps: who did no sin, neither was guile found in his mouth: who, when he was reviled, reviled not again; when he suffered, he threatened not; but committed himself to him that judgeth righteously: who his own self bare our sins in his own body on the tree, that we, being dead to sins, should live unto righteousness: by whose stripes ye were healed" (1 Peter 2:21–24).

One in a position of authority may endure his day in power without these other mentioned elements of authority, I suppose. One who has the position and the power may live it out, and he may—he may—absent these other elements and qualities, act as did Jehoram anciently. This king of Judah, a young man who reigned in Jerusalem eight years without concern for others, without competence, without integrity, "departed without being desired" (2 Chronicles 21:20).

In Loco Parentis

There are several other things I would like to say, and I will undertake for a few moments to add an illustration or two.

When we talked earlier of "in loco parentis"—the school assuming some of the burdens and blessings of parenthood, caring about what kind of people young people are—there came to my mind the day when, representing the educational system of the Church, I went to the University of Missouri as a trustee and sat in a conference with others from across the land. The theme of the conference really was the abandonment of the notion that universities have anything like the relationship of "in loco parentis" with their students.

I never want to forget the anxiety and fervor expressed by the young student president who came to greet a group of these regents, listened to the latter part of a speech keynoting the demise of "in loco parentis," and then came with obvious distress to the podium. There he quickly filled the role of welcoming us and said some words that I, at least, have not forgotten: "If, in fact, you, representing the universities of the land, reject the responsibility to act for us in the role of parents who care about us, then you are entitled to know that that leaves a whole lot of us without any parents at all."

Whatever our position or experience or function is on this campus, we are acting, you and I, as authority figures to youth.

Sister Hanks was helping me recall a phrase from years ago when I spoke to a national group about young people and said of them that we habitually underestimate their intelligence and overestimate their experience. They are bright, most of them, and very able, but they have had little experience. Let me read a few lines from Shel Silverstein:

GOD'S WHEEL

God says to me with kind of a smile,
"Hey how would you like to be God awhile
And steer the world?"
"Okay," says I, "I'll give it a try.
Where do I set?
How much do I get?
What time is lunch?
When can I quit?"
"Gimme back that wheel," says God,
"I don't think you're quite ready yet."
("God's Wheel," from *A Light in the Attic*
by Shel Silverstein, p. 152. Copyright ©
1981 by Evil Eye Music, Inc. Reprinted by
permission of HarperCollins Publishers.)

They are not quite ready yet.

If you have a heart for sentiment, listen to this:

When we plant a rose seed in the earth, we notice that it is small, but we do not criticize it as "rootless and stemless." We treat it as a seed, giving it the water and nourishment required of a seed. When it first shoots up out of the earth, we don't condemn it as immature and underdeveloped; nor do we criticize the buds for not being open when they appear. We stand in wonder at the process taking place and give the plant the care it needs at each stage of its development. The rose is a rose from the time it is a seed to the time it dies. Within it, at all times, it contains its whole potential. It seems to be constantly in the process of change; yet at each state, at each moment, it is perfectly all right as it is. (W. Timothy Gallwey, *The Inner Game of Tennis* [New York: Random House, 1974], p. 37.)

Finally, let me share with you that as a lad, among the books I was reading I was strangely moved by one book and one incident. The incident and the book were later made into a prominent movie. The book was *Keys of the Kingdom*, by A. J. Cronin, a physician and novelist. In it is the incident of a young priest who was assigned to work with an old, worn, unappreciated parish priest who had given his life to Christ, who had served with great unselfishness but was not responded to or encouraged by his hierarchical superiors. The young priest, brilliant, vigorous, talented, saw this and decided to surrender his vocation. He would not be a priest if this was what happened to those who unselfishly, truly served. With these quiet words of encouragement the older priest urged him not to abandon his calling: "You've got inquisitiveness and tenderness. You're sensible of the distinction between thinking and doubting. . . . And quite the nicest thing about you, my dear boy, is this—you haven't got that bumptious security which springs from dogma rather than from faith." (A. J. Cronin, *The Keys of the Kingdom* [Boston: Little, Brown and Company, 1941], p. 144.)

I would fondly wish, though I honestly do not anticipate, that no teacher or worker will remain at BYU, and no student ever depart, filled with "that bumptious security which springs from dogma rather than from faith," who does not have and is determined to stifle in others "inquisitiveness and tenderness," who is not "sensible of the distinction between thinking and doubting."

I bear witness that in my judgment there is no other function more important than to be able to influence—in his or her inner self, in that part susceptible to nobility and decency, that part which in us is better than we know—the great young people who come along in this coarsening world, wondering. We have so many who are so good, and I marvel that they manage it.

I commend you and congratulate you on your election and selection to serve here. I think you are highly honored, and I really don't care—and perhaps you know that I really mean that—whether you are the plumber fixing a fountain or the gardener planting a garden or the president in his office. We are authority figures, and our outreach, or our interest—or our lack of it—may influence these of little experience but of great capacity to learn.

God bless you and sustain you and strengthen you and help you to be, as Brigham Young once encouraged others to be, gentle with opposite or other viewpoints. He spoke of those who would measure their associates by their own length of bedstead and either cut them off or stretch them to fit if they differed in thought or feeling. Be gracious, he said, the whole world is before us. (See *Journal of Discourses* 8:9.) Don't demean by minimal comprehension the message or the God who gave it. If your view is small, be modest and seek to learn.

Generally speaking, I cannot believe there is a faculty or a staff or an administration superior to those at this school; and I have to say that I love it and believe in it and would do anything I could in this world to promote its interests. May the Lord bless you, I pray in the name of Jesus Christ. Amen.

III

Family

CHAPTER 12

Father as Teacher

Tonight I would like to look with you at a significant theme as it is expressed in a familiar source. I am reinforced in my effort by the hope that you are already in a measure conscious of and committed to the theme and that you
may in more or less intensity be familiar with the treatment of
the theme in the source from which I draw.

My purpose is to consider with you the responsibility of fathers to teach their children, and amidst many possibilities to
confine the source materials exclusively to a few pages of the
Book of Mormon.

While I refer only to the teachings of the fathers, I do not,
of course—as the Lord has not, and as life does not—confine
that responsibility and blessing to fathers or in any sense ex-
clude the contributions or responsibilities or demean the importance of mothers. God has put the expectations and responsibilities upon parents. In my home a widowed mother, a true
Saint, carried the burden alone, which gives me a special consciousness of that part of the story. Many others have had and
are having similar experience.

I mean to shine the Book of Mormon light on the commission of the fathers and fathers-to-be to teach and testify to their
own children. For mothers and mothers-to-be, this exercise

Address given in Brigham Young University Last Lecture series 1 November 1973.

may be helpful in clarifying what you need to be looking for and planning for and trying to accomplish.

The vital importance of parental instruction and example is well understood. Wrote George Herbert, "One father is more than a hundred schoolmasters."

The Lord has given some special instruction in the modern dispensation:

> Little children are redeemed from the foundation of the world through mine Only Begotten;
>
> Wherefore, they cannot sin, for power is not given unto Satan to tempt little children, until they begin to become accountable before me;
>
> For it is given unto them even as I will, according to mine own pleasure, *that great things may be required at the hand of their fathers* (D&C 29:46–48, italics added).

Gospel Charge to All Fathers

The assignment and sobering responsibility seem very clear. That instruction was given in September 1830. In May 1833, at the start of a great declaration on parental responsibility, the Lord said:

> Every spirit of man was innocent in the beginning; and God having redeemed man from the fall, men became again, in their infant state, innocent before God.
>
> And that wicked one cometh and taketh away light and truth, through disobedience, from the children of men, and *because of the tradition of their fathers.*
>
> But I have commanded you to bring up your children in light and truth. (D&C 93:38–40, italics added.)

It is interesting to know that this instruction and the chastisement that followed were given to the First Presidency of the Church and the Presiding Bishop.

To Frederick G. Williams the Lord spoke of condemnation under which President Williams continued, and added:

You have not taught your children light and truth, according to the commandments; and that wicked one hath power, as yet, over you, and this is the cause of your affliction.

And now a commandment I give unto you—if you will be delivered you shall set in order your own house. (D&C 93:42–43, italics added.)

Similar messages were then delivered to Sidney Rigdon and Joseph Smith. Then to Newell K. Whitney came the word that he had need to be chastened, "and set in order his family, and see that they are more diligent and concerned at home, and pray always" (D&C 93:50).

In this series of instructions the Lord emphasized, "What I say unto one I say unto all" (D&C 93:49).

In 1831 there had come what is possibly the admonition best known to Latter-day Saint parents:

And again, inasmuch as parents have children in Zion, or in any of her stakes which are organized, that *teach them not* to understand the doctrine of repentance, faith in Christ the Son of the living God, and of baptism and the gift of the Holy Ghost by the laying on of hands, when eight years old, the sin be upon the heads of the parents.

For this shall be a law unto the inhabitants of Zion, or in any of her stakes which are organized.

And their children shall be baptized for the remission of their sins when eight years old, and receive the laying on of the hands.

And they shall also *teach their children* to pray, and to walk uprightly before the Lord. (D&C 68:25–28, italics added.)

To this is added that parents who "humble yourselves even in the depths of humility, calling on the name of the Lord daily, and standing steadfastly in the faith. . . ." shall have great blessings, including this, that they will "*teach* [their children] to walk in the ways of truth and soberness; [they] will *teach* them to love one another, and to serve one another." (Mosiah 4:11, 15, italics added.) So the message is clear; children are innocent, the devil has no accessibility to them until they begin to become accountable, and this that great things may be required at the hand of their fathers. Though children are innocent before

God, they are susceptible to the example and instruction of their fathers. The wicked one can take away light and truth through disobedience and because of the tradition of their fathers.

In Shakespeare's *Henry VIII* are these lines:

> If I chance to talk a little wild, forgive me;
> I had it from my father.

We are told that Diogenes struck the father when the son swore.

Children do listen and observe. On that we must count. But it must be said clearly that experience and records teach us that they do not *always* listen or comprehend or follow the path lovingly laid out for them. Lucifer, Cain, Laman and Lemuel, young Alma and the sons of Mosiah, and many others are sobering witness of this.

But in the same heavenly home with Lucifer was the Christ; in the same family with Cain was Abel; Nephi and Sam were taught by the same parents and in the same household where Laman and Lemuel received tutelage; and it is notable and encouraging that young Alma and the sons of Mosiah later turned completely around from their destructive course.

Thus every father must do all that he can do to raise his children in righteousness. To do less is tragic and foolish in the extreme. It is reported that Samuel Taylor Coleridge once was in the company of a farmer renowned for his productive acres, sculptured gardens, and bright children. Coleridge heard him say that while he hoped his children would grow up to be God-fearing, prayerful, religious people, he would never prejudice them in favor of religion by teaching them religious principles or taking them to church. They must grow up and decide for themselves.

Coleridge reportedly answered the man in this vein: "Bravo. This is a very progressive idea. Why do you not apply it to your fields and orchards and gardens in the future? Do not prejudice the soil to seed or weeding or cultivation, the trees to pruning or thinning, the gardens to bulbs or planting. Why not see if they will just grow up and decide to be what you hope they will be."

So let's look in the Book of Mormon for a few moments at one of its most significant and powerful contributions: the records of fathers who taught their children. Consider Lehi, Alma, and Mormon, and much more briefly three others—Jacob, Benjamin, and Helaman. There is remarkable uniqueness within the uniformity of their teachings.

What did they teach?

—The revealed truth, principles of eternal significance, theology that was basic and beautiful.

—Sound counsel of unassailable practicality and observable effectiveness.

—Values, upon which a life, a culture, a civilization could be built.

—Opinion, occasionally, well labeled, but there is an interesting absence of theories.

—They fervently urged righteousness, and particularly in Alma's case sorrowfully noted their own fallibility and departure from righteous behavior, with the heavy burdens that followed.

—And uniformly they repeatedly bore powerful personal witness, bore their testimonies of Christ and His Father and the eternal plan of salvation, of redemption, of mercy, and of happiness.

Lehi

First consider Lehi. What of his teaching?

By instruction, witness, and example, Lehi gave powerful gifts to his children. Nephi began his record with the remarkable tribute of respect and love: "I, Nephi, having been born of goodly parents, therefore I was taught somewhat in all the learning of my father" (1 Nephi 1:1).

With his son, Lehi shared his great visions and dreams of God, the Christ, the Apostles, the warnings and promises of the Almighty. These were basic in Nephi's earliest declaration that he "had a great knowledge of the goodness and the mysteries of God," and in giving him the foundation for the testimony with which he begins the record: "And I know that the record which I make is true." Nephi later declared that the Lord had blessed him to believe all the words which had been spoken by his father, a statement which he repeated to the Spirit of the Lord: "Yea, thou knowest that I believe all the words of my father" (1 Nephi 11:5).

One of Lehi's great visions, reported to his family and later given also to Nephi, involved the tree and its fruit, the path, the rod, the great and spacious building, the depths of water, and the mists of darkness. Through this vision Lehi's family and all of us learn that there are various responses to the love of God and His efforts to bless His children. There are:

1. Those who do not care or who are cynically and mockingly arrayed against the truth.
2. Those who get feet on the path but find it obscured by the mists of darkness, which are the temptations of the devil, and they wander off and are lost.
3. Those who walk the path holding the rod, partake of the fruit of the tree, and taste its sweetness, but then become ashamed because of the pressure of those who fill the great building—who mock and point the finger of scorn. The building represents the so-called wisdom and pride of the world and its vain imaginations. In the vision, so powerful was the pressure of those in the building that the members of the group who had reached the tree and tasted the fruit fell away in the forbidden paths and were lost.
4. Those who hold onto the rod of iron (the word of God) and press their way forward until they have eaten the fruit, have known its sweetness, and are filled in their souls with exceedingly great joy. In the vision their immediate response was to desire that their families should partake of the fruit also, for they "knew that it was desirable above all other fruits."

Thus Lehi taught his children early that there is opposition in all things; that through the agency of man choices are made which determine the course of life, mortal and eternal; that there is a devil and there will be pressures and enemies and those who succumb to them; and that, notwithstanding that the sweetest of all blessings come through feeding upon the love and the pleasing word of God and sharing it, yet there will be many who disdain it, and many who are misled before they really taste it, and some who wander from the path even though they have known the sweetness of the fruits.

All of these great lessons Lehi subsequently explained in detail to his children, teaching under the revelations of God and the power of the Spirit.

Lehi taught his children the truth about the land of promise and the conditions on which they should enjoy it and through which it should be preserved (see 2 Nephi 1).

To his young son Jacob, who was born in the days of tribulation in the wilderness and had suffered much affliction, Lehi delivered one of the most important, enlightening, and encouraging of truths. Through his travail Jacob had learned "the greatness of God," and was taught that God "shall consecrate thine afflictions for thy gain" (2 Nephi 2:2). Like all else the Father taught, this lesson is true this evening and personal to each of us.

In the same magnificent chapter Lehi gave his son a witness about opposition, explained the true role of father Adam in God's plan, and testified: "Adam fell that men might be; and men are, that they might have joy."

In powerful language Lehi taught that through the redemption of the Messiah men have "become free forever, knowing good from evil; to act for themselves and not to be acted upon. . . . Wherefore, men are free according to the flesh; and all things are given them which are expedient unto man. And they are free to choose liberty and eternal life, through the great Mediator of all men, or to choose captivity and death, according to the captivity and power of the devil; for he seeketh that all men might be miserable like unto himself." (2 Nephi 2:26–27.)

Teaching the coming of a latter-day prophet, blessing his grandchildren before he died, Lehi pleaded with his sons to choose the way of eternal life and not of eternal death. He said:

> I desire that ye should remember to observe the statutes and the judgments of the Lord; behold, this hath been the anxiety of my soul from the beginning. . . .

O my sons, that . . . ye might be a choice and a favored people of the Lord. . . .

. . . Arise from the dust, my sons, and be men. . . .

Awake, my sons; put on the armor of righteousness. Shake off the chains with which ye are bound, and come forth out of obscurity, and arise from the dust. (2 Nephi 1:16, 19, 21, 23.)

To Laman and Lemuel he had earlier yearningly pleaded: "O that thou mightest be like unto this river, continually running into the fountain of all righteousness! . . . O that thou mightest be like unto this valley, firm and steadfast, and immovable in keeping the commandments of the Lord!" (1 Nephi 2:9–10.)

All of this and much more Lehi left his children, bearing his testimony that "the Lord hath redeemed my soul from hell; I have beheld his glory, and I am encircled about eternally in the arms of his love" (2 Nephi 1:15).

His powerful testimony of Jesus and the importance of bearing the message is summarized in these marvelous verses:

Wherefore, redemption cometh in and through the Holy Messiah; for he is full of grace and truth.

Behold he offereth himself a sacrifice for sin, to answer the ends of the law, unto all those who have a broken heart and a contrite spirit; and unto none else can the ends of the law be answered.

Wherefore, how great the importance to make these things known unto the inhabitants of the earth, that they may know that there is no flesh that can dwell in the presence of God, save it be through the merits, and mercy, and grace of the Holy Messiah, who layeth down his life according to the flesh, and taketh it again by the power of the Spirit, that he may bring to pass the resurrection of the dead, being the first that should rise. (2 Nephi 2:6–8.)

Jacob

The power and efficacy and solemnity of Jacob's teaching is well known, but the sweetest and most moving effect of them is in the report of Enos, a not untypical son who heard and saw his father's convictions but did not respond to them until one day, while he was hunting beasts in the forest,

> the words which I had often heard my father speak concerning eternal life, and the joy of the saints, sunk deep into my heart.
> And my soul hungered; and I kneeled down before my Maker, and I cried unto him in mighty prayer and supplication for mine own soul; and all the day long did I cry unto him; yea, and when the night came I did still raise my voice high that it reached the heavens.
> And there came a voice unto me saying: Enos, thy sins are forgiven thee, and thou shalt be blessed. (Enos 1:3–5.)

The rest of the impressive story of Enos in that one short chapter is evidence enough of the foundations laid by a noble father and an unnamed mother, foundations that caused this restless, late-blooming man of strength and faith to spend his life preaching Christ and striving to bring about the welfare of God's children. At the end he said, "I rejoice in the day when my mortal shall put on immortality, and shall stand before him; then shall I see his face with pleasure, and he will say unto me: Come unto me, ye blessed, there is a place prepared for you in the mansions of my Father" (Enos 1:27).

Benjamin

King Benjamin taught his people some of the most moving and marvelous lessons that any prophet has ever shared. His sermon recorded in the first part of the book of Mosiah is perhaps unparalleled among the prophets in its beauty and understandability and importance. But beyond all this he found time to teach his three sons "in all the language of his fathers, that thereby they might become men of understanding; and that they might know concerning the prophecies which had been spoken by the mouths of their fathers, which were delivered them by the hand of the Lord" (Mosiah 1:2). He taught them the value of scriptures and explained the indispensability of the recorded word of the Lord. To his sons he bore this witness of the holy word:

> O my sons, I would that ye should remember that these sayings are true, and also that these records are true. . . . And we can know of their surety because we have them before our eyes.
>
> And now, my sons, I would that ye should remember to search them diligently, that ye may profit thereby; and I would that ye should keep the commandments of God, that ye may prosper in the land according to the promises which the Lord made unto our fathers.
>
> And many more things did king Benjamin teach his sons, which are not written in this book. (Mosiah 1:6–8.)

Alma

To Alma the Younger, grateful recipient of God's forgiveness for his rebelliousness and unfaithfulness, it was left to provide some of the most marvelous and moving instructions and inspiration of the Book of Mormon, and indeed of all history. He taught his sons individually and gave them the benefit and blessing of his faith and of the experiences of his life.

To Helaman he sorrowfully reported the iniquities of his youth and testified of the tender mercies of God. The declaration is moving and instructive and deeply honest.

In the course of his destructive behavior, Alma was turned around by an angel who delivered a message that is of great importance in all times and of especial importance in these times: "If thou wilt of thyself be destroyed, seek no more to destroy the church of God" (Alma 36:9).

Alma described what happened after the angel spoke to him and he had fallen to the earth.

> But I was racked with eternal torment, for my soul was harrowed up to the greatest degree and racked with all my sins.
>
> Yea, I did remember all my sins and iniquities, for which I was tormented with the pains of hell; yea, I saw that I had rebelled against my God, and that I had not kept his holy commandments.

. . . The very thought of coming into the presence of my God did rack my soul with inexpressible horror.

Oh, thought I, that I could be banished and become extinct both soul and body, that I might not be brought to stand in the presence of my God, to be judged of my deeds.

And now, for three days and for three nights was I racked, even with the pains of a damned soul.

And it came to pass that as I was thus racked with torment, while I was harrowed up by the memory of my many sins, behold, I remembered also to have heard my father prophesy unto the people concerning the coming of one Jesus Christ, a Son of God, to atone for the sins of the world.

Now, as my mind caught hold upon this thought, I cried within my heart: O Jesus, thou Son of God, have mercy on me, who am in the gall of bitterness, and am encircled about by the everlasting chains of death.

And now, behold, when I thought this, I could remember my pains no more; yea, I was harrowed up by the memory of my sins no more.

And oh, what joy, and what marvelous light I did behold; yea, my soul was filled with joy as exceeding as was my pain!

Yea, I say unto you, my son, that there could be nothing so exquisite and so bitter as were my pains. Yea, and again I say unto you, my son, that on the other hand, there can be nothing so exquisite and sweet as was my joy. (Alma 36:12–21.)

Surrounding him with this sobering account, Alma taught Helaman three great messages which every faithful father will want to deliver to his own son.

First Message:

And now, O my son Helaman, behold, thou art in thy youth, and therefore, I beseech of thee that thou wilt hear my words and learn of me; for I do know that whosoever shall put their trust in God shall be supported in their trials, and their troubles, and their afflictions, and shall be lifted up at the last day.

And I would not that ye think that I know of myself—not of the temporal but of the spiritual, not of the carnal mind but of God. (Alma 36:3–4.)

Second Message:

Yea, and from that time even until now, I have labored without ceasing, that I might bring souls unto repentance; that I might bring them to taste of the exceeding joy of which I did taste; that they might also be born of God, and be filled with the Holy Ghost.

Yea, and now behold, O my son, the Lord doth give me exceedingly great joy in the fruit of my labors;

For because of the word which he has imparted unto me, behold, many have been born of God, and have tasted as I have tasted, and have seen eye to eye as I have seen; therefore they do know of these things of which I have spoken, as I do know; and the knowledge which I have is of God.

And I have been supported under trials and troubles of every kind, yea, and in all manner of afflictions. (Alma 36:24–27.)

Third Message:

But behold, my son, this is not all; for ye ought to know as I do know, that inasmuch as ye shall keep the commandments of God ye shall prosper in the land; and ye ought to know also, that inasmuch as ye will not keep the commandments of God ye shall be cut off from his presence. (Alma 36:30.)

In a few words with great meaning Alma expressed an attitude and gave his sons direction as to many matters yet to be revealed: "Now these mysteries are not yet fully made known unto me; therefore I shall forbear" (Alma 37:11).

The same wonderful chapter, Alma 37, contains some of the sweetest and finest counsel on record from a father to his son, particularly to a missionary son:

Preach unto them repentance, and faith on the Lord Jesus Christ; teach them to humble themselves and to be meek and lowly in heart; teach them to withstand every temptation of the devil, with their faith on the Lord Jesus Christ.

Teach them to never be weary of good works, but to be meek and lowly in heart; for such shall find rest to their souls.

O, remember, my son, and learn wisdom in thy youth; yea, learn in thy youth to keep the commandments of God.

Yea, and cry unto God for all thy support; yea, let all thy doings be unto the Lord, and whithersoever thou goest let it be in
the Lord; yea, let all thy thoughts be directed unto the Lord; yea,
let the affections of thy heart be placed upon the Lord forever.

Counsel with the Lord in all thy doings, and he will direct
thee for good; yea, when thou liest down at night lie down unto
the Lord, that he may watch over you in your sleep; and when
thou risest in the morning let thy heart be full of thanks unto
God; and if ye do these things, ye shall be lifted up at the last day.
(Alma 37:33–37.)

Alma's choice tribute to his son Shiblon is recorded in chapter 38, including his witness, his personal testimony of Christ
(verse 9), and the remarkable counsel in verses 10 through 14
that contains the important words, "See that ye bridle all your
passions, that ye may be filled with love."

In chapters 39 through 42 of the book that bears his name
it is left for Alma to provide for his son Corianton and all the
rest of us what to me is the most meaningful and realistic counsel ever written for the sinner—that is, for each of us. In it are
all the lessons the counselor should need—that counselor who
is laboring to preserve the spiritual life of the sinner.

Corianton was guilty of unchastity. He was proud and
boastful, not impressed with the gravity of his sin or the seriousness of his position. Alma forthrightly and with great clarity explained his jeopardy; called him to repentance; admonished
him: "Counsel with your elder brothers in your undertakings. . . .
And give heed to their counsel." He spoke the very message of
his heart: "And now the Spirit of the Lord doth say unto me:
Command thy children to do good, lest they lead away the
hearts of many people to destruction; therefore I command
you, my son, in the fear of God, that ye refrain from your iniquities; that ye turn to the Lord with all your mind, might, and
strength; that ye lead away the hearts of no more to do wick-
edly; but rather return unto them, and acknowledge your faults
and that wrong which ye have done" (Alma 39:12–13).

In the midst of this he spoke some of the saddest and most
poignant words that could come to a wayward son from a heartbroken, faithful father: "When they saw your conduct they
would not believe in my words."

The famed chapter 40 of Alma declares the reality of the resurrection for all men and teaches that there is a time between death and resurrection. The prophet declares it with certainty: "There is a time appointed unto men that they shall rise from the dead; and there is a space between the time of death and the resurrection" (Alma 40:9).

In chapter 41 is the prophet's assurance to his son that we shall all be granted the eternal consequences of our desires—happiness and good and righteousness if we wish, evil if that is what we really want. The way is prepared for all, "that whosoever will may walk therein and be saved" (Alma 41:8).

As he explains the meaning of the "natural" or "carnal" state, Alma delivers the declaration, "Wickedness never was happiness" (Alma 41:10).

Those who are in "a state of nature, . . . a carnal state, are in the gall of bitterness and in the bonds of iniquity; they are without God in the world, and they have gone contrary to the nature of God; therefore, they are in a state contrary to the nature of happiness" (Alma 41:11).

He teaches the true nature of restoration—that is, mercy restored to the merciful, justice to the just, and good to those who do good: "For that which ye do send out shall return unto you again, and be restored (Alma 41:15).

In the magnificent finale, recorded in chapter 42, Alma teaches Corianton the relationship of mercy and justice; speaks to him of the plan of salvation, the plan of redemption, the plan of mercy, and the plan of happiness; teaches him of temporal and spiritual death; and bears his testimony that "whosoever will come may come and partake of the waters of life freely; and whosoever will not come the same is not compelled to come; but in the last day it shall be restored unto him according to his deeds" (Alma 42:27).

The summary of it all is in the last three verses of that chapter:

> And now, my son, I desire that ye should let these things trouble you no more, and only let your sins trouble you, with that trouble which shall bring you down unto repentance.
>
> O my son, I desire that ye should deny the justice of God no more. Do not endeavor to excuse yourself in the least point because of your sins, by denying the justice of God; but do you let

the justice of God, and his mercy, and his long-suffering have full sway in your heart; and let it bring you down to the dust in humility.

And now, O my son, ye are called of God to preach the word unto this people. And now, my son, go thy way, declare the word with truth and soberness, that thou mayest bring souls unto repentance, that the great plan of mercy may have claim upon them. (Alma 42:29–31.)

Helaman

Helaman's teaching to his sons consisted partly in giving them the honored names of the early Lehi and Nephi, so that, as he said: "When ye remember your names ye may remember them; and when ye remember them ye may remember their works; and when ye remember their works ye may know how that it is said, and also written, that they were good" (Helaman 5:6). We should note too his wonderful testimony to his sons as to his faith in Christ: "There is no other way nor means whereby man can be saved, only through the atoning blood of Jesus Christ. . . . And now, my sons, remember, remember that it is upon the rock of our Redeemer, who is Christ, the Son of God, that ye must build your foundation." (Helaman 5:9, 12.)

Apart from these references let us note only the effect of a great father's teachings in the lives of his sons: "They did remember his words; and therefore they went forth, keeping the commandments of God, to teach the word of God among all the people" (Helaman 5:14).

Mormon

The last of the father-teachers whom we shall mention is Mormon, whose instructions on faith, hope, and charity are recorded in chapter 7 of the book of Moroni. Mormon taught his son and others:

For behold, God hath said a man being evil cannot do that which is good; for if he offereth a gift, or prayeth unto God, except he shall do it with real intent it profiteth him nothing.

For behold, it is not counted unto him for righteousness.

For behold, if a man being evil giveth a gift, he doeth it grudgingly; wherefore it is counted unto him the same as if he had retained the gift; wherefore he is counted evil before God.

And likewise also is it counted evil unto a man, if he shall pray and not with real intent of heart; yea, and it profiteth him nothing, for God receiveth none such. (Moroni 7:6–9.)

All things which are good cometh of God; and that which is evil cometh of the devil. . . .

. . . That which is of God inviteth and enticeth to do good continually; wherefore, every thing which inviteth and enticeth to do good, and to love God, and to serve him, is inspired of God. (Moroni 7:12–13.)

For behold, the Spirit of Christ is given to every man, that he may know good from evil; wherefore, I show unto you the way to judge; for every thing which inviteth to do good, and to persuade to believe in Christ, is sent forth by the power and gift of Christ; wherefore ye may know with a perfect knowledge it is of God (Moroni 7:16).

Mormon's testimony of Christ was summarized in this: "For he hath answered the ends of the law, and he claimeth all those who have faith in him; and they who have faith in him will cleave unto every good thing; wherefore he advocateth the cause of the children of men" (Moroni 7:28).

Mormon teaches the first principles, the importance of hope, which, along with faith, a person cannot have "save he shall be meek, and lowly of heart" (Moroni 7:43).

And if a man be meek and lowly in heart, and confesses by the power of the Holy Ghost that Jesus is the Christ, he must needs have charity. . . .

But charity is the pure love of Christ, and it endureth forever; and whoso is found possessed of it at the last day, it shall be well with him.

Wherefore, my beloved brethren, pray unto the Father with all the energy of heart, that ye may be filled with this love, which he hath bestowed upon all who are true followers of his Son, Jesus Christ; that ye may become the sons of God. (Moroni 7:44, 47–48.)

Moroni chapters 8 and 9 are letters from father Mormon to his missionary son soon after the latter's calling to the ministry. Disputations have occurred concerning infant baptism, and Mormon answers them plainly. Mormon declares that it is solemn mockery before God to baptize little children.

> Behold I say unto you that this thing shall ye teach—repentance and baptism unto those who are accountable and capable of committing sin; yea, teach parents that they must repent and be baptized, and humble themselves as their little children, and they shall all be saved with their little children.
>
> And their little children need no repentance, neither baptism. . . .
>
> But little children are alive in Christ, even from the foundation of the world. . . . also all they that are without the law. (Moroni 8:10–12, 22.)

Repentance is for those who have the law:

> And the first fruits of repentance is baptism; and baptism cometh by faith unto the fulfilling the commandments; and the fulfilling the commandments bringeth remission of sins;
>
> And the remission of sins bringeth meekness, and lowliness of heart; and because of meekness and lowliness of heart cometh the visitation of the Holy Ghost, which Comforter filleth with hope and perfect love, which love endureth by diligence unto prayer, until the end shall come (Moroni 8:25–26).

As Mormon concludes his last recorded letter to his son, the occurrence of tragic things among his people compels him to speak of the depravity of their behavior and their perversion. They are "without principle, and past feeling" and Mormon cannot commend them to God.

In his love he can recommend his faithful son to God, and pray for him, and trust that they will meet again so Mormon can deliver the sacred records to Moroni. The summation of Mormon's grief is in the recognition that a people who only a few years before had been a civil and delightsome people had become so perverse that the hand of God in judgment could not be stayed from them.

In one of the most beautiful of all passages, Mormon bears
his testimony: "My son, be faithful in Christ; and may not the
things which I have written grieve thee, to weigh thee down
unto death; but may Christ lift thee up, and may his sufferings
and death [and resurrection], and . . . his mercy and long-suffering, and the hope of his glory and of eternal life, rest in your
mind forever" (Moroni 9:25).

CHAPTER 13

Seeing the Five A's

As I have met some of the fine chaplains who represent us across the earth and are here for conference, I have been reminded of some wonderful memories. One of them made me smile as I recalled one of our brethren who had finished his tour in Vietnam and was leaving as we arrived in Saigon. He said, "I am leaving this place with mixed feelings—joy and gladness." Brethren, we think of you with those kinds of mixed feelings, knowing your great contributions across the earth.

I smiled to myself again today as I thought about an afternoon a little while ago at the National Boy Scout Jamboree when, sloshing through the rain, soaked myself, I saw a youngster sliding down a mud bank into a mud puddle. He was as wet and muddy as anyone could get. I said to him, "Son, you don't look too unhappy with the rain."

He said, "No, sir."

I said, "You don't wish you were home, then?"

"No, sir. They would never let me do this at home!"

Address given at general conference October 1977.

A Regular Dad

It is about two such boys and two good men that I'd like to talk tonight, for they form the central theme of my remarks.

The boys are special young men, like all of you, and the men are choice leaders in Church and community. I met one of these fathers and his five-year-old son just a few days ago. The father told me of a recent conversation with his boy in which he explained that elections were coming soon and that he was being urged to run again for the office of mayor. "Shall I run for mayor?" he said.

"Uh-uh," said the lad.

"Well," said the father, "some Church leaders are coming to our stake next week, and they may ask me to continue to serve as stake president. Shall I say yes if they ask me?"

"Uh-uh," said the boy.

"What do you want to me to do?" the father laughed.

His son said, "I just want a regular dad."

The Five A's

The other story was equally interesting and significant to me. The family in this story has a tradition of educational accomplishment, and the father was shaken a bit when his wife brought him their high school son's report card with his first C on it. Dad brooded over the matter, and when the son came home he invited him into the study, sternly confronted him with the card, and said, "Son, what is this I see on your report card?"

"Well, Dad," replied the boy, "I hope you see the five A's."

We can all understand that it may be difficult for a boy to realize that his father can be a regular dad and do other important things too. And it may be difficult on occasion for men to see the A's on the report card when there is a C there. So let me speak a few words tonight to men who once were boys and to boys who are fast becoming men. Men remember being boys, but boys, I'm sure, have a hard time imagining how it will be to be a man. But you boys will become men, you know—some kind of men—and it is very important to you and all whom your life will touch that you be regular boys in every wonderful sense of the term, so you can become regular men.

As men who are trying to do a number of other important things as well as live the gospel we realize that none of our involvements matters much—and accomplishing anything else will not bring much satisfaction—if we have not done all we should at home.

As to the five *A*'s and the *C*, all of us must be reminded that while perfection is a worthy goal and while good grades are important, yet individuals have different capacities and gifts, and imperfection is with all of us; and school grades that represent honest and earnest effort should be acceptable. What really matters, after all, is what kind of people we are. The problems of the world are at root all human problems, and the opportunities in the world are at root all human opportunities. Those who help solve the problems and make the most of the opportunities are those whose priorities are straight, who are mature and strong in character.

Fatherless Boys

There is another consideration we must think of as we talk of fathers and sons. Many boys grow up without a father. My own dad died when I was a little boy, so I am especially aware that many boys have no father at all, or maybe a father who doesn't provide the best example and instruction he could. So in addition to being good fathers to our own sons, true men must reach out to show concern for other boys also. And even boys blessed with wonderful mothers need men to look up to, to love and follow. They need men to teach them how to be men; otherwise they may learn, as so many do, from imitating men who themselves have it all wrong, who may have perverse ideas, who think that manhood rests in muscles or money, in crime or crudity, in drugs or conquests. I cannot prescribe how many of the available meetings and activities we individually should go to, but it should be our first priority to take whatever time is necessary to keep faith with our families and to be a friend to a boy or girl who needs some help.

Support from Church Programs

Use your imaginations with me for a moment. Imagine that I am drawing a star at one end of a chalkboard. That star represents a boy named Alan. I will draw a tight circle around the star representing Alan's good family, including a mother who loves him very much and a dad who talks to him and listens to him and spends quality time with him.

On the other end of the chalkboard I will draw another star representing Dick. Dick is not so fortunate. He doesn't have a family like Al's. If he gets any help, it will have to be from outside his home.

Now draw some lines, radiating like spokes in a wheel, from the circle of Alan's family and from the star representing Dick. Imagine writing on those lines the forces for good that would be available to each of the boys if all of us were doing our jobs well in the programs of the Church: leaders in Primary, Sunday School, Young Men, Young Women, Scouting, seminary; Aaronic Priesthood quorum associates and presidencies; quorum advisers; home teachers. Melchizedek Priesthood quorum and Relief Society leaders would be there also, of course, for both Dick and Al, because while the best of families needs all the sustaining support it can get, a boy without a father to guide him is in even greater need of friends, especially those who could help him form an image of what a good man should be.

All of these forces for good would be coordinated by a strong bishopric who pray humbly, plan wisely, organize carefully, delegate with confidence, and efficiently check up, and who would thus have time to give the personal attention that young men and young women need and that they say they appreciate more than time spent in more formal associations in which others than the bishopric could as well lead out.

A Regular Boy

What happens when what we have been imagining actually occurs? Let me tell you about one young man I know personally who got that kind of attention and made an appropriate response.

Not long ago and not far away a boy entered a pharmacist's shop, told the proprietor that he was Bob Brown, son of Mrs. Helen Brown, and inquired whether there was any possibility for him to work at the pharmacy to pay for medicine that the store owner had supplied to the family but for which he had not yet been paid. Mr. Jones didn't really need any additional help, but he was so impressed by the unusual conscientiousness of this seventeen-year-old high school boy that he made arrangements for Bob to work at the store part-time on Saturdays.

That first day of diligent work greatly impressed the businessman, who at the completion of it handed the young man an envelope containing twelve dollars—the wages agreed upon. The boy took two one-dollar bills from the envelope and asked Mr. Jones to give him change for one of them. Bob put the other dollar bill and twenty cents in his pocket, deposited the eighty cents change in the envelope with the ten-dollar bill, and handed the money to Mr. Jones to apply to the family account, asking if that division of wages was agreeable to the pharmacist.

Mr. Jones tried to insist that Bob keep a larger portion of the money. "You'll need some money for school," he said, "and besides, I've already decided to increase your pay in the future. Why don't you keep at least half of the twelve dollars?"

"No, sir," said the seventeen-year-old. "Maybe later I could keep a little more, but today I would like to pay the ten dollars and eighty cents on our bill."

At that moment some of Bob's friends came by and invited him to attend a movie with them. He said he couldn't, that he had to go home. They continued to tease him to go with them until finally he informed them firmly that he didn't have any money and couldn't go with them. Mr. Jones, observing all of this, was about to intervene again to offer money to Bob when one of the boys who had playfully jostled him heard the twenty cents rattle in Bob's pocket. The bantering began again, because obviously he did have some money. Quietly Bob finally said: "Look, guys, I do have a little money but it isn't mine; it's my tithing. Now take off, will you, please. I need to get home to see how Mom's doing."

When Bob and the others had left the store, Mr. Jones went to the telephone and called a physician friend. "Doctor," he said, "I have been filling your prescriptions for years and have long admired your reputation as a fine surgeon. I've also known you are a Mormon bishop, but I have never had any interest in your religion. But I now have one of your boys working for me who is so different that I need to learn about a religion that can produce a young man like that."

Arrangements were made, and the pebble dropped into the life of Mr. Jones by Bob Brown began the extending circles that to this point have gently washed the druggist and members of his family and many others into a warm, loving life as fellow citizens with the Saints in the household of God.

Somehow, early in his life Bob has mastered principles and developed character that set him apart from most others. He is a regular boy in every choice sense of the description. Can anyone doubt that he will be an equally fine man, a good husband, a regular dad, a concerned leader who will help many others?

Responsibility for Family

The Church must and always will continue to place great emphasis on the family, because strong, loyal families are the heart of society. No nation will ever be stronger than the strength of its homes. No agency or institution can do what the home should do.

But we must take people—boys and girls, men and women—where they are, as they are, in the imperfect conditions that so widely exist, in the personal imperfections which are universal. We cannot escape responsibility for our families and others whose lives we might touch, nor can we in good conscience ever cease pulling for them and praying for them and trying to help them. If they make wrong decisions, follow the false programs that many of their peers pursue, still we will love them and suffer with them and work with them and wait for them, even as the father in the Lord's parable waited for the prodigal, who finally came to his senses and headed home: "When he was yet a great way off, his father saw him, and had compassion, and ran, and fell on his neck, and kissed him" (Luke 15:20). We will watch and pray, even as the Lord himself waits with godly mercy, as He declared through His prophet twenty-seven hundred years ago: "And therefore will the Lord wait, that he may be gracious unto you, and therefore will he be exalted, that he may have mercy upon you" (Isaiah 30:18).

As you young men (and the fine young women you will one day have the privilege to marry) accept your responsibility to strengthen the families and build sound relationships in the homes where you now live, and as we who are adults seek to help you, all of us are under sacred obligation to reach out in friendship and love for each other and for others—young associates, young brothers and sisters—who do not have in their homes or their lives what so many of us are blessed, or could be blessed, to enjoy.

Two Examples

Now let me give you two examples of the application of all of this as I have been blessed to observe it.

Only a few days ago in Arizona, as I was at the pulpit in a conference meeting, a tiny boy came walking down the aisle and up on the stand, perhaps searching for a mother in the choir, maybe just investigating. He wasn't making any fuss, but he was a delightful little boy and I couldn't refrain from pausing a moment and talking with him. I asked him his name and where his mommy and daddy were, and at that point a tall, handsome young man stood in the chapel and advanced to retrieve his child. When the father took his son in his arms in front of the pulpit he kissed him, and I had to swallow a quick lump in my throat. There was no embarrassment, no spanking, no yanking, no anger. There was just the gentle kiss and a loving hug in those big strong arms, and for all of us present a warm, tender, memorable experience from a fortunate youngster and a wise, mature, regular dad.

Recently I visited the junior Sunday School meeting in connection with the stake conference to which I was assigned. As I entered the room I saw a little girl who was crying and looking very lost and very, very frightened—apparently her parents had deposited her and gone on to the meeting with the big people. But in a moment a loving young teacher reached her, knelt by her, put her arms around her, and comforted her. The sobs turned to sniffles, and peace began to enter a little heart.

Just then the second act in the drama began. Another youngster appeared and started to cry also, fearful, and feeling alone as the other had. The young teacher, still holding the first little one, reached the second child, knelt by her, and enveloped her in her arms. As she did I heard her say to the first little girl, "Ellen, this young lady is frightened and lonesome. Will you help me make her feel welcome?"

The first youngster, her sniffles barely dried, nodded, and the two little children, in the safe haven of the teacher's arms, supported each other and soon both were quieted. The teacher put three chairs together and sat between the two of them, a hand gently resting on each.

When I left that morning I thought I had seen as clearly as I am capable of seeing how the Lord expects us to treat each other, and how wonderful it is to have someone who has lived a little longer and learned to love, to reach out and help us, and then help us help others.

In the scriptures is a magnificent sermon in a single line that by extension can be a reminder of our responsibility towards others. In quoting it I interpolate an additional word: "For how shall I go up to my father, and the lad [or lass] be not with me?" (Genesis 44:34.)

God bless us, young men and women, to be what God permits us and expects us to be. In the name of Jesus Christ. Amen.

CHAPTER 14

Daughters of God

I thought this morning of the young man who came home bringing his report card, which was not quite as good as usual.

His dad said, "Son, is this another report card that takes you to the top of your class?"

The son said, "No, sir, I'm sorry; this leaves me second."

The father said: "Second? Second to whom?"

The boy answered, "Mary Jones."

"Second to Mary Jones, a mere girl?"

Said the boy, "Dad, girls aren't so mere anymore."

Well, I think they are not, and I believe I will couple with that little introduction an assignment Sister Hanks gave me once on a time to learn a little quatrain that had come out in the newspaper:

> "It was in women's liberation
> That my freedom began,"
> Said the Fuller Brush lady
> To the Avon man.

Some things change with the times; others remain steadfast.

Address given at Melbourne area conference February 1976.

All God's Blessings in Time

I have the great responsibility in the Church of being managing director of the Melchizedek Priesthood MIA, which includes, as you know, all single people in the Church eighteen years of age and older. And so I was especially touched, as some of you must have been in your hearts, to hear President Tanner's reference to that choice group of ladies in the Church for whom the timetable, at least so far, has not been as they would wish it.

I had the remarkable blessing of living in the home of a lady, a great lady, a grand lady who, after her husband's death—my father's death—lived without a companion for forty-five years until her death. I grew up in a home where there were three wonderful sisters. I found and married a wife of comparable quality, and we have four daughters. So there is in me some sense not only of committed responsibility, assigned responsibility, but of personal interest and deep involvement in the lives of those whom God has especially blessed, as he has you.

It would be a wonderful thing if there could come to pass for each of God's choicest daughters all the fulness of blessing that each would wish and that we would wish for them. But it is a fact that not all have all those blessings in this world. It would be, again, wonderful if we could control this situation, but we cannot. Perhaps in the passing of time there are those of you here who fit the description of not having had the timetable work out quite as you would wish it, or of having had other experiences, such as my mother's, that make your situation less desirable than you wish. We would like you to know that the Church officially, and we who serve personally, are deeply conscious of that reality. We pray for you. We have a magnificent group of people who are working prayerfully to try to be helpful. We want you to know there is a place for you and for others who may not be here tonight.

For all of God's daughters there will be the opportunity to enjoy all of God's blessings—sometime, somewhere. There *is* a place in the Church for you. There *is* a life of worthwhile quality for you. So as we speak tonight of mothers and daughters, we are conscious that not all here are mothers, and in truth not all may become so in this life. But all are daughters, daughters of God, and have the absolute assurance that in His eyes and in His plans there will be a fulness of individual opportunity. I keep in my office a little framed plaque that someone that I love inscribed, and to which reference is made perhaps as often as anything else among the personal treasures which are available for visitors to see. It reads: "To believe in God is to know that all the rules will be fair and that there will be wonderful surprises." So I believe and so I testify: I know that this is true.

Make Good, Constructive Lives

One early spring evening as I walked from the Church offices toward my home in Salt Lake City, I overtook a bent figure slowly and carefully picking her way over the sidewalk. I recognized that the person ahead of me was my fifth-grade schoolteacher, who was now an elderly lady, and my very good friend ever since I was her pupil in a classroom. We stood and talked a time on the corner, held hands, joked a little. And then as we parted she said, "Now, Marion, don't you forget our appointment. I'm depending on you to keep that appointment." I assured her that if I were anywhere on earth from which I could travel home to keep that appointment, I would do so.

She was talking about her funeral service, at which I long ago had been asked to speak. Within a few days of that conversation, a telephone call from her sister in California informed me that Carol Bird had died there while on a vacation and that she had left instructions about her funeral service. In those instructions she said there was one thing she'd like Elder Hanks to say, and that was that while she hadn't enjoyed some of life's blessings she would have dearly loved to have—she hadn't married, had not had a family of her own—she had nevertheless lived a happy and full life. She had been privileged to love and be interested in many children of other people. She had served in her community, had enjoyed music and other cultural blessings, had loved and read many books, and had been privileged to have many wonderful, close friends. She had experienced a great blessing of membership in the Church, had lived the commandments of God, and had great love for God and Christ and great faith in their promises. She said she'd like Brother Hanks to say at her funeral that she believed absolutely in God's love and that she would have a chance to enjoy all of His blessings someday if she proved worthy of them.

Accordingly I said that at her funeral service a day or two later and testified of her great contribution in my own life. She had been like another mother to me—that interested and that involved as little triumphs came along, which she would acknowledge with a note or a telephone call.

Now my testimony to you is that Carol Bird's faith was based on sound principle. It would be wonderful if every girl could enter into a good marriage with a choice, clean son of God, have a lovely family, and bring up happy, faithful children. This is our objective and ideal and is, of course, the proper goal of every normal girl in the Church. But sometimes this does not happen, as it did not to Carol Bird. What then? Then we must do what she did, of course, and make good, constructive lives for ourselves. Every person is an individual with a chance to make the most of the opportunities available. Our own salvation will come in obeying those two great basic laws taught by Jesus Christ: to truly love God and serve Him with all we have, and to love His other children, our brothers and sisters. When we serve others we not only do something useful but we also obey a commandment of God and we involve ourselves in activity that is fruitful and rewarding for us.

"It's All Right"

Sometimes affliction comes into our lives. One day I learned of the illness of a choice young lady who was attending Brigham Young University. She was a very good student, with many talents, but she had contracted a form of cancer when she was only twenty years old. Before she died I visited Teri a number of times, and we became good friends. She was not thinking then about the things most young ladies are normally thinking about at her age. Instead her mind was filled with very serious things. She desperately needed to know for herself that God lives and that His love was not being withheld in some personal way. She was anxious to have a testimony of Jesus Christ.

I sat at her bedside with her mother, read scriptures to her, and talked with her about the Lord and the trials He went through. And I quoted to her His first words after His identification of himself as he arrived on the American continent after His resurrection and ascension: "I have drunk out of that bitter cup which the Father hath given me" (3 Nephi 11:11).

It seemed to bring Teri great comfort to hear my testimony and to know for herself, through the Spirit, that it was true. Her life was in the hands of a loving Father and a loving Lord who understand our needs and who want to help us. I called her on the telephone periodically. I sent her a dozen roses not long before the end, and the day before she died we had a telephone call from her. The last words I ever heard her say were words of gratitude, and then: "Brother Hanks, it's all right. I know it's all right."

The scriptures teach us that Christ is in heaven with our Father, speaking for us and loving us and understanding us, our advocate and representative. He became a son of Abraham, born with flesh and blood in this world so that He could be a merciful and faithful friend to all of us—"touched," as the scriptures say, "with the feeling of our infirmities . . . in all points tempted like as we are" (Hebrews 4:15). He himself has suffered, being tempted, and so is able to give help to all of us who suffer or are tempted. "Though he were a Son, yet learned he obedience by the things which he suffered" (Hebrews 5:8). These were the things my dear young friend needed to know as she prepared to meet her Savior and her Heavenly Father. And before she died, she had received that comforting blessing of a sure testimony. She was not afraid.

Now, I don't mean to be at all negative or overly somber tonight. I don't believe that we should live our lives in fear or worry. But it is true that there is opposition in all things, that the rain falls on the just and on the unjust, and that we individually are therefore assured that we will have our share of life's complexities, that we will be tested in this world.

"Everything That Money Could Not Buy"

Having been left a widow, my own wonderful mother was forced to provide for six children. She had to work very hard; all of us children learned to work very hard to help each other go on missions and to school, and we learned to make do with what we had. I know now what I sometimes shamefully and tearfully realize I did not know clearly enough then: that there were many things Mom did without in order that we might have what we needed.

One of the loveliest moments of my life came at her funeral service when somebody who knew her very well said of her, "This noble lady gave her children everything that money could not buy." And so she did. He was speaking of love and faith and unselfish care. He was talking about prayer and laughter and courage and good example. He was talking about singing and about reading and about happiness. He may not have known that he was even talking about making stockings out of flour sacks for children to wear to school, dying them black, the seam neatly done, as Mother could do it. He may not have known that he was talking about the very soles we wore on our shoes, which she put on, on the old shoemaker's last down in the basement. He may have been talking, though he didn't know it, about the little guitar she made out of a cigar box, which was the first musical instrument I personally learned to play.

Well, Mother knew trouble, and I know a little bit about it because of her. So what I am about to say I say in that context. It is said not with any wish to emphasize sorrow or trouble or deprivation or separation but with the desire to recognize that these are part of life and that a person does not commit his faith to the absence of them but rather commits his or her life to constructing a foundation upon which to meet them with courage and with that kind of dignity and integrity that I saw in my mother's life.

I am saying that the Lord has warned us that even the best life will have trials, and that we should do everything in our power to prepare ourselves, through faith in God and a knowledge of the gospel and through righteous living, to meet whatever condition life does bring. Jesus said, "Be patient in afflictions, for thou shalt have many; but endure them, for, lo, I am with thee, even unto the end of thy days" (D&C 24:8).

Eternal Family Relationship

I said in the beginning that not all of you lovely ladies and young ladies here are mothers, but all are daughters; we are all children of our Heavenly Father. We have a common goal and purpose that has been born in us. We've all had an earthly mother who gave us life. We are all God's spiritual children in a gospel family—in the family of the Savior, who, through His atoning sacrifice, gave us immortality and made possible for us life eternal, which is life with God, and life with loved ones from this earth in an eternal family relationship.

If you have the blessing now of living together as mothers and daughters, you're very fortunate indeed. It's wonderful for me to see how my wife and four daughters love each other and enjoy each other. Two of those girls are married and have children of their own. They love to visit their mother and to talk with her. Two are in the university, one about to be married. She especially needs to be able to talk with her mother and to receive counsel from her.

A Guide for Growing Up

As a girl is growing up (and I talk now for a moment to you girls) she should be preparing herself to live a constructive, happy life. The counsel Sister Tanner and Sister Brown have given us is such good and sensible and farseeing advice. A young lady should be taught to live the way Heavenly Father wants her to live. When I was a young man, I read something that had been written to help girls in the Church live that way, and I've always loved it. In fact, as a young man I memorized it. Let me repeat just a part of it to you. Some of you will recognize it as the old Gleaner Sheaf. It tells what a good Mormon girl will do to bring her to later life, to marriage, to home, to a family in that condition which she'll be grateful for and which the Lord expects.

The Gleaner Sheaf starts with that section of the Twenty-fourth Psalm which begins: "Who shall ascend into the hill of the Lord? or who shall stand in his holy place? He that hath clean hands, and a pure heart; who hath not lifted up his soul unto vanity, nor sworn deceitfully." (Psalm 24:3–4.) On that magnificent invitation are these commitments:

> First, I shall bring a clean body—nothing forbidden shall enter it—no corruption shall touch it. It is my surety of eternal joy.
>
> Second, I shall bring . . . a pure heart. From it shall flow high ideals, pure thoughts, clean speech, righteous actions. By the pure eye of faith I shall see God.
>
> Third, . . . I shall bring a humble, obedient spirit.
>
> I shall obey God's law with delight.
>
> I shall honor my womanhood.
>
> I shall intelligently, diligently, and prayerfully perform my duties.
>
> I shall know God.
>
> Fourth, . . . I shall bring an honest mind.
>
> I shall not bear false witness.
>
> I shall speak truly.
>
> I shall honor my word.
>
> I shall learn the truth and the truth shall make me free.

It finishes, you may recall, "Thus, bearing my fourfold sheaf, I shall hope to ascend into the hill of the Lord and stand in His holy place; then shall I receive the blessings from the Lord, and righteousness from the God of my salvation." (From the "Gleaner Sheaf," *M-Man Gleaner Handbook,* 1969–70, pp. 9–10.)

I cannot think of a more wonderful guide to growing up than that, for God's choice daughters. Keep your body clean. Keep your heart pure. Develop a humble, obedient spirit. Be honest, and fill your mind with thoughts and dreams that are wholesome and clean and uplifting and will be self-fulfilling. As you prepare for marriage in later life, remember that God has given you certain special gifts, which you must develop and appreciate and use for righteous purposes. He has given you a lovely face and form and the power to create. You have a mind which can learn and think and be used to help and teach others.

Perhaps most of all—I wonder if you yourselves know it— he has given you a marvelous gift of sweetness and beauty and of faith, a gift which is special. Men do not have the gift in the same measure, I am sure of that. President Joseph F. Smith once said: "Women can approach nearer to the Lord than men can, as a general thing. Or my mother did. I could not do as my mother did." And he was the President of the Church. That's a wonderful tribute to this gift of faith, which pure women have. My mother had it, my wife has it, my daughters have had it since they were little girls. Many times I've had the blessing of kneeling in humble wonder as a tiny girl talked with her Heavenly Father. Girls and ladies, I repeat, this is a blessing God has made available to you that you can have. Be grateful. Use and protect this gift to bring a wholesome, faithful influence into the lives of others.

You girls can be especially important in the lives of the young men with whom you associate. If you will keep your body clean, your heart pure, your mind honest, and your spirit in tune with Heavenly Father, you'll help them stay clean, go on missions, and serve the Lord.

Mothers Are Special

For a moment I speak to you wonderful ladies who are mothers now. God has blessed you with a magnificent responsibility. No one in a home is as important as Mother. Fathers are very important, of course, but mothers are special. Almost the last words of Christ on the cross were of His mother. Every decent man treasures and honors his mother, and so does every decent woman.

President McKay said this wonderful thing about mothers, influenced, I'm sure—as were so many things he said—by his own choice mother and his love for her: "The noblest calling in the world is that of mother. She who rears successfully a family of healthy, beautiful sons and daughters deserves the highest honor that men can give."

A woman in a home fills a number of responsibilities. You know, of course, that she is the heart of the home; she is wife, partner, friend, companion, sweetheart, mother, homemaker. Each of these is a major role in the lives of the members of her family. A young girl growing up should consider what a very big undertaking it is to accept such responsibilities. Every one of them requires preparation and prayer and character. Be wise in your preparation and humble in your prayers. Try to build that character that is expressed in unselfishness and consideration, in tenderness and a warm heart, in a good disposition, in good humor.

A Mother's Faith

I heard a noble mother speak once in a stake conference in response to invitation. I'll never forget her. She and her husband and twelve-year-old son lived on a ranch fourteen miles away from the place where they worshiped every Sunday. Saturday night the telephone rang and the twelve-year-old came to his mother with the news that it was Bruce Brown who was asking if he could go with Bruce and another friend and their fathers on a hunting and shooting trip the next morning. He wanted to know what he should tell Bruce.

The mother, as she stood at the pulpit fighting a problem of a lump in the throat, said, "My first impulse was to respond: 'Of course you can't go. Tomorrow is the Sabbath; tomorrow morning is priesthood meeting and Sunday School, and you have obligations.' But I didn't say that." She said she was also tempted to say, "You wait till your father comes in and ask him. He'll have an answer for you." But she didn't say that, either.

Somehow, she found the wisdom and restraint and faith to say: "Son, you're twelve years old. You hold the priesthood of God. You can make up your own mind about that."

He turned away without another word; she went with a prayer in her heart—a prayer with which mothers and fathers, I testify, are familiar: "Lord, Lord, please"—to her own room and knelt down and talked with the Lord. Nothing more was said about the incident.

Father came in, the three of them had their family prayer, went to bed, awakened early the next morning, and prepared for and then went in to priesthood meeting and Sunday School. They parked their pickup truck across the street in a parking lot and were crossing toward the chapel when a truck drove by with guns slung in the window, snowmobiles in the back, and two boys and two laughing men in the front.

The lady at the pulpit then had her hardest moment. She said, "I had hold of the hands of my two men, and as the truck passed the one on the right said, almost inaudibly, 'Gee, I wish . . .' and my heart clutched a moment; then he finished: 'Gee, I wish I could have convinced Bruce that he and Bob ought to be in priesthood meeting this morning.' "

And then we found out the reason for the big lump in the speaker's throat. She said: "We've been particularly grateful we were able to be with him that Sabbath morning, because it was the last Sunday we had him in this world. He was killed in a farm accident that week."

Thank God for a mother's faith, for a mother's wisdom, and a mother's love. There is no more honored place than a mother's, and certainly no more sacred responsibility.

Do you remember the words the Apostle Paul wrote to Timothy, his young protege and brother and missionary companion, encouraging him from a distance? Speaking of the young man's faith, he said it "dwelt first in thy grandmother . . . and thy mother . . . and I am persuaded . . . in thee also" (2 Timothy 1:5).

A Mother's Prayer

I add just one somewhat ancient memory, at least it is old for me. In a stake conference I attended many years ago in a small Utah town, a young man, recently returned from a mission, bore his testimony. He said he had just one thing to say. He really didn't wish to talk about his mission then. He said, "I'm willing to say I worked hard, and if I did some good it will show up in my life and the lives of others in the years to come. What I do want to do is take this moment to thank Mother, to thank my mother."

He then went back to a night when, his father having recently passed away, his baby sister also became desperately ill. He was in his early teens. He had suffered, as the family had, from the tragedy of the loss of the father. But as the little girl worsened and worsened, and as fasting and prayer and the blessings of the priesthood seemed not to be rewarded, he became more and more anxious in his heart. Still he had faith that she would recover.

Then the baby died. And he went into his room and, although only a boy, was angry with God and said he would never think of or talk to God anymore. He couldn't imagine having anything to do with a God who would do what He had done to their family, to his little sister who was so innocent, and to his dad whom he loved so much, and to his mother whom he worshiped. He was awake the rest of the night, thinking of himself and consumed with anger.

Dawn and then early morning came and brought with them an uneasy feeling in him for which he couldn't really account. After a while there came a knock on the door, and he knew why he had this special unease. He went to the door to open it. His mother said, "Tommy, it's time for family prayer." And he replied, "I'm never going to pray again!"

She said again, "Son, it's time for family prayer," and he said, "Mother, I'm not coming!"

"Tommy," she said, "you're the only man I have in this house, and if I ever needed a man, I need one now. Your little brothers and sisters are waiting, Tom."

He walked with her, but he was full of bitterness. As they knelt down he said to himself, "I wonder what she's going to thank God for this morning."

He found out. Out of her broken heart she taught her children the gospel. She taught them what it means to live and have problems and have faith. He now stood, a fine, strong, valiant young man, tears coursing down his cheeks, thanking God for his mother and the faith she displayed that hardest morning of all. From her he learned how to be a man; and so—to the measure I've learned it—did I at such a mother's knee.

And so, pray to God with your children or your parents, difficult as it may be for you, imperfect as your situation may be. God bless you. God bless you to learn and live and, with this special gift of God's spiritual influence, share and teach His truth. As I testify to you, there is something special about you, or can be. In the name of Jesus Christ. Amen.

CHAPTER 15

Boys Need Men

I wonder how many of you young men and men who are a little older have heard the story of the man in the brown leather jacket.

A famous surgeon received a phone call one night from a doctor friend who said he had a young child on the operating table and needed the surgeon's help in order to save the child. It was a long drive across town to the hospital, and the surgeon drove as fast he could with safety. As he pulled up to a stop sign a man wearing a brown leather jacket opened the car door and slid in beside him with his hand in his pocket as though he had a gun. The man was excited, demanded the surgeon's car, and obviously was in no mood to discuss the matter. The surgeon stood helplessly on the highway as the man in the brown leather jacket sped away in his car.

By the time the surgeon finally arrived at the hospital, it was too late. The child had died only moments before. The other doctor asked the surgeon to come with him to meet the child's father in the hope that together they might offer him words of comfort. As they entered the waiting room, the father came forward. He was the man in the brown leather jacket.

It occurs to me to wonder whether any of us here tonight

Address given at general conference April 1974.

are, in a different sense, men in brown leather jackets, who, through our lack of wisdom—perhaps not knowing it, certainly not wishing it—keep spiritual help from reaching our children when they need it. Or if we are young, we are tempted to follow a course that could damage the children that we will one day have.

Models of True Manhood

This great meeting tonight is not only exciting and encouraging in its evidence of the tremendous priesthood potential in the kingdom of God; it also manifests the capacity of the Church to exercise a powerful influence in helping to meet one of the most vital needs in the world today, and that is supplying models of true manhood for boys who are on their way to becoming men.

The absence of fathers from their homes, for one reason or another, and the lack of father image and influence in the lives of boys are obvious factors in the large troubles that face our society. My firmly held conviction is that in the homes of the Church, and through priesthood leadership in the Church, the problem is correctable; the challenge can be met, if we will.

Only God knows the worth of a boy, but we too are fathers, and we have an inkling. Not only is a boy priceless on his own account but every individual boy is a kind of omnibus carrying with him all the past that has gone into his making, all the potential in him for influencing the present; and he has, in addition, the sobering reality to face that he carries within himself the seeds of the future. Under every normal circumstance there will be one day those who call him father, and to them and their future he has a great and solemn responsibility.

Boys Learn from Men

Boys need men to learn from, men to be with who understand their need for activities that are challenging and are socially and spiritually constructive and that stretch them and give them a chance to learn manly skills; men to love and who love them; men who are models of what a man ought to be. The father should be the first line of strength, and a boy blessed with such a father is fortunate indeed. Of course, even such a family can use all the supportive influence it can get from good men who genuinely care.

But what of the boy who has no father, or whose father is not presently supplying what a father uniquely can give? To help him, the Lord has provided what I believe to be the finest program the world has ever known—a program of bishops and counselors, advisers, teachers, Scoutmasters, leaders, home teachers, coaches—strong men who really care. If the Lord's program is effectively operating, literally no boy in the whole Church should be without the blessing of choice men in his life, and every boy will, in fact, have several good men actively concerned for his well-being. I rejoice in the wonderful influence of mothers and other noble women in guiding boys—and no one in all the world is better qualified than I to understand that—but it takes men to make men. Even mothers cannot do it by themselves, and certainly none should have to undertake the effort alone; nor can schools or other institutions supply the need. Boys need men!

Implications for Fathers

The implications of this for fathers and for men who hold the priesthood are clear indeed. In many homes, in every neighborhood, in every community, in every ward and branch of the Church, there are boys who need the help of men, mothers who need men to help their boys.

Is it fair to ask what will happen if boys don't get what they need from good fathers or conscientious men whose blessing it is to help them? The answer is that they must improvise or learn from other youth as ignorant and inexperienced as themselves. They will learn on street corners or in school corridors where success may be measured in terms of physical, sexual, or economic prowess instead of in terms of character and quality relationships.

Now, brethren, if we need to do better than we are doing, and wish to do better, what program shall we follow? There is time here tonight to consider only the beginning of one answer among many, but that is a vital answer and it needs to be understood.

Teaching Our Own Children

How foolish we are if we reserve to ourselves, or for others than our own children, the knowledge and testimony of the gospel we have gained! They, no less than others, need and deserve this from us.

Is it possible that some of us are in some measure men in brown leather jackets in this matter?

Do you remember that many of the most powerful teachings in the Book of Mormon are from fathers directly to their beloved sons? Lehi, Jacob, Benjamin, Alma, Helaman, Mormon, and others all taught wonderful lessons to their own sons.

Do you recall Alma's son Corianton and the sad mistake he made? He was proud, stubborn, willing to excuse himself because many others had also sinned. Alma plainly identified the seriousness of his son's actions, called him to repentance, taught him the meaning of Christ's atonement, gave him a path to follow, and spoke the message of his heart: "And now the Spirit of the Lord doth say unto me: Command thy children to do good, lest they lead away the hearts of many people to destruction; therefore I command you, my son, in the fear of God, that ye refrain from your iniquities" (Alma 39:12).

In this marvelous lesson for sinners—and those who seek to help sinners—are some of the saddest and most moving words that I know from a faithful father who had tried to do missionary work in the very area where his son had been immoral. The result? "When they saw your conduct, they would not believe in my words" (Alma 39:11).

Nephi's Love for His Father

There are other relevant accounts in the Book of Mormon, of course, like that of the boy who heeded his father's teachings and who made up his mind early in his life about what he really wanted. He wrote these words (you know him!): "I, Nephi, being exceedingly young, nevertheless being large in stature, and also having great desires to know of the mysteries of God, ... I did cry unto the Lord; and behold he did visit me, and did soften my heart that I did believe all the words which had been spoken by my father" (1 Nephi 2:16).

Nephi performed many great tasks, and one I remember well was his help to his father, who had murmured when the company lost its hunting equipment and faced starvation. Nephi, you will remember, had himself been blessed with marvelous spiritual experiences, but he loved his father so much that, instead of criticizing or taking over, he helped him regain his self-respect and confidence by going to him and asking Lehi to inquire of God where he, Nephi, should hunt. With that support, the older man found his faith and was again able to lead his people. The story itself is a minor incident in the Book of Mormon, but the lesson is not minor. It is no small thing to re-establish confidence and faith in a man at a critical point in his life when he has failed and is full of self-doubt.

So the scriptures are one remarkable and perhaps largely untapped source of strength for choice young men on their way to adult influence and responsibility, and for those who are now charged to guide them. How well are we using the source?

Liability in Failure

Fiorello La Guardia, an Italian immigrant to the United States, became one of the most respected and influential mayors in the history of New York. Early in his life, while he was a magistrate, a man convicted of theft was in his courtroom. The young judge felt compelled to impose a sentence of imprisonment. But when the man explained that he had stolen food to feed his impoverished family, the judge suspended the sentence and then levied a fine on every person in the courtroom for living in a city where a man had to steal bread to feed his family.

One wonders if some such liability may not, in justice, one day be imposed upon parents and teachers and other adults in the Church who have failed to feed our young the bread of life for whatever reason.

Automobile Without Key

Perhaps both boys and men will understand the analogy of an automobile which a young man desperately wanted and which his father promised him on his birthday if he merited it. "Just go with sensible people and do sensible things," said the father, "and on your birthday I'll see that you get the kind of car you want." The automobile was described in detail, with all the equipment a boy could imagine. So he went with sensible people, and did sensible things, and prepared himself, hoping almost beyond hope for the big day. It arrived. He looked out of the window of the house and saw the car of his dreams sitting there. It had everything on it which he in his imagination had conceived. He could scarcely contain himself with love and appreciation. He ran from the house, looked it over, and then went back to his dad for the key.

"The key?" said the father. "Oh, the key. Well, I'll tell you. The car is yours. I've been preparing you for it for a long time. It is very valuable and very important, and I know you'll make very good use of it, but for now I'll keep the key. I'll let you know when you can use it. You can tell everybody it's yours, but don't use it."

Boys need more than a promise and more than a name; they need to be permitted to test their strength, to use their abilities, to use their priesthood.

Responsibility of Young Men

You young men, of course, have a very great responsibility in these matters also. Many of you have been wonderfully blessed with gifts from the Lord and with opportunities to enjoy and use them. Your sense of appreciation, your respect for the blessings of God, your mature acceptance of responsibility, and your wonderful service, your sense of humor—these all strengthen and encourage us and make us very proud of you.

A Father's Support

Now let me finish, if I may, with two very brief accounts of two great fathers.

A young lad stood at the pulpit one Sunday trying to give an assigned talk, but he could not get the words out. His spiritual giant of a father walked from the congregation to stand beside his son, put his arm around him, and said: "I know Larry has prepared his talk and that he'll be able to give it. He is a little frightened, so I'll just speak to you for a moment and then I know he'll be ready." The father stood by his boy with his arm around him, and in a moment the lad gave his talk. And many in the congregation wept.

A while ago I met a special boy, and this week I had the privilege of spending some time with him and his family. This boy has a form of muscular atrophy. He is a remarkable young man, loved by everyone in the ward. He has always wanted to do the things the other fellows do. He has succeeded in Cub Scouting. He is now a First Class Scout and is progressing.

While Jay was a deacon, he passed the sacrament with the others. He can't walk or stand on his feet, so his dad lined up with the other boys, holding Jay with his strong arm around his waist and helping him hold the tray, since his hands are not strong enough to support it. Jay's father thus assisted his son from row to row as he passed the sacrament. Jay did a great job as a deacon collecting fast offerings too. His dad carried him from door to door. Can you imagine that scene on the doorstep?

This young man bears a strong testimony; his attitude and outlook are amazing. He gives talks and does well. He has sung in church, and always when he does these things his dad is there to hold him in his arms and stand by him and support him.

In all my life I never heard a sweeter story nor a more moving one. God bless such a father, and God bless such a son, and God bless us who have so much and who have yet a little time, that we may take another look at our boy or at the boy who needs some additional help outside his home. God bless you boys to appreciate your dads, to be patient and gracious and forgiving. God bless us all, boys and men, now and in the future, always to act in a way that will help others enjoy the special blessings God wants them to have.

The Unspoken Sermon

Fathers, priesthood leaders—young men need models. The unspoken sermon is heard most clearly and learned most strongly by those near at hand. It is not through definition or diatribe that young men acquire values. "They do not learn ethical principles; they emulate ethical (or unethical) people. They do not analyze or list attributes they wish to develop; they identify with people who seem to have them." (John William Gardner, *Self-Renewal: The Individual and the Innovative Society* [New York: Harper and Row, 1963], p. 124.) What boys need is not lectures about notions of love, human relationships, or God, but to be exposed to unconditional love, to unselfish service, to the reality of God in reverence and worship and humble prayer. And that is why they need models of what a man at his best can be.

And since none of us fathers is perfect, will you young men, as I sit down, hear these words of Moroni: "Condemn [us] not because of [our] imperfection . . . but rather give thanks unto God that he hath made manifest unto you our imperfections, that ye may learn to be more wise than we have been" (Mormon 9:31).

And to those a little older, these words from ancient times: "For how shall I go up to my father, and the lad [is] not with me?" (Genesis 44:34.)

In the name of Jesus Christ. Amen.

CHAPTER 16

Fitting into Your Family

No doubt everyone would like to be part of a perfect family and live in perfect harmony in a perfect home. Yet no one is, or does, or can, because such blessings do not exist. There are no perfect families or homes, but there are some very good ones; and those who experience such circumstances are very fortunate indeed.

Others have learned or are learning to cope with a home situation other than the "traditional" family—husband and wife together in a permanent relationship, Dad the major breadwinner, Mother in the home, the two sharing together responsibility for the care and well-being of the children. Society seems to have changed to a major degree this definition and ideal. Divorce afflicts many families; single-parent households proliferate; and so do dual-career (or dual-job) parents with latchkey or farmed-out children. Poverty, abuse, alcoholism, drug use are too evident, and many households must cope with physically, mentally, or socially handicapped members.

Coping and Improving

How can teenagers and younger children survive in such

New Era article June 1991.

imperfect circumstances, and maybe even help to improve them?

I am one who grew up in a single-parent home under very strained economic circumstances. My father died suddenly when I was two years old, leaving my mother with six young children. That she coped and how she coped with that situation seems a miracle to me now as I watch so many other courageous mothers (and some fathers) struggle with similar tough challenges. Some parents—and some children—seem to have an even more difficult set of circumstances to deal with.

One such person I know, an attractive young convert to the Church, found her way to sanity and peace through the Master. She is very fortunate. After a young lifetime of bad choices and trouble, she is now in a home where she is really valued and esteemed and where she has been taught by loving foster parents her relationship with the Savior. She has begun to know and appreciate Him, to find meaning in life, and to develop a sense of responsibility.

On my office wall is a statement that was lovingly lettered and bordered with delicate flowers, then graciously framed behind glass and delivered to me by a teenaged young lady who came to understand her value to the Lord as she followed counsel and began to make wiser choices:

> Though Christ a thousand times
> In Bethlehem be born,
> If He is not born in thee
> Thy soul is still forlorn.

"One Room at My House"

One of my most memorable experiences was with another young lady convert to the Church who had found in a Latter-day Saint fellow student, and in the home of this new friend, a spirit and a caring family relationship she had never known in her own family. She said that since her baptism things had not materially changed in her home; there was still abuse and argument and conflict and alcohol and foul language and a hateful spirit. "But," she said, "there is one room at my house where I can go and shut the door and read the scriptures and listen to good music and pray and feel the Spirit of the Lord. In my little room I can have that blessing. One day, if the Lord will help me, I will marry a man and establish a home where we and our children can have the Spirit of the Lord always and everywhere."

Sometimes, as in her case, there seems to be little one can do to change and improve circumstances that tend to smother self-esteem and productive use of our energy. But even then we must not surrender the possibility that if we are thoughtfully prepared and patiently willing, and if we are faithful and humble, we just may one day make a difference. If we seem unable to effect a change for the better in others, we must still prayerfully consider the vital importance, now and over a lifetime and eternity, of our individual attitude towards our own personal health and well-being—spiritual, mental, physical, and emotional.

One Can Still Choose

One of the most powerful lessons to come out of the incredibly vicious experiences in the concentration camps of World War II is taught by Dr. Victor L. Frankl, a physician and psychiatrist who was in those camps for three grim years, in his book *Man's Search for Meaning*. His father, mother, brother, and wife, along with millions of others, died of starvation or privation or abuse or were sent to gas ovens in camps, their only offense being their race, which was unacceptable to their depraved tormentors.

Yet in these bestial camps, where unspeakable brutality worked to strip prisoners of every possession and value and shred of dignity, quiet heroes arose who exercised the one human freedom of which they could not be deprived, and that was the capacity to choose the way they responded to the wickedness of their persecutors. And that choice for some of them was to walk through the huts in the concentration camps bringing comfort to others, on occasion giving away their last small piece of bread, and jeopardizing their lives in so doing. This "inner decision" permitted those few who made it to retain their human dignity even in foul circumstances. While only a few managed to rise above their degradation and suffering in preserving and exercising their right to choose their attitude, these few were proof enough that "man's inner strength may raise him above his outward fate."

And such "spiritual freedom" is exercised not only in concentration camps. In obscure rest homes, institutions, neighborhoods, Boy Scout troops for the handicapped, and a multitude more of unsung places, courageous individuals quietly and unselfishly serve others under adverse, even hopeless, conditions.

For us such courage involves faith—faith in a mortal and eternal future, faith that the best in us is better than we know, confidence in ultimate justice and in a loving, personal God. It requires faith that though life and a future may seem at this moment to hold little promise *for us,* yet life and the future still hold significant *expectations of us.*

On my office wall is another boxed declaration of good cheer coming from an unidentified source. Many have found comfort and hope in its message: "To believe in God is to know that all the rules will be fair and that there will be wonderful surprises."

Some of those surprises await us in the joy we can *bring to* extended families and *gain from* them; some in activity and service in ward organizations and worship; some in obtaining employment and devoting perhaps unexpected diligence to it; some in education available to the willing in nearly every community. There can be wonderful surprises for one who unselfishly serves in helping the handicapped and the needy, the poor and the elderly and the lonely.

Every ward or branch is an extended family, and every ward or branch family has members who are, or feel they are, neglected, unnecessary, not really respected or wanted. The difference a small handful of interested ward family members can make in extending love and emotional support is tremendous. The bishop, as father of the ward, would be grateful beyond measure for a few young people who took seriously their membership in the family and made the "inner decision" to reach out unselfishly and share a little of their time and concern.

I cannot keep far from frequent remembrance the feeling of sadness and frustration that came when I learned that not far from Church headquarters in Salt Lake City a very elderly lady, active in serving others all of her life, was eating Corn Flakes for every meal because she could not shop or cook for herself and had no one to help her. In that same neighborhood and Church family there were able, intelligent young people who were attending classes and Church meetings and planning and pursuing parties and service projects with no knowledge of the needs of or any apparent interest in helping others in their ward family. When the facts were brought to their attention about the choice elderly lady and her Corn Flakes, they immediately moved into action and did something about the situation. Her life and theirs became immediately more happy and harmonious even though she, and some of them, were not living in the ideal family home circumstances they would have wished for.

Be Guided by the Best in You

This same happy blessing could be experienced in every quorum and class and Young Women and Young Men group in the Church if all of us would permit this "best in us" to guide our lives. It will be the blessing of every individual who will undertake to peel off the outer layers of shyness and self-interest and lack of confidence and invite to the surface the noble instincts and generosity of spirit that each possesses as a heritage from God, the Heavenly Father of all the human family, and from His Son, Jesus Christ.

We can start by feeling and expressing to our Eternal Father our gratitude for being part of His eternal family, and part of His great Church family which extends to far corners of the earth, and part of a ward or branch family. The family we were born or adopted into and the future family we will establish should also be of the greatest concern to us.

Those of us who are lucky enough to belong to one of the good if imperfect families we talked about before can thank

God and renew our best efforts to be a contributing citizen in a home where friendship and values and traditions and discipline exist, and where we can make a significant contribution if we are willing.

Those of us whose families are not what we wish they were can be thankful to parents who through God's gift have given us life, and we can do everything possible to minimize conflict and enhance harmony in our homes. Small miracles do in fact sometimes occur in situations where there just doesn't appear much probability that one young person can make a difference.

I once heard in a stake conference the testimony of a humble leader who spoke of an incident involving his young son that had caused the father to significantly change his life overnight. He had gone to pick up the lad and his belongings from the home of a family who had provided a place for him to stay while he participated in a baseball tournament that had lasted several days. The young man had seemed reluctant to go with his father to the home of his benefactor, and the father had begun to wonder if the people had mistreated his son. He was almost belligerent as he knocked on the door, the boy half cowering behind him. Once inside, however, it was evident that the earlier apprehension could not be valid; the lad was warmly greeted by the host family and he obviously loved them very much.

Back in the automobile, the puzzled father had asked his son to explain his strange behavior. Now the father, weeping at the pulpit as he spoke in conference as a stake leader, shared his son's answer: "I was afraid you might forget and swear in their house, Dad. They don't swear at their house; they are really nice people. They talk nice to each other and laugh a lot, and they pray every time they eat and every morning and night, and they let me pray with them."

Said the father, "It wasn't that the lad was ashamed of his dad; he loved him so much that he didn't want him to look bad."

This father, having resisted a generation of earnest people who had tried to help him find a better way of life, had been touched by the sweet spirit of his own young son.

Lessons from Lehi and Sariah's Family

For me, one of the most real and authentic portrayals of family as it often is comes from one of the best-known scriptural accounts, the story of Lehi and Sariah and their family.

Lehi, the father, was a wonderful person, as was Sariah, the mother, but each was also subject to some imperfections. Lehi, a good and faithful man, weakened and "murmured" when he was faced with possible death from starvation or anarchy in the desert. Sariah became deeply concerned with the safety of her sons on an errand their father had appointed them to undertake, and "complained against" Lehi for jeopardizing the lives of her boys. (See 1 Nephi 16:20; 5:2–3.)

The family had other challenges. Some of the sons were rebellious and became a serious problem during the journey and for the rest of their lives. Laman and Lemuel "did murmur in many things against their father. . . . And they did murmur because they knew not the dealings of that God who had created them." (1 Nephi 2:11–12.)

Actually, this was a refugee family who had to leave everything behind as they fled for their lives into the wilderness, taking with them only such provisions as they could gather. They lived in tents as they traveled.

Nephi began this account of their lives with the well-known words: "I, Nephi, having been born of goodly parents"—an appropriate beginning! Yet it is probable that every thoughtful, sensitive person who ever shared those words with a class of students has been aware that there would be those present whose home circumstances would not qualify for such a beginning. Those favored with "goodly parents" could rejoice and be made to feel glad with proper attention to their blessings. But what of those present whose experience contained at least some element of broken homes and broken hearts and single parents, and in some cases poverty and abuse and distress?

How would some of these listeners respond to the declaration of Nephi's good fortune as study was begun in this book that they should learn to love? I myself have been in that circumstance as a teacher many times, determined to approach this situation with honesty and integrity and yet with compassion and concern for the real circumstances of life for promising young people.

Notwithstanding his good fortune, the remaining lessons of the very first verse in the book reveal that Nephi had been subject to "many afflictions in the course of [his] days" but that he had been "highly favored of the Lord in all [his] days," which he explains by saying that he had been blessed with a "knowledge of the goodness and the mysteries of God."

That is, he had been taught the truth about God and understood the loving relationship of our Eternal Father to us, His children. He had suffered many afflictions, but they were not evidence to him of any displeasure on the part of his Heavenly Father; they were part of living and spiritual maturing.

Getting to know this Book of Mormon family tempered quickly for certain students the potential anxiety of hearing about somebody who does everything right and who enjoys a situation that is just right in every way with everything going perfectly well. In the class, continuing reference would be made to the good fortune Nephi enjoyed in having good and caring parents, while it would be noted that some of the brothers and other members of the extended traveling family chose different and sometimes even evil courses, not those desired for them by the Lord and laid out for them by their parents.

With life comes agency, and the chance and responsibility to set our own individual course and to be accountable for it. Perhaps the greatest lesson we can learn from Lehi's family is that lesson—that we are individually able to choose a course of decency and integrity and wholesomeness; that "I, John (or Dorothy) will one day be a parent, and I am determined to be a 'goodly' one. I am determined that my children will have good parents, and so I will prepare myself and choose friends (for friends may be as important as family) who will help me succeed in that effort, and I will prepare to marry a husband or wife with whom I may share that sacred responsibility."

Parents owe much to children, and children owe much to parents, and future parents owe much to those whom they will bring into the world. Remember that "all the rules will be fair . . .

[with] wonderful surprises," and leave with your Heavenly Father the questions that may disturb you about parents and families who are not perfect, and about "eternal families" and other matters which an individual cannot effect for herself or himself but which in God's good time will be answered on the basis of God's love and man's continuing eternal agency.

CHAPTER 17

Priesthood and Partnerships

Years ago I heard the story of the president of a railroad who was on a hunting expedition out in the boondocks when he got lost. He almost froze, but fortunately he found his way to a little way station of his own railroad. Inside he found a young man in a cubbyhole sending out wires.

The small waiting room was freezing. Not identifying himself and in his rough hunting clothing, he tried to persuade the young man to start a fire in the stove. The young man, not knowing that he was talking to the president of the railroad, declined, saying, "I am too busy sending wires to start fires." The president then said, "Please send one wire to my office." He wrote, "By return wire, fire the man who runs this way station," and signed it with his name and title. The young man looked at it, burst quickly from the room, grabbed the coal bucket, and said, "Sorry, sir, I am too busy building fires to send wires."

I have felt like that this week, trying to distill into a few moments so significant a subject as marriage and what relates to it, but it has been enjoyable.

I think I may have heard substantially every problem you have had to listen to. In the last two years as a temple president I have had a graduate course in the tribulations of good people. It is a remarkable place to be and it needs no exposition of its

Address given at the Association of Mormon Counselors and Psychotherapists 4 October 1984.

beauty and joyfulness, but it also is a collection point for personal challenges, particularly if one is willing to listen; and I am, as occasion permits. It is also a marvelous place for sanctuary from coarseness and crudity and for the containment of attacks upon virtues and values in which we earnestly believe—attacks in constant process in much of the television and video material available all around us. Walking through the airports of Asia, for example, is in itself an education in deliberately avoiding moral pollution. We are all susceptible, and the resistance effort has to be calculated, deliberate, persistent, and consistent. The temple is a real sanctuary.

For what I have to say today I offer, as a kind of support, a letter I received several years ago from a psychiatrist, a strong and noble fellow with whom I was, as it were, exchanging referrals. In those times there were few who would listen and few who believed in what some of those experts had to offer, and I both was interested and believed in some of them whom I knew well. They would send people to me to be taught the fundamental principles of faith and repentance, and I would send people to them when I felt those people needed the kind of special help they could give—which in a sense also involved faith and repentance but was given from their expert and highly qualified point of view. I have great respect for people who are in your professions, because sincere and earnest people are desperately needed in them, and I assume you are both professionally competent and sincere; if you are not, you shouldn't be doing what you are doing.

I simply read, without pride or apology, what the doctor wrote, what he felt was needed:

> The need for wide dissemination throughout the Church of your observation on marriage is becoming more critical each day. You have indicated in the past you may write a book on the subject. Even a booklet would help. The inundation of professional offices by families in trouble is a tragedy because it is preventable if an adequate education program can be installed to identify marriage for what it is: one of the hardest jobs for any individual to undertake, requiring tolerance, patience, and planning as well as love instead of the romanticized concepts which are found even in many of our Church publications. It is heartbreaking to see so

many fine young people destroyed on false illusions of what marriage should be. A book or booklet would be real helpful. I hope it will be available soon.

Your perceptions of my sense of reluctance will be supported by the fact that I have never written either the book or the booklet. In a sense I am sorry for that. Many good books and booklets have been written, and the library in my house has a suitable store. The fundamentals of which I will speak may be, in some sense, treated here much as they are treated elsewhere, but I would hope I may speak them with some special sense of what people in the Church can and should learn, and also of the resources available to us. I keep thinking of what Conrad Hilton said when someone asked him his biggest problem in the hotel business: "Getting people to put the curtain inside the tub." That may almost capture the homely nature of what I wish to say to you.

Let me share a few lines from Ogden Nash at his best. He defines marriage:

> Just as I know there are two Hagens, Walter and Copen [for you younger people, Walter Hagen was a great golfer], I know that marriage is a legal and religious alliance entered into by a man who cannot sleep with the window shut and a woman who can't sleep with the window open. Also, he can't sleep till he has read the last hundred pages to find out whether his suspicions of a murdered eccentric's recluse secretary were right. And she can't sleep until he puts out the light which, when he finally does, she's still awake. . . . That is why marriage is so much more interesting than divorce because it is the only known example of the happy meeting of the immovable object and the irresistible force. I hope husbands and wives will continue to debate and combat over every thing debatable and compatible because I believe a little incompatibility is the spice of life, particularly if he has income and she is patible. (*I Do, I Will, I Have: Selected Poems of Ogden Nash* [Boston: Little, Brown & Co., 1975], p. 248.)

The Best Thing by Far

Let me also quote from sociologist Jerry Talley of Stanford

in a recent issue of *U.S. News and World Report:* "Despite the risks, Americans remain the marrying kind. Eventually more than 90 percent of the population will marry. Even those who have endured the trauma of divorce usually make at least one more attempt to achieve wedded bliss. Although people may be disappointed in a marriage partner, they are not generally disappointed in marriage." Many other interesting things have been said on this subject: J. P. Marquand, for example, is quoted as saying, "Marriage is damnably serious business, particularly around Boston."

Well, it is serious business, and it is the basis for much that is meaningful in our religion as in our lives. I share what Sir Arthur Bryant said, as extracted from a London newspaper: "Though life in this transitory world can never, for anyone, as in fairy stories, be free of threat and trouble, the companionship of two partners, tried in the fires of life and brought together by true and lasting love, can be and is the best thing by far that life offers a man and a woman."

My wife, Maxine, and I were once at the home of Robert Burns in Scotland. Under glass on his desk was a little single-sentence note he wrote to a friend in 1789: "That you may have a safe journey and a happy meeting with that dearest of all connections, your fireside circle, is the sincerest wish of your obliged humble servant, Robert Burns." I have had that in mind ever since—"that dearest of all connections, your fireside circle."

A Family Forever

In a beautiful sealing room in the temple one day I talked with a little boy dressed in white who was ready to join his parents and siblings in the sacred ordinance. I said to him, "Why is your family here in the temple?" He said, "To be sealed." I said, "What does it mean to be sealed?" He said, "To be a forever family." "Oh," I said, "you're going to be a family forever? You must have a good family, a happy family, if you want to be with them forever. Do you have a happy family?" (His parents and brothers and sisters and others were there.) "Yes, sir." This fine lad had already begun to understand two of the most important principles anyone could ever know: (1) that our Heavenly Father has provided for marriage and family ties which may be established permanently, to endure forever, and (2) that a marriage whose eternal continuation we can joyfully look forward to must be a good marriage here. Such a marriage is the heart of a happy home and family.

There is another truth of which I also would wish to testify: that the principles of the gospel, particularly those of the temple, are the best possible basis on which to build a strong marriage, and such a marriage never just happens. The sealing ceremony in the temple is to us beautiful and indispensable, but it does not automatically assure a successful marriage. Such a marriage is brought about not by circumstance or chance but by two mature, loving adults who are able and willing to learn the principles upon which a genuine and durable marriage may be fashioned and who, day by day, year by year, earnestly make the effort, building on the solid foundation of the covenants of the temple.

Eternal Marriage

I note these five basics: (1) temple marriage as the basis for (2) a happy eternal union (3) built on the solid foundation of gospel covenants (4) by two mature adults who are learning and growing together, and (5) with the priesthood as the authority through which these covenants are administered and as a commission for leadership in the home in the spirit and after the pattern of the principles which were central in the life of the Savior. The "Holy Priesthood, after the Order of the Son of God," I am saying, is not a commission to superiority or dictatorship or domination. It is a commission in one instance to seal by God's authority, and it is—and for all of us ought to be understood to be—a commission for leadership in the home, in the spirit and after the pattern of the principles and life of Jesus Christ—"The Holy Priesthood after the Order of the Son of God."

I believe deeply that honorable marriage with honorable

people involved, wherever and however the wedding ceremony is performed, is acceptable to God. I believe God honors honorable marriage and blesses it with His love and Spirit. But He himself has established and made available to some, and given them the responsibility to teach others, a "more excellent way," a more excellent hope. There is a best way to start such a significant and demanding enterprise as marriage. He would like us all to know about that and choose it. That is the reason for missionary work. That is in my judgment the major reason for the expansion of temples. Of eternal marriage, the scriptures teach us that marriage is ordained of God for His children, and we who truly love a husband or a wife and live in a respectable, respectful, growing, developing relationship could not contemplate an eternity without marriage and family. Much of everything lovely and eternally significant relates to those who are closest and dearest to us, and we could not really think of heaven absent their association and their love.

This week I chanced upon some Whitman lines that I will share: "Oh, to make the most jubilant song. It is not enough to have this globe or a certain time. I will have thousands of globes and all time."

The Lord declared that whatsoever He does shall be forever. His way of everlasting marriage is filled with hope and promise and is designed to lead to happiness here and to an eternal stewardship like His own. In the beginning after the earth was prepared, God brought man and woman together in the garden, and the first wedding occurred. They were not yet mortal. Death had not entered into the world, and no time limitations were placed upon their marriage. God declared, "Therefore shall a man leave his father and his mother, and shall cleave unto his wife: and they shall be one flesh" (Genesis 2:24). When Christ lived among men He quoted this commandment and added, "What therefore God hath joined together, let not man put asunder" (Matthew 19:6). He gave His disciples power to bind in heaven that which is bound on earth. Paul later declared that "neither is the man without the woman, neither the woman without the man, in the Lord" (1 Corinthians 11:11).

In the time of the restoration of the gospel came a renewed understanding of temples and temple worship. The power to bind and seal in heaven has again been entrusted to chosen servants of God. Eternal marriage, temple marriage, marriage of the highest promise, is again performed for time and all eternity by authorized officiators in the holy temples of the Lord. Thus the "more excellent way" is given its base, which can weld, blend, build, and bless with an eternal marriage that is indispensable to our eternal happiness.

Parley Pratt said that Joseph Smith had influenced him in a way he could not have imagined:

> It was from him that I learned that the wife of my bosom might be secured to me for time and all eternity; and that the refined sympathies and affections which endeared us to each other emanated from the foundation of divine, eternal love. It was from him that I learned that we might cultivate those affections, and grow and increase in the same to all eternity. (*Autobiography of Parley Parker Pratt* [Salt Lake City: Deseret Book, 1938], pp. 297–98.)

But an *eternal marriage* will have to be a *happy marriage,* creative, progressive, gracious. Sometimes the distinctive elements of temple marriage are thought of as resting exclusively in duration and authority. Of course, everyone who comes to the temple to be married understands that it is done by God's authority for time and eternity. But the remarkable revealed ceremony at the altar in the temple contemplates much more than this. Wonderful promises are sealed upon a man and a woman in a temple marriage, blessings related to the solemn commitments the two make to each other and the promises that they make individually and as a couple to the Lord. The commitment of each with the other is total and permanent, the whole person "as is" for the whole journey.

Now, of course, neither will remain as he or she is. That is not meant to be. They will grow and develop in a multitude of ways—that is, they *can;* but the pledge they make to each other is without condition or reservation. On this solid foundation the newly formed family undertakes to build a strong and loving union that will grow more wholesome and more glorious forever.

Liberty and Union

How will they do this? The personality and the individuality and uniqueness of each partner to the marriage must be understood, accepted, protected, and preserved if there is to be happiness; but this liberty must be enjoyed in the spirit of a deep commitment to the building of the union, not chiefly in the spirit of self-concern, self-satisfaction, self-determined expectations. You are probably acquainted with the Daniel Webster saying that to me has more to do with marriage than with politics, though it has a lot to do with both. Said he, "Liberty and union, one and inseparable, now and forever."

Emerson with all of his mighty intellect didn't seem to quite understand that, or at least he unbalanced it with the emphasis on the individual's needs and expectations and rights of fulfillment. Lincoln understood it better. Lincoln understood that unless there is a strong union there cannot be any independence and liberty. Now, he of course was talking politically, but his great mind and great heart would have understood that, like the states and the union over which he presided, unique, separate, special individual human beings brought together in this most total, intimate, and close relationship called marriage are not obligated to surrender. They make an alliance. They do give up some freedoms in order to establish and perpetuate a union, but that union becomes the base upon which their individuality may truly be accepted, appreciated, and expressed in the sense God intended it to be, bearing in mind that each of us has been around a lot longer than the total of his or her birthdays. We are eternal persons, and this personality therefore is eternal. "Liberty and union, one and inseparable, now and forever."

Henrik Ibsen's *A Doll's House* has a scene in which Nora, self-sacrificially, has done something to sustain her husband, Torvald, but he, bland and inconsiderate, doesn't really appreciate that. Indeed, at the height of that dramatic moment he says to her, "Before all else you are a wife and a mother." Her answer is, "I believe that before all else I am a . . . human being."

Now, nothing I know of in eternal marriage—and certainly not in the temple where those covenants are made—in any sense mitigates or vitiates that critical truth. You who know what you should know about marriage—and perhaps have been married long enough to become philosophical and a little whimsical—will be aware that you have not plumbed the depths of this other individual. You will have that interesting day when your heart and your tear ducts and your center of exultancy and the smile muscles and all the rest will mingle in a high, holy moment when you look at her or him and marvel. You will have learned how much deeper and better and more decent and full of faith she is than you are. And there will come the marvelous recognition that, knowing all you know, you still have not penetrated the depths of this person.

A human being is sacred, for one reason because he or she is always more than a human being, an eternal child of God.

As they are married in the house of the Lord, two human beings have a new life opened to them offering many relationships and unities which can and are meant to develop into a union.

Partners

Among the new relationships in marriage—in the sense that they never have existed before—is a *partnership* to which the two entering it bring assets and in which they recognize a need to grow with the problems, challenges, and conflicts; but the two become partners in the warm, sweet, wonderful, sharing, learning, growing sense of marriage. Partners. Real *partners*. Equal partners. Sharing, valued, respected, admired partners.

Companions

Such partners become *companions* in a special sense, whether they are in the same room or a world apart. They are married twenty-four hours a day. They care about each other's whole person and whole future, each exhibiting good humor, a good disposition, and a genuine consideration of the other's needs and desires. They set out to make it a happy life. They laugh a lot and cry a little. They are warm, considerate, and thoughtful. They show this in the note, the telephone call, the kind word, the sensitive response, the tremendous excitement of heading home to her when the work is done or the trip is over—back home to her and them and your place—and the wonderful excitement they feel when you are coming home.

Get together a group of grown children with their own children and listen to what they remember, and watch how they behave when their partner is arriving. Elder Matthew Cowley wrote a beautiful little piece on the "eternal triangle." The triangle is man, woman, and God. My "companion wife" is one with whom I break bread, that being the very meaning of the word. The root of the word *companion* is bread, and the implication obviously is that being together to break bread will be warm, rewarding, exciting, pleasing, and thoughtful in its preparation and its sharing.

Sweethearts

Through a few words of covenant the basis is laid, but that does not accomplish the job of making the two become *sweethearts*. Married people are sweethearts in a special creative union, blessed with a powerful chemistry that draws them together, sometimes from next door, sometimes from a world away. The sexual union is one of the many unions or unities in marriage which is critical and significant, a divinely bestowed blessing. *It is not the only flower in the garden.* To be what it is meant to be it must be sustained by other fundamental qualities—by respect, integrity, and loyalty. To be able to give oneself with a complete confidence and trust and to receive the other joyfully and gratefully is a blessing that grows in meaning forever.

One of my saddest, heartbreaking moments in many hours of counseling—mostly listening, trying to help a little—came when a beautiful well-groomed, well-dressed woman, the wife of one of my closest and best-loved friends, sat across the desk from me and asked me to speak to her as if she were a bride. She was desperate. Her marriage had no meaning. She and her husband were not really partners. They had made a lot of money and she could spend it, but there was no sense of sharing, nothing left of their beautiful months in one room with a let-down bed. "We are not companions really," she said. "He has his shotgun, his golf clubs, his friends, his handball gloves. We are not really sweethearts anymore, either. *We have nothing left to express.*" I swallowed a tear, and I feel like crying now as I recall the interview. Married all those years, with beautiful children, everything anyone could want, and they had ceased sharing, ceased being companions, ceased being sweethearts.

I never apologize for a personal example, although this one comes with some unease because it requires a great deal of trust in your good sense. On Christmas Day some years ago, when all our children were still at home (we had four teenage daughters, the oldest about to move into her own life, and their little brother), I gave their mother a beautiful white nightgown and said to them: "Now, I don't know that you are able to understand this, but you will remember it, and one day you will understand it. Your mother and I have been married many years and have been blessed with you five and some whom we have lost along the way. A marriage of this most intimate and total and close relationship has brought us our own peace. Having been through all of this together and knowing each other as we do, she is more pure and more beautiful to me today than she was the day I met her or the day we married."

The sweetheart relationship is appropriately sustained by character, quality, consideration, the capacity to repent, and the capacity to forgive. The complete trust that some have the capacity to enjoy and many others don't—that beautiful sweet thing that has been minimized, maligned, and tragically imposed upon through the centuries—is a plant established by God's good grace which ought to flower and grow with all that sustains and blesses it.

Friends

The two become *friends* in the special way that married people should be best friends, showing the considered kindness, the thoughtfulness, the support. Married people should be best friends because, in truth, no relationship on earth needs friendship as much as marriage does.

As I walked up the aisle in the auditorium at a university recently, I stopped and said to a young man sitting on the edge of the row, "Who is that beautiful girl sitting by you?"

"My best friend," he said, right off the top of his head.

"Oh, and is she also your wife?"

"Yes."

I spoke to her. "Is that true? Are you his best friend?"

"Yes."

"And is he your best friend?"

"Yes."

I said, "Do you know how lucky you two are to be married to your sweetheart who is also your best friend?"

They said, "We know."

Friendship blows away the chaff, rejoices in the uniqueness of the other person, listens patiently, gives generously, forgives freely, and is loyal. Friendship may indeed motivate one to cross the room to say, "I'm sorry, I didn't mean it," or "I didn't understand. I love you." Friendship will be more important than winning an argument or proving something. Friendship will endure our immaturity and our callousness. We are all both adult and child; so much of our response is childish in a nonconstructive sense. Friendship will not pretend perfection or demand it. It will not insist that in thought and feeling both respond in exactly the same way in every situation; but it will be understanding and supportive, repentant, and forgiving, respectful, trusting, and trustworthy. Friendship will say: "I am your husband, I love you. We are married. I am occasionally responsible for behavior that isn't quite consistent with the level of my understanding, but I love you and I am proud of you. I'll speak well of you, and I will not betray your trust. I will delight in your uniqueness. I am your best friend."

Covenants and Commitments

A good marriage doesn't just happen. Temple marriage is not isolated. It serves both as a culmination of other ordinances and as the foundation for family and eternal future. No one can enter into a temple marriage without first having been to the temple to receive his or her own blessings, to personally make sacred covenants with the Lord. These covenants center in principles that are basic in a truly Christian life and in the formulation of good marriage and family. The covenants we make in the temple, like the other sacred covenants of the gospel, commit us to the Lord Jesus Christ and His loving example. In the temple—think now of your experience—we make commitments to follow Christ in doing God's will and keeping His commandments, in valuing others and unselfishly serving them, in loving God and our fellowman. We pledge complete fidelity to moral principle, self-control, devotion to the cause of righteousness and truth; and all of this happens through the priesthood, the Holy Priesthood after the Order of the Son of God.

A thoughtful understanding of this single reality should automatically eliminate any false perceptions of superiority or inferiority. Men and women are of equal value before God and therefore should be equally valuable in the eyes of each other. A true devotion in following the example of the Son of God will never permit notions of domination or dictatorship or possession or control. It will never justify unrighteousness, abuse, foul talk, or discourtesy. Christ's way is the way of persuasion, longsuffering, meekness, kindness, love unfeigned, pure knowledge, unselfishness, gentleness, mercy.

It is simple to see, isn't it, that the kind of marriage we are talking about doesn't just happen. Nobody can pronounce happiness. No one can pronounce the quality that forgives and thus expresses real love. These are elements in lives that have to be brought to the union by those involved, grown in and developed in—through the course. The foundation can be laid in the house of the Lord. The marriage can be pronounced by the authority of God, but it must be fashioned by two who are wholesome, who are prepared emotionally and practically, and who are honest. It requires being *ready* to go to a temple, being mature enough to *make* and *keep* promises and to *receive* holy promises and *qualify* for their fulfillment.

Wherever one is with respect to marriage—years from it, close to it, deep in it—the same basic principles should be understood. Keep the commandments. Be honest. In this most close and intimate relationship one is committed in the most serious and sacred decisions of life. Temple marriage is much more than the experience of the temple, the sacred ceremony, the authority by which it is performed, and the wonderful promises sealed upon the participants. It involves our attitudes toward God and each other, toward marriage, toward children, toward family. It involves our preparations, our worthiness, our ability to learn and grow and graciously endure.

Vision of Continuity

The inspiration for all of us is the assurance, deeply impressed upon the hearts of decent people who live as they should, that heaven will be heaven for us because this one we love the best will be there. A few days ago my wife and I sat in a room with our five children and their eternal partners and their sixteen children. Twenty-eight of us were joined in a circle of affection and appreciation. That circle established at an altar in the holy house of the Lord only a few short years ago has expanded miraculously. I sat marveling. Now, I don't know what you may know, but I know enough to be aware that when a magnificent phrase like "eternal lives" is repeated, it refers to that kind of life which exaltation expresses—that is, a creative life, a godlike life on a godlike level with the Almighty. I looked at twenty-seven other people, realizing that my wife and I hadn't had a child for twenty-four years and would not again in this world. Yet twenty-eight of us were in the room, and there were others yet to come. If God is willing, the two of us may even live long enough to see the next generation. This stewardship of ours is expanding eternally, like the stars of the heavens and sands on the seashore. We little specks, twenty-eight of us, are important individuals, producing life.

One who never knew his father can get excited about that. One who loves a mother can appreciate that. I get interested in a thirteen-year-old boy who joined the Church—a drover, a roughneck, with crude language and all the rest, who became a grandfather to me; and an eighteen-year-old girl who stood on a street corner knowing that what the elders were saying was true and also knowing her father would never permit her name to be said again in his house when she joined the Church.

What an exciting, remarkable vision it is to perceive continuity into the past and into the future: that all of us will find a place, ultimately, a loving place under the holy influence of Him whose sons and daughters we are spiritually and whose holy life and sacrifice brought us the blessings of these excellent hopes.

I say to you that of course the plan of God will be fair altogether, as He is fair. Those who earnestly desire the eternal blessings of marriage and family, but who through no fault of their own are deprived of this blessing here, will ultimately have an opportunity to enjoy it. The Holy One of Israel standeth at the gate and "employeth no servant there" (2 Nephi 9:41). The judgments and decisions of eternity will be stamped with His approval, with His justice, and blessed with His influence. It is my absolute conviction that no one will be forced into an eternal relationship that is not wholesome and desirable, nor deprived of a joyful, eternal relationshp which they desire and have done their part to qualify for. The plan provides for vicarious blessings to those who have no opportunities to enjoy them in this world. So also will it provide for those who are deprived of the blessing they deserve and desire.

Doctrine of the Priesthood

The glorious promises of God are summarized in a magnificent verse of scripture: "Then shall thy confidence wax strong in the presence of God; and the doctrine of the priesthood shall distil upon thy soul as the dews from heaven. The Holy Ghost shall be thy constant companion." (D&C 121:45–46.)

What is the doctrine of the priesthood? Is it the doctrine of command, of domination? Who will observe the kneeling at the altar of two who take each other by the hand and look to the Lord Jesus Christ as they make covenants—every one of which looks to Him as the Holy Exemplar—and think it gives some kind of domination? No one with any sense, in my judgment.

Regularly I get the privilege of looking young men in the eye and charging them to understand that simple thing: that the priesthood is a called commission to serve in the spirit and after the pattern of the Lord Jesus Christ as applied to their home in all the challenges they will have. The doctrine of the priesthood is a doctrine of agency, of learning, teaching, blessing, receiving, storing, acting in the ordinances, becoming a Savior to our people, creating.

Key to Attaining Good Marriage

I testify to you that God is fair, good, and just, and that we don't deceive Him any. We are dealing with realities—including the people who walk through the temple with their broken hearts or with whom I counsel every day, as there is time. Often their problem is not a failure to understand law. Their problem is that they do not know who they are, or they have met and been involved with others who don't know who they are. The fundamentals of the gospel are real and true and are applicable and appropriate for all of God's children.

My prayer is an earnest one for you. Either personally or in counseling, repentance and forgiveness are all-important—so important that your life depends upon it, as mine does. And so I urge you, if you have reservations, consider the simple, sweet truths in an "excellent way" of marriage that doesn't remove responsibility from the individuals involved but indeed gives them a base upon which to build, formulate, and fashion. This can be done by two mature adults who really want to and who can learn—not being blessed with perfection. There are no perfect marriages, but there are some very good ones, and they are always the product of two mature individuals who learn fundamental principles and build on them an unselfish, strong union.

IV

Choices

CHAPTER 18

The Message We Deliver

I would pray for clear vision for all of us and particularly for me in this few brief moments.

It isn't long since I was present in a meeting at a great school in our section of the country in a civic enterprise and heard the president of that university make a very intelligent though somewhat academic talk. He was part of a panel of outstanding people; the others were all businessmen. One of those businessmen, a graduate of that school, was reportedly the youngest head officer of an important business institution in the United States, and one of the youngest in the world in that position. His company deals in the billions of dollars. He and others had given excellent talks, but especially he. This young man was the chief executive officer of his corporation, an appointment he received following the resignation of his predecessor to become a cabinet officer in the United States government.

When the talks were over there was a period for questions. Since he had talked about ethics and morality in business, this question was directed to the businessman: "Suppose a ship loaded with your products pulled into a major harbor and you learned in a private way that it would be required of your company to pay a large amount of money for the privilege of un-

Baccalaureate address given at Ricks College 24 April 1979.

loading that ship in that harbor, and the unloading would need to be done quietly, otherwise it would not happen. What would you do?" This young man's answer was immediate and unequivocal: "We would endeavor to unload the cargo without paying the bribe. If we could not, we would withdraw the ship from the harbor without unloading it."

Those present sat and looked with that sense of appreciation that comes when you know that you are hearing the truth and that truth declares a sacred principle.

Moral Teaching in Universities

A question was thereafter directed to the educator. "We have heard, doctor," it said, "about the high ethical and moral standards these businesses represent, and we are thrilled by the realization that they are telling the truth. One of them assured us he really would order that ship out of that harbor without unloading its cargo. Now, doctor, do you teach these ethical and moral truths in your university?"

Now I watched the man who a few minutes previously had ridden high on the eloquence of his language and position. I saw him cast his eyes down and heard him say: "No, we do not. And you are going to ask why, so I will tell you. We are not permitted to teach those things in our school."

I could scarcely believe it, but it was true. Perhaps just coincidentally, he had resigned his position at the university that afternoon. (The newspapers would report this the next morning.) He said, "We don't teach those principles," and he added a thought: "Teaching people, helping people to learn, preparing people without teaching those principles is like trying to teach mathematics without numbers."

I thought of that a few hours ago for the first time in quite a long time as I considered the blessing of studying and teaching and serving at this school. That is a rare blessing which many of you appreciate now and which I pray the Lord all of you will appreciate in far greater measure as you live out your lives and experience some of the pressures of this interesting and complex world.

A Life Rich and Rewarding

I have two things to do today. First, to read a brief statement which I have written; second, to illustrate that statement in simple fashion and much less formally. To make the illustrations adequate to this significant occasion I invite you humbly to listen carefully to these several simple paragraphs that will give meaning to what is thereafter said. I am not much interested in simply telling stories and not at all interested in telling them to entertain, but I am interested in illustrating principles in a way that can be understood, and I will attempt in this brief few minutes to set the stage for doing that.

I come to you today with the conviction that when all is said and done what really matters for all of us and for this world is *the kind of people we are.* Christ settled that for sure for me when He replied to some who claimed place because they were Abraham's seed that God could of stones raise up descendants to Abraham (see Matthew 3:9).

We are not exempted, you and I, from the storms of this world. We are only assured that if we build well we shall stand. Nor are we promised salvation on any but the basis of personal preparation and performance in manifesting our desire and willingness to accept the priceless gift of the atoning sacrifice of Jesus Christ. Life is not meant to be easy, but it *is* meant to be rich and rewarding, and much of its richness is found in meeting with faith and courage the frustrations and afflictions and temptations that come with living. We are meant to discover along the way the limitless opportunities life affords for doing the good and the holy. We are here to meet our responsibilities and to live up to our opportunities and to develop our capacities, to see and speak and serve and become.

Getting information is important, but it is less important than cultivating a sense of appreciation. Information rests mainly in the mind and may be stored like grain in a silo. Appreciation includes emotion and touches also the heart and the spirit. It has been said that "mankind will not die for lack of information but it may perish for lack of appreciation." In our best and loftiest moments we are discovering and expressing that which in us is better than we know, which is more than merely human, and which has relationship to the God who made us.

History is unfinished. Our individual future is unfinished. The future is not "out there" someplace. It is within us, being shaped and formed and determined day by day. Others have noted that the whole life of an individual is nothing but the process of giving birth to himself or herself. And it is said poignantly, "We should be fully born when we die."

But the tragedy is that some of us die before we are thus born. We never come fully alive. That mortal process of gestation and maturation toward a larger and loftier life takes place on the level of our existence as unique individuals, as *persons* charged with the responsibility to grow and to develop and to use the gifts God has given us. But each of us lives simultaneously also on the other levels—as spiritual beings and as social beings, by nature responsive to moral values and to all living things. When Christ replied to the lawyer's question about the great commandment (see Matthew 22:37, 39), he quoted the ancient records that were written long before His mortal ministry: "Thou shalt love the Lord thy God with all thine heart, and with all thy soul, and with all thy might" (Deuteronomy 6:5); and "Thou shalt love thy neighbor as thyself" (Leviticus 19:18).

Thus the three relationships that must be right for a healthy, happy person are with himself, his neighbor, and his God.

Then, to illustrate.

When you and I settle for something less than we could have in terms of our relationships with ourselves and with others and with God, we inevitably shrink. We suffer a shriveling of the spirit. This we may try to mask with belligerence or cynicism or sin or indifference. We pretend that we don't care.

"My Life Is My Message"

In India my wife and I went to a large, beautiful area in the center of which is a tomb. The tomb is the resting place of Mahatma Mohandas Gandhi, and on it is written an interesting set of lines. Some of them talk about not failing to keep pledges.

Another talks of his life and repeats his expression, "My life is my message."

I declare to you today that, for you and for me, when we are not doing what we should, when we are only partially alive, when we are not responding to the best in us, when we are not growing but are settling for something mediocre and merely adequate in terms of what we could be, then we are delivering a message; and the message is not worthy of us, not wholesome, not hopeful, not happy, and not healthful.

My invitation to you today is to consider to what extent your life and the message that life is radiating reflects credit upon your origins, your heritage, your possibilities, your responsibilities. If you would feel inclined to be uneasy or dissatisfied at any answer you would have to give, if you would not really be inclined to defend as adequate to your own heritage and possibilities the message your life is giving, then the question you must entertain is, What can you do? What shall you do about it?

I answer by saying, check your attitudes. Please do. Three times in one chapter in the sacred record the Savior of the world addressed the same question to certain people whose attitudes were negative, destructive, arrogant, and who were ignorant of the greatest truths, though they were very learned in many other ways. Concerning their relationship with John the Baptist, who had preceded Christ, He three times asked, "What went ye out for to see?"

What did you expect? What were you looking for? You see, one fact was as true then as it is now; it was true before then and will be forever true. It is that we are inclined to find what we are looking for. If we look in places where foul language and evil ideas and inappropriate behavior are present, we shall find them. And if instead we have other places and other persons and other objectives in mind, we shall discover them.

Let me share the latest thing I have learned, or relearned. Brother Holland and I were in an airport, forced to wait a little time while the airplane came and prepared to leave. Several persons came to talk to me while he was busy with others. Among them was one whose dear one was dying in another city across the land and might not live until we got back to Salt Lake City, so I made a telephone call then. On the phone I talked with a lovely person I had known long ago, wife of a wonderful man I had known. In the airport I had learned that he had long since been gone from the roots of his early life; and she, torn as beautiful, pure, loyal women are between following an errant husband and following the path that earlier they had mutually chosen—weeping and heartbroken, and alternately, I am sure, ebbing and flowing—followed him, and watched their beautiful children also follow that path. Now dying, she thanked me, seemed to know all the things I would like to say without my saying them, responded in gratitude, bore a testimony, and said: "I feel all right because I love the same God you love, and I know He loves me. The mistakes I have made I no doubt will have to recover from, but I have made them in anguish trying to do the right thing."

We met others at the airport, and I won't pursue the individual concerns or involvements, but I thought to myself a strange little thought which you may remember if you remember nothing else. As we rode here from the airplane, laughing a little and enjoying the friendship and love of good people, there crossed my mind something I used to say once in a while: If you want to understand a crooked stick, you can try very hard to describe it and may not succeed. Instead if you would like to understand it and have others do so, lay it alongside a straight one.

Think about that.

Attitudes Make Choices

I am in the company of good people; not pretentious people, any more than I desire to pretend to be what I am not, but good people, people who are really trying, loving good humor, decency, integrity, clean language, honorable marriages and loyalty in them, and the other things that a crooked stick often doesn't honor. Laying a crooked stick by that is to me the most significant and powerful preachment I know on companionship, on places to be, on things to read and watch.

Check the attitude. There is no incompetence, *no* incompetence, so significant in this life as a bad attitude.

At the root of the crooked sticks, of people with sad problems because of bad attitudes and therefore bad choices, is a question, and it may be or it may not be anticipated. What is wrong with people in the prisons? Is it that they don't know what is right and wrong? Do they not know the law? I tell you that some of them know more about certain elements of the law than practitioners in the profession do. I do not generalize, but I know enough cases to say that in many instances they are not where they are because they do not know the difference between right and wrong. They are there because they lack knowledge of one other thing. They do not know who they are.

Let me share with you just a couple of lines that you will appreciate in this context. Socrates wrote a long time ago, "The ignorance which causes vice and immorality is not ignorance of moral principles or laws but an ignorance of self." To which Kierkegaard added many centuries later, "There is nothing of which man is so afraid as of getting to know how enormously much he is capable of doing and becoming." That is one of the saddest and truest things I ever read.

A Matter of Identity

The other night I arrived home to hear my wife listening to a cassette of *Fiddler on the Roof*. She was excited. She had something to share. I knew it would be good, and I was excited too. She stopped the cassette, partially rewound it, and then said, "Do you recall hearing this line?" Tevye is explaining about tradition and how his remarkable people, the Jews, have endured and survived the centuries of oppression and disaster visited upon them. At the beginning of his explanation is this sentence, which I didn't recall having heard before. Why could they do all of this? He answers: "Because of our traditions every one of us knows who he is and what God expects him to do."

What I have said about prison and prisoners can apply also to the simplest of places and sorrows. Perhaps I shouldn't mention these examples, but I think I will. Those of us who eat a little too much or drink a little too much or sleep a little too much or work a little too much or do something else to excess—is it because we don't know the simple rules or laws of life? Do we not know, for instance, that if we take in more calories than we use we are going to gain weight? Yes, we know that. And yet we go on doing it. Why? Because we don't know the law? Does it seem sensible to say, "No, it is because we have forgotten who we are."

We are all going through an identity crisis, and we never get over it, in my experience. We are discovering, rediscovering, who we are. And since we are all imperfect we can be comforted by a wonderful statement in the Doctrine and Covenants. "Seek ye earnestly the best gifts," says the Lord (and He mentions various gifts), "always remembering for what they are given; . . . they are given for the benefit of those who love me and keep all my commandments, and him that seeketh so to do, that all may be benefited that seek or that ask" (D&C 46:8–9).

Does that strike you with any kind of a feeling up the spine or in the viscera? Those who keep all God's commandments *"and him that seeketh so to do."* There is room in the kingdom, room on the path to salvation, room in the highest and holiest of creative associations and opportunities for those who are not perfect but who really seek, ask, want, and try to do the right thing.

All Children of God

I spent last weekend in Texas in the middle of a disastrous flood as the guest of a rabbi, who is now retired from his life-long labors in that capacity. It was a civic assignment that took me there, and I didn't have the comforting anticipation of the brotherhood that always awaits us when I and the other Brethren go to visit a stake president or a bishop or anyone else in the Latter-day Saint fold. I had never met the man and knew nothing about him. He didn't look what I might have anticipated. He was tall and slim and in very good physical condition, although he is old enough for his retirement. He was warm and outgoing and very soon responsive, and we became friends and then brothers—enough to shed a tear on parting and to look to a time of reunion.

Feeling perfectly comfortable in doing it, the night before we left I said to him: "May I try out a couple of stories on you? I have heard them, I have loved them, I have shared them, but I have never had a chance to get from someone I trusted, as I now do you, the answer from the Jewish heart. Will you tell me whether these things are valid?"

I told him the wonderful story of the Half Hallels. I had heard or read it someplace, and had asked another rabbi in military uniform in a place called Nha Trang, Vietnam, to tell me about the Half Hallels. He rejected me, he rebuffed me—he thought I was insincere, I guess, or that I wanted to argue—and he hurt me deeply. He didn't want to talk about it. I was a little concerned therefore about asking my new friend, but I finally said, "Will you tell me?" He said, "Tell me what you have heard about it."

I said I had been told that there is a tradition among the Jews that in the last few days of the Passover they say or sing only half hallels—short prayers, short songs of praise. They deliberately shorten them. The reason they do this goes back to the time when the children of Israel escaped from Egypt through the Red Sea, while the Lord rolled back its waters, and the pursuing Egyptian army, going through the same access route, were caught in the middle when the waters were loosed. The Israelites, safe on the opposite shore, began to sing hymns of praise and say prayers of gratitude to God, but God stopped them and said, "How can you rejoice and sing hymns of praise when so many of my children are drowning in the sea?"

My rabbi friend said, "I have never had anyone who wasn't a Jew ask about that before. That is true. That is our tradition."

I think it is a beautiful and inspiring tradition.

I said, "One more, Rabbi."

At a national conference I met a seventeen-year-old boy who said he was going to be a rabbi. He was the brightest, best-educated, most brilliant young expresser of his thoughts that I have ever met. We came to know each other. I was the older person, a kind of mentor to a group of young folks whom I had never met before that occasion. As the days went by I became more and more respectful of this young man's abilities but concerned about his sincerity.

A death in my family occurred and I had to leave the conference. On the last night I found Bernard, and we sat and talked for a few minutes. I said to him, "Tell me, my special young friend, why are you going to be a rabbi?"

He responded: "My father is a rabbi. My uncles are rabbis. It is a tradition in my family."

I said, "That isn't enough, Bernard."

Shocked, surprised, he said, "What do you mean?"

"That isn't enough reason for you to be a rabbi."

He knew by now of my own feeling for him and his people. He thought for a moment and then he said, "Do you know the wonderful writings of Hillel and Heschel and others?"

I said, "Some of them."

He said, "They and others like them—they are reasons why I want to be a rabbi."

I said, "They are marvelous people, but they are not enough reason. Why do you want to be a rabbi?"

He thought for quite a while before he replied: "Long ago in a tragic time, a terrible time, a group of Jewish people were rounded up, imprisoned, many of them murdered. Their rabbis were imprisoned with them. In a prison dungeon a guard came, found the Jewish people singing and dancing in their own magnificent, peculiar way, and smashed the rabbi to the floor. Standing over him, he said: 'You fool. Don't you know you are going to die? Don't you know that I can kill you at any moment? Why are you dancing and singing?'

"The rabbi through bloody lips said, 'We are dancing and singing because in a world where people are being killed by other people we can still choose to be killed rather than kill other people.' "

I said to my young friend, "That is a very good reason to be a rabbi. I hope you will never forget it."

When I shared this with my rabbi friend in Texas he shed a tear and said, "That too is a magnificent and true story out of the tales of the Hasidism." (These are the Jews who wear the black clothes and hats and have the ringlets and have among them some wonderful men and women.)

There are a thousand ways to say it, and I have chosen these out of recent experience: We are all children of God. We are something a little more than human, you and I. We may forget it, and sometimes we may not act to the level of our highest humanity. But the truth is that there is something in us that is better than we know, for which we should be reaching and for which we should be grateful to God.

Sensitivity to Others

But I said we live on several levels simultaneously. We also live as neighbors. I want to illustrate that with one simple story.

A man stood in a stake conference to meet his obligation as a great leader in the stake. He was also an outstanding leader in government and industry. He had only five minutes, he said, and would share one event that he remembered more compellingly than any other. As a young college student in Depression times he had had to work to pay his way and couldn't quite make it. He was eating one meal a day. He found a benefactor in those Depression times, a professor who helped him by getting him employment at helping to read papers from his classes.

The essential to the story is that the professor had left a foreign land in times of war, had lost his wife and family, had left behind any mirth that may have otherwise graced his life, and was a very dogmatic, insistent teacher in the field of physics. He found little to laugh at and little to be compassionate about with students who were not serious enough to suit him. He insisted that they work beyond the level of other students in comparable classes. He had the reputation of being demanding and a bad marker, and the majority of students avoided him. A few sought him out because he also had the reputation as the teacher who, when they were through, would have shared most and prepared them best.

Tests were completed at the end of the school year. The man at the pulpit said, "I with others rejoiced and relaxed and went down to get on a streetcar to ride to town." On that streetcar, standing in the aisles, some of the other young men who had gone through a rough final exam in his class began to mimic the professor's strong Polish accent. They bad-mouthed him all the way downtown, the one improving on the other in his lack of grace and his intensity of criticism. "It became a riot," said the man at the pulpit. "I didn't want to participate. He was my benefactor. Furthermore, he was the best teacher I had ever had. I didn't like his tests, I didn't like the hard work, but I liked what I had learned and the way I felt about it. So I kept still until finally they egged me on and egged me on; and they became ugly about it, and so, uncomfortable as I was, I joined them. I said a few choice words of criticism and unkindness and mimicked the professor.

"I was first off the streetcar. I walked back through the line of passengers to the back door, and stepped down on the step which would open the door automatically when the streetcar came to a halt; and as I stood there on the step, the person sitting in the seat just behind the safety railing—the person behind the newspaper—lowered the newspaper a little and I looked into the big, brown, tear-filled eyes of the professor.

"He said not a word, but his eyes spoke a bookfull: You too! These others maybe I could understand, but *you?* And the paper was slowly raised."

The speaker continued: "I have not forgotten that awful moment on the streetcar, and I am still ashamed. I have diligently tried to make no more memories like that one."

Oh, please, in our homes, in our relationships may we not be young and vital and vivacious and intelligent and fun and all the rest—yet have good manners and graciousness and a sensitivity to the fact that other people need to know they are valued, that we value them? Anytime we bring that into question, we hurt, we destroy.

Of Beauty and Strength

Let me finish by calling to your attention something else that is sweet and beautiful. We are spiritual, you and I. We are members of an eternal family, and we are also individuals, *persons* with special talents who can learn to play a viola so beautifully, or a trumpet, or a violin, or to lead, or to sing. We can, if we want to, festoon our minds with poetry that we can repeat under our breath, share with others. Can I chance the latest I have learned? I hope I learned it. I'll try it publicly. You listen carefully:

> In the sudden mirror in the hall
> I saw not my own self at all;
> I saw a most familiar face,
> My father stood there in my place,
> Reflecting in the hall lamp's glare
> My own surprised and watery stare.
> In thirty years my son shall see
> Not himself standing there but me.
> —T. S. Eliot

That needs some consideration and some thought. I want to share the conviction and the experience, limited as my own capacities may be, that make me exult in the presence of beauty and strength and tenderness and graciousness, make me proud to be a human being. Oh, do not misunderstand. As we heard this marvelous solo today I thought about Pablo Casals. Who is he, cellists? Perhaps the greatest cellist who ever lived, still alive, possibly the finest cello teacher who ever lived. He is ninety-five, and the other day I read that he said he spends an hour or so every day looking at the flowers; and sometimes, he said, "I cry."

I share what only you and no others have heard and what I conclude with. I do this because I felt a little twinge as I talked about beauty and strength. Would some of you think, if your own body is imperfect or you feel that your capacities are limited, that I didn't mean you? Louise Lake has been in a wheelchair for nearly forty years. She was honored at this school not long since. I am humbled to be one graced with friendship with Louise. For the forty years I have known her that body has grown more and more difficult to live in. She cannot move her lower limbs at all, has scarcely been able to for forty years. She was a beautiful, lovely, wonderful young mother when polio hit her. Suddenly she was totally incapacitated. She fought, fought to the point where she became "Handicapped Person of the Year" in the whole United States, traveled around the world helping handicapped people, inspiring them. Gradually that body has grown less and less responsive to her own needs. I go to her place occasionally when she needs a blessing or the company of a friend. Again, I share here what is very sacred and very personal.

In her presence, as with Elders Matthew Cowley and Harold B. Lee and others, I have felt almost lifted off the floor with her faith—not some kind of an unnatural or strange experience. She laughs, she smiles, she talks a little about her problems. She is normal—except in that body and except in what God has done, and she cooperating with Him, in strengthening a spirit. She wrote this in her journal, and I would like you to hear it. It says a multitude of things that I need not repeat.

> I have not been pleased with this inconvenient, twisted body. I have been commanding it to function for years but not appreciating its struggling efforts to perform and its great worth to me. I have realized since that blessing [referring to a blessing I had given her] what the past performance of this incapacitated body has really been to me. It has been magnificent, and I say that humbly. My prayers for bodily strength to meet the day's activities have been gloriously answered. It has been cooperating with my spirit's decisions and assisting me for years. It has carried me as I have traveled in the service of my fellowmen. Oh, I know we can progress with the aid of a healthy tabernacle, but in physical misery and discomfort the spirit can be refined to spiritual heights more rapidly and thus permit one to rise to greater calls in the service of the Master.
>
> Overnight, as it were, I have come to respect and cherish this body. More than ever I desire to increase in faith that I may, as soon as I grow worthy, experience the reuniting of my spirit and my renewed flesh and bones. I want no other body—just this one, cleansed and strengthened and spiritually refined. It is part of me.

You are so beautiful, so strong, so promising, and you no doubt have many problems among you of which I do not know. Please, please know that you are precious beyond your capacity to comprehend, special children of God, blessed with different gifts and problems but all bearing the image of the Lord. I rejoice in this chance to be with you.

God bless you and yours and the future in which you have a chance to do what this world needs so deeply to have done. God bless you. I bear witness that this is His work, that He lives, that we are His children, and that what we do is very important to Him. In the name of Jesus Christ. Amen.

CHAPTER 19

Trust in the Lord

The motivation for my preparation this morning came from a recent brief excursion through the pages of the day's newspaper. There, mingled with the ordinary reports of trouble, were several heart-warming accounts of human concern and unselfishness: a high school group giving hard-earned vacation money to an ill classmate; two workmen suffering serious injury to save the life of a colleague; blood donations oversubscribed for a stricken mother; a noble young follower of Christ giving his life attempting to rescue a companion.

Affliction and the Source of Comfort

These particular events were reported because they were exceptional. The news media, like history, often emphasizes that which is unusual or sensational. But it was historians who reminded us that "history as usually written is quite different from history as usually lived. . . ." If the whole story were told, "we should have a duller but juster view of the past and of man." Behind what they called "the red facade of war and politics, misfortune and poverty, adultery and divorce, murder and suicide, were millions of orderly homes, devoted marriages," strong, lov-

---

Address given at general conference April 1975.

ing families, and inspiring examples of goodness, courage and kindness. (See Will and Ariel Durant, *The Lessons of History* [New York: Simon and Schuster, 1968], p. 41.)

In our own communities—in our own neighborhoods— there are many such instances, unsung and unreported. An invalid quietly suffers through weeks and months, through recurring birthdays, with vital energy limited, and still radiates confidence in the love and purposes of God, lifts those who come to lift, helps those who come to help, and brings joy and light to the world around her. A loved one keeps watchful, tender vigil, ministering to needs, foregoing pleasures or physical freedoms, uncomplainingly sacrificing personal desires to give help where it is needed. A young father stands at the funeral of his wife and bears thankful testimony that they have found in their period of lengthy affliction that Jesus Christ and His strength are sufficient for any need.

Whatever Is Good Comes from God

What motivates people to unselfish, courageous actions? Are there wellsprings of strength and consolation accessible to those who suffer, or are alone, or afraid, or steeped in sin, or depressed? Whence comes the moral energy for good and lofty acts—for improved lives?

The scriptures answer:

"I say unto you that whatsoever is good cometh from God. . . . If a man bringeth forth good works he hearkeneth unto the voice of the good shepherd, and he doth follow him." (Alma 5:40–41.)

As life supplies its store of tribulation, we need the consolation that comes with knowing that God is good and that He is near, that He understands, and that He loves us and will help us and strengthen us for the realities of a world where sin and affliction exist. And while I'm talking about principles this morning, I am not really thinking in the abstract, but I'm thinking of many noble souls who have met difficulties with courage, like my mother and many others who had few other resources to rely upon—who had little but ingenuity and will and courage and faith. I'm thinking too of a more recent scene—a beautiful young face whiter than the hospital sheet upon which she lay, her sorrowing parents nearby grieving as a relentless disease consumed her life. Comfort came to them in the quiet knowledge of the nearness of a Savior who himself had not been spared the most keen and intense suffering, who himself had drunk of the bitter cup.

From this source—from God and Christ—wisdom and strength can be found that will make endurance possible and relationships generous and helpful, that will lead to abundance of life and to everlasting life. God will "temper the wind to the shorn lamb" and help us to endure all things and to continue to maintain integrity in the face of the siren song of invitation to "curse God and die"—die spiritually, die as to things pertaining to righteousness, die to hope and holiness and faith in a future where there is no corruption and no pain.

Knowledge of God Is the Greatest Treasure

Christ came that men might have life abundant and life eternal, and He declared: "This is life eternal, that they might know thee the only true God, and Jesus Christ, whom thou hast sent" (John 17:3).

And that knowledge, I testify, is the most important treasure one can possess or seek. From Hosea comes the word of the Lord: "The Lord hath a controversy with the inhabitants of the land, because there is no truth, nor mercy, nor knowledge of God in the land." And again, "For I desired mercy, and not sacrifice; and the knowledge of God more than burnt offerings." (Hosea 4:1; 6:6.)

Not long thereafter the Lord said through Jeremiah: "Let not the wise man glory in his wisdom, neither let the mighty man glory in his might, let not the rich man glory in his riches: But let him that glorieth glory in this, that he understandeth and knoweth me, that I am the Lord which exercise lovingkindness, judgment, and righteousness, in the earth: for in these things I delight, saith the Lord." (Jeremiah 9:23–24.)

All the prophets taught this truth about God, and their

prime purpose was not to argue or try to prove the existence of God but to be His witnesses, to testify that He lives, and to make His will known among mankind. Christ revealed the Father in His life and teachings. Through His Son the Father was not only bringing salvation and making eternal life possible for everyone but also was offering the ultimate opportunity for us to know God himself.

Power of the Holy Spirit

The influence of the Holy Spirit, we declare and testify, is a supreme blessing, for to "know the love of Christ, which passeth knowledge" and thus to "be filled with all the fulness of God" (Ephesians 3:19) is the source of the greatest comfort and consolation in this world, and the greatest motivating power for good. How do we gain this indispensable knowledge? The "works of the Lord, and the mysteries of his kingdom" can only "be seen and understood by the power of the Holy Spirit, which God bestows on those who love him, and purify themselves before him; to whom he grants this privilege of seeing and knowing for themselves" (D&C 76:114, 116–17).

As a Little Child

As a guest in the home of a choice young family only a few days ago I was invited to offer prayer as we knelt together at the day's beginning. Loving parents, who knew of my experience with our four little girls, suggested that their three-year-old would like to pray first, as she regularly insists on doing. The tenderness of the moment increased as a six-year-old brother undertook to help her when she faltered.

The purity and openness of little children in their relationship with the Lord points the way for all of us. If we would seek the Lord, we must put off the "natural man" and become "as a child, submissive, meek, humble, patient, full of love, willing to submit to all things which the Lord seeth fit to inflict upon [us], even as a child doth submit to his father" (Mosiah 3:19).

It is written: "None shall be found blameless before God, except it be little children, only through repentance and faith on the name of the Lord God Omnipotent" (Mosiah 3:21).

What, then, is our course? In our own dispensation the Lord has told us: "Verily, thus saith the Lord: It shall come to pass that every soul who forsaketh his sins and cometh unto me, and calleth on my name, and obeyeth my voice, and keepeth my commandments, shall see my face and know that I am" (D&C 93:1).

Of the Church in an earlier age, Mormon wrote: "They did fast and pray oft, and did wax stronger and stronger in their humility, and firmer and firmer in the faith of Christ, unto the filling their souls with joy and consolation, yea, even to the purifying and the sanctification of their hearts, which sanctification cometh because of their yielding their hearts unto God" (Helaman 3:35).

By the revelations of His mind and will through the Holy Spirit, the Lord will give us understanding and knowledge. But we must qualify for the blessing. As we learn to love Him, to purify ourselves before Him, to yield our hearts to Him, and to walk in the light of His Spirit, we can become again like a child and know Him. He "waits," Isaiah wrote, "that he may be gracious" unto us, and is "exalted, that he may have mercy" upon us (Isaiah 30:18). The Lord delights to bless us with His love.

We know that the Lord needs instruments of His love. He needs a Simon Peter to teach Cornelius, an Ananias to bless Paul, a humble bishop to counsel His people, a home teacher to go into the homes of the Saints, a father and mother to be parents to their children. But it is also the privilege of every child of God to seek and know for himself the comforting personal assurance that comes with confidence in the wisdom and character of a beloved Heavenly Father.

Enduring in Faith

There is, of course, much more to be said. Problems and difficulties occur in everyone's life, and the solutions we wish and pray for do not always come about. The power that remade

Paul, that poured in love and washed out hostility and hate, did not save him from the great travails, including Nero's dungeon and a martyr's death. Christ lived in him, he said, he had found the peace of God that passed all comprehension. Nothing—not tribulation, distress, persecution, famine, nakedness, peril, sword, death, life, angels, principalities, powers, things present, things to come, height, depth, nor any other creature—nothing could separate him from the love of Christ, from that love of God which is in Christ Jesus, our Lord (see Romans 8:35–39). Christ died on the cross and won His victory; His disciples and followers also have been subject to the brute forces and foibles of this world, yet through enduring faith they have shared and will share in that victory.

Like Habakkuk of old, we may in our anguish feel that we could bear anything if we could only understand the divine purpose in what is happening. The ancient prophet learned that the righteous live by faith and that faith is not an easy solution to life's problems. Faith is confidence and trust in the character and purposes of God and in the ultimate triumph of His holy will. Habakkuk declared: "Although the fig tree shall not blossom, neither shall fruit be in the vine; the labour of the olive shall fail, and the fields shall yield no meat; the flock shall be cut off from the fold, and there shall be no herd in the stalls. Yet I will rejoice in the Lord, I will joy in the God of my salvation. The Lord God is my strength, and he will make my feet . . . to walk upon mine high places." (Habakkuk 3:17–19.)

Our religion is "not weight, it is wings." It can carry us through the dark times, the bitter cup. It will be with us in the fiery furnace and the deep pit. It will accompany us to the hospital room and to the place of bereavement. It can guarantee us the presence of a Master on the rough voyage. It is, in short, not the path to easy disposition of problems but the comforting assurance of the eternal light, by which we may see, and the eternal warmth, which we may feel.

"The Lord is good: Blessed is the man that trusteth in him" (Psalm 34:8).

In the name of Jesus Christ. Amen.

CHAPTER 20

Choices They Made

I appreciate the beautiful music and the tender prayer, and particularly the feelings of exultancy of spirit and equally great sobriety that comes as one looks into this assembled body of students. With all of that, I confess that I believe and have trust in good humor. Just this morning I recalled a panel or two from the Beetle Bailey comic strip that seem appropriate. Sergeant Snorkle has been at the men, and Lieutenant Fuzz is explaining to him that you can't do that anymore. He says, "Sergeant, this is a different generation. You have to explain things to them, quietly."

The next panel shows Sergeant Snorkle with a grenade in his hand, saying, "Men, I just pulled the pin on this grenade. Ordinarily, I'd say, 'Duck,' but Lieutenant Fuzz says—"

And the lieutenant screams "Duck!" and dives for the ground.

There is a time in the learning process when we'd better *move*. I'd like to accelerate that this morning, if I'm fortunate.

Pursue Spiritual Values

In the scriptures are these interesting instructions:

Address given at Brigham Young University devotional 18 January 1977.

Seek not for riches but for wisdom, and behold, the mysteries of God shall be unfolded unto you, and then shall you be made rich. Behold, he that hath eternal life is rich. . . .

If thou wilt do good, yea, and hold out faithful to the end, thou shalt be saved in the kingdom of God, which is the greatest of all the gifts of God; for there is no gift greater than the gift of salvation. . . .

Therefore, fear not, little flock; do good; let earth and hell combine against you, for if ye are built upon my rock, they cannot prevail. . . .

Look unto me in every thought; doubt not, fear not. (D&C 6:7, 13, 34, 36.)

We are taught to look to God in faith, to seek wisdom, to do good, and to hold out faithful to the end. We are to pursue the high and noble values of the Spirit, give our lives freely to them, and do this with courage and devotion on the road which stretches out before us, whether in common paths or lofty ones, whether with public acknowledgment or in the quieter and narrower circles of our homes, whether with a full basket of present blessings or the postponed but certain assurances of forever. In faith seek, serve, and endure. And for those who do, the promise is eternal progression and eternal life—life with God, a life of divine quality. Creative, learning, progressive life, loving life, with dear ones.

What are those values of the Spirit which, if sought and served, open to us that kind of life? For the Christian—for the Latter-day Saint Christian—there is one foundation, one beginning: To know our Heavenly Father, the only true God, and His holy Son, Jesus Christ (see John 17:3). Repentance, obedience, and walking in the light of the Spirit increase our faith and build upon that foundation. But where does this lead us? What values become our inspiration and guide in our daily lives? To what ideals shall we give more than lip allegiance? How do we express in living the native nobility that sometimes pushes itself up through the crust of our pride or fear or selfishness or self-satisfaction or sin?

Make Noble Choices

There is a story I have long wished to tell here and have repeatedly, sometimes at the last moment, not told. And I will tell it today on that beginning. It is the story of Tycho Brahe, sixteenth-century astronomer, and it is also, as you shall see, the story of certain others—some of whom you know or of whom you have heard.

Tycho Brahe, you may know, was a Danishman born to high station, which absolved him from having to earn a living. He studied to be a lawyer, but early in his life his interests led him into astronomy. In fact, he discovered a previously unknown star and became famous for it. King Frederick was a patron of science and the arts and all things good, and seeing the great strength and potential of this man he made it possible for Tycho Brahe to do what he might not otherwise have been able to do. There was provided for him, on an island, a magnificent working place which he came to call Uraniborg. It was all that he could wish. And his great intellectual capacities made of Uraniborg a university of the skies.

But King Frederick died, and young Prince Christian came to power, bringing with him courtiers to whom the senseless survey of the stars seemed only to pour lots of Danish money down a useless drain. Two pompous officers knocked at Tycho's eastern gate one day. "We are sent," they said, "to see and to report what use you make of these estates of yours. The uses now! Show us the *uses* of this work of yours."

When he had done so they asked, "And this is all?"

"Not all, I hope," said Tycho, who had marked the accurate positions of hundreds of stars, "for I think before I die I shall have marked a thousand."

You can almost see their smirk. "To what end? When shall we reap the fruits of all this toil? Show us its uses."

Tycho responded (and I am reading from this marvelous book called *Watchers of the Sky* by Alfred Noyes): "In the time to come, perhaps a hundred years, perhaps a thousand, when our own poor names are quite forgotten and our kingdoms dust, on one sure certain day, the torchbearers will, at some point of context, see a light moving upon this chaos. . . . We are like men that hear disjointed notes of some supernal choir. Year after year we patiently record all we can gather. In that far-off time, a people we have not known shall hear them, moving like music to a single end."

The officers could not understand this life that sought only to bear the torch and hand it on, and so they took back a report that all these foolish dreams of this foolish man were of no avail and might, in fact, even be used against the crown in some time ahead.

So Tycho lost his patronage, lost his place, was exiled, the question tinging through the world of science: "To what end? Show us its uses."

"Will you go on, Tycho?" he was asked.

He answered: "Yes, I still hope, in some more generous land, to make my thousand up before I die. Little enough, I know; a midget's work. The men that follow me with more delicate art may add their tens of thousands; yet my sum will save them just that five and twenty years of patience, bring them sooner to their goal, that kingdom of the law I shall not see. . . . Many of you will see them. . . . The victors may forget us; what of that? Theirs be the palms, the shouting and the praise; ours be the father's glory in the sons."

Tycho Brahe's choice, you see, was a choice of values, some of which did not demonstrate their validity or fulfill their full promise in his lifetime. Yet humanity has lived long enough since his contributions to begin to understand. His choice you will recognize to be the choice of every child of God of high or lowly station who has found (or been found by) noble pursuits and has selflessly served them. It is the story of Abraham Lincoln. It is the story of my custodian friend, who for several years has carried his bright and beautiful but terribly physically handicapped son in his arms to the doors of the people to collect fast offerings, through the aisles to serve the emblems of the sacrament, through the trails to earn merit badges—even on the dance floor he has carried his boy, so that he could soar a time in spirit where his sorrowfully afflicted and undeveloped little body could not itself go.

Tycho's choice was the choice of Albert Schweitzer, and of Tom Dooley, the jungle physician; of the unsung LDS plastic surgeon I met in Samoa, where for several weeks each year he spent twelve to fourteen to eighteen hours a day performing his miracles for the severely handicapped. It was the choice of the missionaries I read about years ago—the missionaries of the

Christian Alliance Church who, in Ecuador, facing death by the people they were trying to teach, went to their deaths singing the great Christian hymn based on a prayer of Asa of old, who led a greatly outnumbered Judah against her enemy, crying, "Help us, O Lord our God; for we rest on thee, and in thy name we go. . . ." (2 Chronicles 14:11). In that attack in Ecuador the men were killed; the women and children were spared. And after a few short months the women, who had returned home for a time, went back to teach the same tribes who had killed their husbands.

It was the choice of a young Latter-day Saint medical family whom I'm sad to say I do not know, but whom I honor greatly—whose wife and mother recently died in missionary service in Samoa. Not having been able to reach Dr. Ashby, I hope I am not presumptuous in sharing one short, sacred portion of a letter he wrote to his friend, President Holgar Peterson, who shared it with me. He talks of his wife's death in Samoa:

> I wish I could describe to you all the beauty, friendship, and love that were evident at the service. The chapel was filled to overflowing with family, missionaries, friends, nurses, doctors, government officials, pastors from other churches, and many who'd known Lily and been touched by her spirit.
>
> Garlands of orchids, wreaths of hibiscus, bougainvillea, and many other flowers freshly picked covered her casket. I was privileged, as few husbands are, to be asked to speak at my wife's funeral. I told a little about her life, her spirit, her love of living and doing and getting things accomplished, her testimony of the gospel, and her joy in our mission.
>
> After the chapel service, the casket was placed in a hospital ambulance (there are no hearses in Samoa), flowers were placed all over the ambulance, and it then drove slowly through Apia and out to the burial site. Everywhere we drove, all activity stopped, all traffic pulled over to the side, and the long line of vehicles drove slowly by. We drove for about fifteen minutes to a group of hills outside of town, and the casket was carried to the grave site. This particular area is somewhat out of the way, and new footpaths had been cleared the night before by members of the Church. We climbed a very steep hill, with everyone helping each other up, and found ourselves in a beautiful area which had been freshly prepared. Several other old graves of missionaries who had

died while on their missions in Samoa were nearby. The graves were mostly dated around 1880 to 1900, and Lily's was the newest in many decades. The grave site was dedicated in Samoan by the counselor to the Stake President.

There has never been any question in our minds about completing our mission. Lily was once concerned that her death might prevent this; but we talked about this at length beforehand, and knew that our call was as a missionary family, so we knew we would be able to complete the work we had been called to do.

This is the year 1977, when choices are still being made by noble people who somehow have a sense of a divine direction. Seemingly, not all of us feel that, though I suspect and believe we might if we sought it.

This same choice has been that of a treasured friend who for over a score of years has carried with her uncomplaining heart and all the strength she possesses the increasing responsibilities of caring for a dear husband who is wasting, inch by inch, with a tragic disease. So chose my beloved missionary assistant, so chose many others like him who, with everything to live for, made their anguished resolves in favor of their country and her commitment and gave everything they had in incredibly heroic actions on hillsides or in jungles in South Vietnam.

And so, in quieter ways, the choice demonstrates itself. We do not, in our pride and the rush of our lives, often see it going on. We may sense it, we may be aware of it, we may even feel compassion for their lives of courage and service, but then something happens—maybe death comes and reveals the strength and beauty. Then we see, and our hearts are lifted and we become honored afresh to be humans, because *they* were humans—*are* humans. It happens in countless places. Some of you here have already, partially at least, qualified. And many others of you know those who do, who have made the choice too, like the New Testament writer, and have walked with "angels unawares" (Hebrews 13:1). I know that among us there are many who make the very difficult choice to meet life's challenges with that singleness of purpose and that courage and that faith which cause the good things in this world, the noble and holy things, to happen.

There are a hundred other examples, but I choose to close with a testimony and a quotation from the man who led me to the Tycho Brahe story, though he is long dead. I read from a commencement address given by Benjamin Nathan Cordoza, great justice of the United States Supreme Court, in which he referred to Tycho Brahe, a reference that prompted me to find him and read of him. Justice Cordoza finished that address with these words:

> You go forth today [he said to a group of young servants of God, prospective rabbis in that case] as preachers of the eternal values. You will find mockery and temptation on the highways, and for the values that you hold to be eternal many a tinsel token will be offered in exchange. Sycophants and time-servers and courtiers and all the lovers of the fleshpots will assail you with warnings that you are squandering the happy days under the sun, and will ask you to tell them to what use, just as in the Danish city of Uraniborg, city of the heavens, the messengers of the Danish king taunted and challenged and drove into exile that other watcher of the skies.

I testify to you in solemnity—but I have to add with exultancy of spirit, because the idea thrills and lifts me and makes me wish to qualify—that there are with our firm foundations many diverse values of great importance that require the service, the devotion, the selflessness, the life commitments of those whose eyes see beyond the present and the limitations of mortality. I pray God that this story I've waited a long time to tell may comfort some and encourage many and, if I could be so bold, inspire a few to do better. God bless us all that, by living more courageously, we may build more strongly—on that foundation of faith, repentance, obedience, and walking in the light of the Spirit—that wholesome habitation which may in fact come out of the materials of the humblest home, that life which may come out of the makings of the humblest circumstances, a life that is worthy of who we are and whom we love and what we can be. In the name of Jesus Christ. Amen.

CHAPTER 21

Agency and Love

I desire to speak of the value of our free agency and of the love that preserved it for us and which should motivate and direct our use of it.

Many years ago I was introduced to an idea which at first seemed only an exercise in imagination, or perhaps a peg on which to hang a story. But the thought has returned occasionally since then as I have traveled the earth, often separated from family and other loved ones.

Suppose that everyone in the world received simultaneously the word that the inconceivable was about to occur: civilization as we know it was about to end.

What would happen?

Well, for one thing, the streets would be a maelstrom of frantic people trying to get to a telephone to talk with someone. Every line would be jammed and every telephone booth besieged by people trying to reach someone to say "I love you." There would be other messages also. "I'm so sorry," would be one of them, or "Forgive me."

Everyday Relationships

The condition of the world about us assures us that the un-

Address given at general conference October 1983.

thinkable could happen; but rather than pondering the possibility of such a cataclysm I am thinking of our daily walk and our everyday relationships. Those who love should manifest their love while there is a chance to do so. If we are waiting for some later time, some period when all imperfections are corrected and when all frustrations pass away, we are not wise. Resentment or pride or selfishness or impatience can lead us to miss what life is meant to be, and can be—and *is* for those who love and serve. To postpone loving and giving until some time of perfect freedom from problems is a great mistake. That will not happen. It is not for this world.

He First Loved Us

We *should* be earnestly seeking and striving to correct and improve our own attitude and our own behavior. God has so ordained it. He loves us and believes in us and has done and will do anything He can to help us, but He will not impose on our free agency. "We love him," says the scripture, "because he first loved us" (1 John 4:19). He does not love us because we love Him; He loves us unconditionally. But His love does not take the course of negating or smothering our privilege to choose, or our responsibility to account for what we choose and to experience the consequences. Indeed, it is written that He weeps for the bad judgment of His willful and disobedient children: "Behold these thy brethren; they are the workmanship of mine own hands, and I gave unto them their knowledge, in the day I created them; and in the Garden of Eden, gave I unto man his agency" (Moses 7:32). And again, "And . . . the God of heaven looked upon the residue of the people, and he wept" (Moses 7:28).

We had that agency when we were with God before this world was. In the heavenly council of which the scriptures teach, another plan as well as God's was presented: Lucifer was permitted to offer his program. It is vital for us in our leadership and our relationships to remember that God so loved us that He would not shield us from the perils of freedom, from the right and responsibility to choose. So deep is His love and so precious that principle that He, who was conscious of the consequences, required that we choose. Lucifer had no love in his heart, no real concept of freedom or respect for it. He had no confidence in the principle or in us. He argued for forced salvation, for imposed survival, for an agency-less round-trip to the earth and back again. None would be lost, he insisted. But he seemed not to understand that under his plan none would be any wiser, either, or any stronger, or more compassionate or humble or grateful, or more creative.

We understood before we left that premortal state that freedom is a precarious, difficult environment. We knew that to love would make us vulnerable to heartbreak and pain and disappointment. But we had learned that the alternatives to love and freedom of choice cannot provide the climate for growth and creative capacity that can eventually lead us to a stewardship like our Father's. The unselfish love of God's firstborn in the spirit helped us understand when He, knowing the personal cost ahead for Him but also the eternal significance for all of us, volunteered for His role of redemption.

We Go On Choosing

We chose then; and we are, in consequence, on this earth still choosing.

Recently I listened to a lovely young lady, just emerging from her teens, as she spoke in a stake conference—her first address ever. She had never known a true family of her own. She had experienced many temporary homes, made many mistakes, suffered much heartache and hopelessness. Then an older Church couple found her, and loved her, and taught her. Her prepared talk was witty and interesting, but when she laid it down and bore witness through tears it became magic.

"No one ever helped me to understand that I was worth anything," she said, "that I was special in any way. And then the missionaries taught me about Jesus Christ and His love, and the God who sent Him. They taught me that Jesus died for me—for *me*. I am valuable! I am valuable! He *died* for me."

The lesson of God's great love and wisdom seems lost on many who are on this earth because of their choice but who do not understand. Our responsibility is to help them. But we must ourselves pray and strive earnestly that we do not obscure its meaning. If we do not really love and really believe in free agency, we may be inclined to impose our will on others for what we think is their best good. If we love enough, we will not do that, even at the risk of failure.

Instruction and rules and training and discipline are essential, of course. From our Father's example of godly love and patience we should be motivated to stretch to any lengths to teach, to persuade, to encourage, to help. But in matters of conscience and faith, if we truly love we will never seek to impose our will and deprive others of their agency. That is, after all, Satan's way. He is still permitted in this world to pursue his own rebellious approach. Since his encounter with earth's first family, he has waged war unceasingly upon God's children.

A scene to give us pause is portrayed in the book of Moses: "Satan . . . had a great chain in his hand, and it veiled the whole face of the earth with darkness; and he looked up and laughed, and his angels rejoiced." But it is written also: "And . . . angels descend[ed] out of heaven, bearing testimony of the Father and Son; and the Holy Ghost fell on many." (Moses 7:26–27.)

The contest for the souls of men continues. We go on choosing.

The loving Father who at such great cost has preserved our agency in and out of this world has made every effort to help us use it well, but He has made it plain where the responsibility now lies: "I have set before thee this day life and good, and death and evil; in that I command thee this day to love the Lord thy God, to walk in his ways, and to keep his commandments and his statutes and his judgments, that thou mayest live and multiply. . . . I call heaven and earth to record this day against you, that I have set before you life and death, blessing and cursing: therefore choose life, that both thou and thy seed may live." (Deuteronomy 30:15–16, 19.)

Touched by Others' Infirmities

It is written that "God so loved the world, that he gave his only begotten Son, that whosoever believeth in him should not perish, but have everlasting life" (John 3:16).

That holy Son died for us and gave us the wonderful example of His life, and nothing in that life touches my heart with greater impact than the manner in which He chose to live among us. It is written:

> Forasmuch then as the children [that is, we] are partakers of flesh and blood, he also himself likewise took part of the same. . . .
> For verily he took not on him the nature of angels; but . . . took on him the seed of Abraham.
> Wherefore in all things it behoved him to be made like unto his brethren, that he might be a merciful and faithful high priest in things pertaining to God, to make reconciliation for the sins of the people.
> For in that he himself hath suffered being tempted, he is able to succour them that are tempted. (Hebrews 2:14, 16–18.)

Through that love it now is that "we have not an high priest which cannot be touched with the feeling of our infirmities; but was in all points tempted like as we are, yet without sin" (Hebrews 4:15).

Jesus has the feeling of our infirmities; He understands our temptations. He came not as an angel but in flesh and blood, that He might be a merciful and faithful advocate for us with the Father.

Would we improve our individual performance in relationship with others if we truly had the "feeling of their infirmities" and truly sought to be a faithful and merciful high priest, or Relief Society teacher, or friend, or wife, or husband?

The intensity and integrity of God's love and Christ's love are beyond our comprehension, but we are here to learn, and we must try.

Only Christ was sinless in this world, and this is why repentance must always company with faith as first principles. God's plan and Christ's sacred gift prepared the way for us to improve, to grow, to change, to learn wisdom and mercy and forgiveness. Out of the wise use of our free agency proceeds every other wholesome quality and every blessing.

Love Is the Basis

It is my deep conviction that any act or program or rule planned or performed without love at its heart, love as the spirit of it, or which curtails the agency of our Heavenly Father's children, is not worthy of God's kingdom or of His leaders or people.

Repeatedly He has protected our eternal agency, thus helping us to qualify, through opposition and in the face of alternatives, for the sweet blessing of eternal creative service. But we must choose—and be held accountable.

All of this came together for me in a very personal way in Manila in the Philippines when a telephone call from my wife reached me in the middle of the night in a hotel room telling me that our only son had suffered a severe accident that threatened his mobility and perhaps his life. He was being flown home for surgery.

About the time of his anticipated arrival home, I telephoned. There was a brief delay, then the sound of my wife's voice, quiet and subdued. "Your four sons-in-law are standing around your son administering to him," she said. "Paul has anointed him, and John is about to give him a blessing. He was worried because you're not here. This will be the first administration he's had from anyone but his father; but he's comforted now." I joined them in that prayer of blessing on my knees in a lonely hotel room half a world away, a room suddenly made sweet and warm.

Whether or not that day ever occurs in our lifetime when the telephone lines may be especially busy, we should be thinking of the love we have and should express, and should manifest it for those nearest us, and for those round about us, and for all others. And especially for our holy Savior and His Father.

Well may we sing, "I stand all amazed at the love Jesus offers me."

In the name of Jesus Christ. Amen.

CHAPTER 22

"I Will Look unto the Lord"

In the early days of the Restoration the Lord commanded one of His servants to "declare glad tidings" and to do this "with all humility, trusting in me, reviling not against revilers" (D&C 19:29–30). In the constructive spirit of that directive I desire to bear my testimony about the vital effect in our lives and the lives of others of the day-by-day decisions all of us are making—and where we can find help in making them.

A teacher once wrote of the unanticipated consequences of some of our decisions. We didn't really ever intend those consequences, but we followed the paths that led to them. "He who chooses the beginning of a road chooses the place it leads to," the teacher said. "He who picks up one end of a stick, picks up the other." And it is not only our own course we are affecting when we choose the beginning of a road; we inevitably travel with others, and sometimes we bring anguish and distress to those we love and to other innocent persons.

President David O. McKay taught us: "Next to the bestowal of life itself, the right to direct that life is God's greatest gift to man. . . . Freedom of choice is more to be treasured than any possession earth can give." (Conference Report, April 1950, p. 32.)

Address given at general conference October 1986.

Sources of Help in Choosing

The oppressing presence of problems all about us—personal, family, and in our society—accentuates the peril as well as the privilege of free agency. The ancient Psalmist surely seems to be singing to our time: "Have mercy upon me, O Lord, for I am in trouble" (Psalm 31:9). Why is there so much trouble? "With all that fairway," someone asked, "why do we spend so much time in the rough?"

Part of the answer is that without opposition and testing, free agency loses its meaning. Opposition, tribulation, afflictions, the refining fire, are part of the eternal plan.

Much that happens to us in this life we cannot control; we only respond. But much of the pain we suffer and inevitably impose upon others is self-induced through our own bad judgment, through poor choices. Where can we look to for help?

The ancient prophet Micah perhaps surprisingly seemed to rule out the nearest and most normal sources of assistance—family, friends, and leaders. Some of us have perhaps experienced a measure of the deep disappointment that he felt because of Israel's rebelliousness when he declared that "the good man is perished out of the earth." He spoke of princes and judges asking for rewards, and of great men uttering "mischievous desire." For Micah, the source of help was clear and sure: "Therefore I will look unto the Lord," he said. "I will wait for the God of my salvation: my God will hear me." (Micah 7:2, 3, 7.)

Jeremiah issued a warning to "the man that trusteth in man, and maketh flesh his arm, and whose heart departeth from the Lord" (Jeremiah 17:5). Other prophets have similarly spoken.

Does this mean that we may never have confidence in the integrity of others? Must we never trust parents or friends or caring counselors or humble servants of God? This is obviously not the meaning of the scriptures, which themselves are the record of revelation and inspired instruction; what they are emphasizing is the *care* we must exercise in *choosing* counsel or example.

There is accessible, for those who will accommodate it, much that is *not* uplifting or wholesome, which sometimes seems so perverse in its portrayal of marriage, of the family, and of personal integrity that the undiscerning might be led to believe that this is the normal way for people or families or neighborhoods to behave.

Only last week a comment was made by an assistant United States attorney general after she had witnessed a popular play in which drug use was made to appear acceptable and even desirable: "We perpetuate the falsehood that drugs make you cute, bold, insightful, philosophical or chic," she said (Lois Hight Herrington, quoted by Godfrey Sperling, Jr., "Tolerance for Drugs Is Undermining U. S. 'War' Commitment," *Deseret News,* 24 September 1986, sec. A, p. 9). And the columnist, in quoting her, added an interesting line: "Our society still sanctions the use of alcohol. There is really no more dangerous drug—and certainly none that has done more damage or wrecked more lives over the years—than alcohol." (Sperling, sec. A., p. 9.)

But for most of us also sound sources of wise guidance are available if we will look for them. There is great power in trust and love, and, of course, we must learn to trust because our confidence in the integrity of man supports our confidence in God. Yet in matters of lasting importance one must not rely on "the arm of flesh" at the expense of looking to the Lord in scripture and in prayer.

Dire Consequences—An Example

In World War II I had an experience aboard a United States naval vessel in the South Pacific that was a powerful example of the virtue of wise choices and the peril of making decisions that are immature or impetuous, or are made in the heat of emotion, or that go thoughtlessly along with the crowd.

The young man aboard my ship was obviously special. He was modest and able and promising, and it was a blessing to be with him on the few occasions when our particular duties during wartime made it possible to be together. But circumstance dictated that much more of the time and attention of my young associate was spent with others with whom he worked intimately in the compressed life of a crew aboard a ship at sea. These associates had life-styles and a view of values that were far removed from those to which this choice lad was accustomed. Gradually the circumstances and the daily pressures began to take their toll on a not yet fully stable young man.

One day, in a far-off port, I observed him almost furtively preparing to go ashore in the company of some of those experienced individuals who were taking him into town for one of their "good times," as they supposed. In the navy these periods off duty were ironically called "liberty."

I had a brief moment with him as he went over the gangway, and I tried to warn him that this adventure was perilous and that these men meant him no good. His furtiveness turned to defiance, and he plainly told me that he was a big boy now, able to make up his own mind, and that he would do as he chose.

The consequences of the decisions he made that day—and those that were made for him when, through his companions' iniquitous "help," he had lost the power to think for himself or govern his own behavior—were different than he ever intended or could imagine. In his immaturity he rebelliously chose the beginning of a road without thinking where the road would lead him. The place at which he arrived in the next few hours was one which in his right mind he would never have chosen.

When he returned to the ship, overleave overseas in wartime, out of control, and in the custody of the shore patrol, he became subject to severe discipline. I cannot forget his tearful anguish as he awaited his ordeal. He could not even remember anything of the most serious of the tragedies that had happened to him. All he could recall was lifting a glass his companions pressed on him, not knowing that they had drugged the drink; and then all was blank. They had proceeded to take him on their rounds with them.

The charges against him, indelibly imprinted on his previously perfect service record, were heartbreaking. I won't forget his tearful anguish as he said over and over, "What will I tell my mom? What will I tell my girl?"

He had time now—and the disposition to listen and to

think. We read together the sweet counsel of the Lord concerning Christ's atoning sacrifice and His mission of redemption and of forgiveness and mercy (see Alma 42).

About two thousand years ago the Apostle Peter wrote in remarkable detail of our times and what is transpiring in them as individuals, young and old, are sometimes led into tragedy by others who have no wholesome interest in their happiness or their future. These "others," and the results of their evil influence, are clearly described. I pray that some who sorely need it, or some who can help those who sorely need it, will hear these remarkable words:

> The Lord knoweth how to deliver the godly out of temptations, and to reserve the unjust unto the day of judgment . . .
>
> But chiefly them that walk after the flesh in the lust of uncleanness, and despise government. Presumptuous are they, self-willed, they are not afraid to speak evil of dignities.
>
> . . . of the things that they understand not; . . .
>
> Having eyes full of adultery, and that cannot cease from sin; beguiling unstable souls: . . .
>
> These are wells without water, clouds that are carried with a tempest; . . .
>
> For when they speak great swelling words of vanity, they allure through the lusts of the flesh, through much wantonness, those that were clean escaped from them who live in error.
>
> While they promise them liberty, they themselves are the servants of corruption: for of whom a man is overcome, of the same is he brought in bondage. (2 Peter 2:9–10, 12, 14, 17–19.)

I have never been able to refer to those powerful words without thinking about a clean young man of strong promise who followed bad counsel and bad example into tragedy, with compromise to conscience and with heartbreak to himself and to those who loved him. We cannot with impunity follow the example or heed the counsels of unwisdom or unrighteousness, or of ignorance or immaturity or ego or greed or bravado. There is no bravery in evil, no true courage in behavior that can only result in deep disappointment. There is no lasting joy in the euphoria resulting from substances taken into our bodies which ultimately sabotage our self-control, overcome our capacity to think for ourselves, and move us to act in ways incompatible with our best understanding.

"Counsel with the Lord"

We see much that is glorious and reassuring in good human beings, but mortal men have limitations. None of us has ever met a mortal in whom we could comfortably rest our salvation. Only one qualifies for that trust, and He is the Holy One of Israel. His love for us was and is so great that He volunteered for the unspeakable burden of carrying the weight of our sins. He is our Mediator and our Advocate with the Father. I repeat the words of the prophet Micah, who spoke truthfully and faithfully long ago when, in a time of great trouble, he testified: "I will look unto the Lord; I will wait for the God of my salvation: my God will hear me" (Micah 7:7).

All of us have much to learn and need good counsel. And beyond sound human help, beyond the "arm of flesh," it is written: "Counsel with the Lord in all thy doings, and he will direct thee for good" (Alma 37:37). "He will console you in your afflictions, and he will plead your cause" (Jacob 3:1).

Mormon's last words to his son are my prayer for my children and grandchildren also, and for the children of men everywhere:

"My son, be faithful in Christ, and may not the things which I have written grieve thee, to weigh thee down unto death; but may Christ lift thee up, and may his sufferings and death, and [resurrection], . . . and his mercy and long-suffering, and the hope of his glory and of eternal life, rest in your mind forever" (Moroni 9:25).

In the name of Jesus Christ. Amen.

V

Relationships

CHAPTER 23

The Three Relationships

Let me begin by quoting some lines from *Julius Caesar*. At this point Brutus and Cassius and their associates have killed Caesar. Mark Antony's oration has been completed, and with his concluding remark, "Now let it work," he has set the mischief afoot which in his mind will mark Caesar's assassins as murderers rather than patriots. Now the battle has been joined between Octavius Caesar and Antony and their armies on one side and Cassius and Brutus and their armies on the other. Cassius, misled into thinking that the battle has been lost, has taken his life. Brutus, who actually had been prevailing over the armies of Octavius, comes on the scene, sees Cassius dead, and says, "Friends, I owe more tears to this dead man than you shall see me pay." Then he turns to his friend and says, "I shall find time, Cassius, I shall find time."

We have just been through a season celebrating the birth, the life, and the mission of another and vastly more important monarch, who also was slain by conspirators. It may well be said of Him by many of us, if we have not yet come to that point of tear-shedding in contemplation of Him and His life and love and gift, that we shall find time.

Address given at Brigham Young University devotional 17 January 1978.

I have been wondering what the season may have brought to you. What happened to you, if anything very special? What have you learned or renewed, or intensified in conviction?

I thought I might share the experience I had this Christmas, because while it involved much that was old and warm and wonderful and comfortable and traditional, it also brought some new and real and lovely and tearful and special times. My experience brought me a reintensified assurance of the three basic relationships that have to be right if life is to be good and our contributions adequate to the Lord's expectations for us. Those three relationships were, of course, specifically taught by the Lord himself, who spoke of a "first commandment" that involved our loving God with everything we have—heart, might, mind, and strength—and a "second commandment" like unto it, which requires that we love our neighbor as ourselves. On these two laws, these two commandments, these two principles of eternal validity, all else hangs. (See Matthew 22:37–40; Mark 12:29–31.)

Paul knew that. Paul was trying to teach Timothy, his young brother in the gospel, as I would testify to you, when he wrote: "The end of the commandment [that is, as I understand it, the objective as well as the consequence of obeying God's commandment] is charity out of a pure heart, and of a good conscience, and of faith unfeigned" (1 Timothy 1:5). Rearrange those just a little and he is saying exactly what the Lord taught us, as I read and understand the record. Faith in God, charity out of a pure heart for our fellowmen, and that good conscience which will produce the pure heart, or spring from it—these are the basics. These are the relationships. These are the indispensables of love.

Relationship with Self

What of our responsibility and the possibility of loving ourselves? We know ourselves so well, you and I, that we find it difficult to really comprehend and to accept that invitation. Love God and love your neighbor as you love yourself. The beginning of love of self is to know that God loves us and that we are His.

There are mentioned in chapter 26 of the book of 2 Nephi some of the basic thou-shalt-not commandments taught to Moses on the Mount, and then these words are recorded: "For none of these iniquities [our breaching of the commandments] come of the Lord; for he doeth that which is good among the children of men; and he doeth nothing save it be plain unto the children of men; and he inviteth them all to come unto him and partake of his goodness; and he denieth none that come unto him, black and white, bond and free, male and female; and he remembereth the heathen; and all are alike unto God, both Jew and Gentile" (2 Nephi 26:33).

I recently sat across the desk from a beautiful young lady whose story I do not wish to repeat in any detail. I will simply say that her life had been very seriously intruded by sin and sorrow of major kinds. She had given up, surrendered, cut herself off from her future, and thought there was nothing at all left for her here or hereafter. Again, the detail would enhance the impression, but I give you only the end.

We had talked a long time, and I had tried the best I could by reference to the Bible, the Doctrine and Covenants, and the Book of Mormon to teach the principle of repentance and to talk of God's love. I had read the verse I have just quoted and knew I was not reaching her; the interview was about over, and I knew she would pass on to the same terror and tragedy she then had in her heart—no hope, no future, no real belief that God would ever have anything more to do with her. Then I read aloud some words from 2 Nephi to which I invite your prayerful attention: "Seeing that our merciful God has given us so great knowledge concerning these things, let us remember him [the one of whom we are speaking today], and lay aside our sins [there is no fooling around with that commandment], and not hang down our heads, for we are not cast off" (2 Nephi 10:20).

We read another verse from this marvelous Book of Mormon, which we are learning over the years to begin to appreciate. This is the last recorded communication from a great father to a choice son, in which the summation of his deepest and sweetest and warmest convictions was declared: "My son, be faithful in Christ [that is the beginning, the center]; and may not the things which I have written grieve thee, to weigh thee

down unto death; but may Christ lift thee up, and may his sufferings and death [and words that mean His resurrection], and
his mercy and long-suffering, and the hope of his glory and of
eternal life, rest in your mind forever" (Moroni 9:25).

Let not the things, the message, the mission, the gift of
Christ weigh you down and grieve you, but may He lift you up
and make to rest in your mind all the warm, wonderful blessings
available to you.

On the other side of the desk I saw curtains part that had
been closed tight, tears come, a heart open, conviction be re-established, repentance radiate, and forgiveness be accepted. I
wish every person in all the world could hear her words, because
at some time they need to be heard by everybody. She said, "I
know I will still be lonely sometimes, but I believe I will never
feel alone again." Certainly we will be lonely too, sometimes.
But we need never feel alone. God does love His children.

Recently I read in a book a statement about life's injustices. I
thought of the Apostle Paul, who knew quite a lot of this world's
injustices and imponderables. He was a very brilliant man; he
knew life's miseries, its inequities, its inhumanities that men put
upon men. Yet it was Paul, with that for background and knowledge and experience, who said to the Romans: "The Spirit itself
beareth witness with our spirit, that we are the children of God:
and if children, then heirs; heirs of God, and joint-heirs with
Christ" (Romans 8:16–17). He also said that we are the offspring of God (see Acts 17:27–29), and much more that reas-
sures us.

Paul knew problems enough, and he ultimately lost his own
life in the cause of the Lord. But Paul knew what each of us
must know, that God is our Father and really loves us; and so,
because we know who we are and care about what happens to
us, we can love ourselves.

The love we are commanded to have for ourselves, the self-
esteem we must have in order to be happy, is not and cannot be
based on perfection. It comes as we realize who we are, to
whom we belong, the extent of our limitations and sins and ignorance, and our need for His love and mercy. It comes as we
learn His word, feel His Spirit, and understand His fatherhood
and His loving kindness. It comes as we keep His commandments. And then we may make the transition, loving ourselves

not in the arrogance God could not brook or in the pride He commands against but in a sense of self-reverence and self-knowledge because we know to whom we belong.

Relationship with Others

With that esteem for ourselves, that love, we can then reach out to our neighbor. Only then can we really love him, I believe. There will be no confusion; we shall not condition our love for him on his perfection, but we shall love him because we know who he is and care about the quality of his eternal spirit. We shall strip off the facade, the veneer, that "muddy vesture of decay," as Shakespeare spoke of it; we shall see each other at heart level and do what we can to qualify as neighbor to our neighbor. Much of what the Lord said expressed His expectations of us in our relationships with others of His children and our need for an attitude and a relationship that is good and wholesome.

I love the statement Jesus made to the scribes and Pharisees. We know that we must keep all commandments, even the smallest, but He himself qualified some things as weightier than others. "Woe unto you, scribes and Pharisees, hypocrites! for ye pay tithe of mint and anise and cummin, and have omitted the weightier matters of the law, judgment, mercy, and faith" (Matthew 23:23). These He interpreted at lengths I cannot take time to do today, but I call to your attention something Christmas reinforced for me.

I have thought over the years that *judgment* may mean *justice*, or the idea that we must be just and merciful and confident in God, and just and merciful and confident with each other. But during the Christmas days I began to think about the way we live, the thoughts we invite or make welcome, our personal choices, our priorities, our loyalties, our love, the use of our time; and it occurred to me that Jesus was talking about *judgment:* good judgment, quiet judgment, slow judgment, compassionate judgment, righteous judgment, fair judgment, merciful judgment.

The scriptures give us many examples, and I offer this suggestion. The Savior expects us not to judge each other—for we are told that with what judgment we judge, so shall we be judged (see Moroni 7:18)—but in our judgments to be all those things He would wish us to be to our brothers and sisters.

What of mercy? This is the subject of much meaningful consideration. I offer you only the great example that has touched my heart and my mind all my life, the example of a man beaten by robbers and left at a wayside, passed by some who might have been thought willing to help, and helped by one who was not then ethnically acceptable to the Jews. The Samaritan stopped to help, doing all that could ever be expected and then much more. And that marvelous story was thus ended by the Savior: "Which now of these three, thinkest thou, was neighbour unto [that man]? . . . He that shewed mercy on him." (See Luke 10:30–37.) Mercy was interpreted by the Lord to mean a sense of relationship, responsibility, and compassion, and acts of benevolence and graciousness and neighborliness to our brother, whoever he is and whatever his serious needs.

To finish this brief moment on our relationship with others, note that the Apostle Paul and the Lord talked of faith, or the confidence that we have in our Father and in His Son, and hear this one example.

The story, of which I share only the headline, is of a beautiful soul in a troubled body. I shall only tell you that my wife and I met her as she received an award designated for one who had done the most to help the handicapped. From the moment of her birth, she had suffered a serious lack of normal physical blessings, but she had a great heart, a great spirit, and a great soul. In accepting the award, she recalled the day when she had run home from school crying because thoughtless, careless children had called her "hunchback" and other names. Her great father had held her in his arms and rocked her on his lap and wept with her as he impressed on her the importance of this day in her life.

"Elayne," he said to her, "today you decide. Your life can be all that God intends it to be. When they called you those names the boys and girls were in a sense telling the true facts. You do have a hump on your back and you have other problems that have made your life difficult physically. But, Elayne, as you were forming in your mother Heavenly Father knew that would be so.

He sent a beautiful, special spirit, one that could handle the problems this little body would have. Now, Elayne, what they said about you is in a sense true, but it wasn't fair and it wasn't kind. If all your life you will be more fair and more kind to others than a few of them will sometimes be to you, then you will have a happy, warm, fruitful life, lack nothing, and be everything God intended."

And that beautiful little soul, who stood there with an oxygen tank behind her to help her breathe, who had to be helped to the platform, bore testimony of gratitude and love for God and her fellowman. She said, "The only real justification that I have for receiving this award is that I can say to you in honesty that all my life I have tried to be more fair and more kind to others than a few of them have sometimes been to me."

Relationship with God

Let me now bear testimony about the third relationship, the relationship we have with God. Christ started there with the first commandment and then added "love thy neighbor as thyself." But the sequence may not be all that conclusive. If we cannot regard ourselves with esteem and respect, lacking the perfections as we do, but knowing who we are and that we really care and are making an effort, the chances of our reaching out to God, and to a neighbor who is also imperfect, seem small. They all go together.

On an airplane recently I read a book by Loren Eiseley. Eiseley is an anthropologist, a naturalist, a writer, and an evolutionist who believes sincerely in the theories of organic evolution that men have developed, and as one of the most wise and sensitive among men in his profession he is an exciting witness. I do not wish to discuss the theories of evolution but only to share a theme that runs throughout Loren Eiseley's book and then concludes it: "I have come to believe that in the world there is nothing to explain the world, nothing in nature that can explain the existent from the potential."

I do not intend to do more than extract a few sentences for their implication and meaning. I neither defend nor question what he is saying, but simply read it. "We all flounder, choosing to close our eyes to ultimate questions and proceeding instead with classification and experiment." He talks then about Sphex wasps, which have a literally incredible capacity to do things they have never seen done, in a way that is so magnificently complex that one marvels how they come to know how to do it. He traces the wondrous way in which an adult Sphex wasp finds the quarry, stuns it without killing it—knowing the way to do that with her own weapon—puts that quarry in the nest she has dug under the ground, and lays her egg in the quarry, which remains alive but insensate. The offspring, once born, eats upon, without killing, the food it has been provided until its own strength is adequate. It then exits its tomb and begins its life, possessed somehow with the specific capacity to do what its predecessor has done. Eiseley quotes the French entomologist Henri Fabre: "It is not in chance that we will find the key to such harmonies. The man grappling with reality fails to find a serious explanation of anything whatsoever that he sees."

Eiseley finishes with a line that I share: "Though shorn of knowledge, willing to accept the dreadful otherness of the biblical challenge, 'your ways are not my ways,' I had come to feel at last that the human version of evolutionary events was perhaps too simplistic for belief. . . . I had spent a lifetime exploring questions for which I no longer pretended to have answers or to fully accept the answers of others." (*All the Strange Hours* [New York: Charles Scribner's Sons, 1975], pp. 241, 245, 246.)

Having spent a lifetime of devoted and productive scholarship, Loren Eiseley does not say that he discounts all that he and others have struggled to discover, but simply that the answers are not all there. The answers are beyond the finiteness of this earth.

Let me conclude with one of those answers that I am so prayerfully anxious to share. A letter came at Christmastime, and I would not for anything betray the confidence it so warmly radiates. I will simply tell you that the person who wrote it is a graduate of this institution. He writes from prison, where he is immured for a very serious crime. He has lost it all. He is brilliant and lettered, his name can be read here and there, he has done very well in the educational world, he is very young, with everything ahead of him; and this act, or series of acts, took him away from his own guided conscience and alienated him from others and ultimately from God, from the Church, from the things so dear and precious. Now he writes from a prison, and I ask you to listen with your hearts and your heads to these few sentences. He talks of a happy situation inside that sad place. He has been assigned a place in the prison that permits him to help others.

> What all of this represents is a miracle, I can put no other label on it. I have had a job that has allowed me to keep my mind active, and I have won the respect of people who trust me. The tears come frequently, but in my job setting I can let them. I have a room not unlike a college dormitory room, and it is private— single accommodations. There I can let the emotions vent, can pray, study, and write. The time is tortuous nonetheless, but not beyond my capacities to bear *because compensatory blessings were granted.* I do not understand all this, but I am grateful.

He mentions a member of the prison professional staff who has helped him. "She knows me and accepts me. I feel better about myself than in all my life. She has helped to heal me. For the first time my spirit feels free to be itself. She had a very difficult life too. [She] has made me see that adversity can be turned to advantage."

The letter continues:

> Perhaps it is this last thought that is the most forceful image I have of Christ. He took the cause of adversity and made it the blessing of advantage. I see him on the cross blessing the thief, forgiving the murderers of his own life. I read over and over about the difficulties and the costs of his associating with the poor and the outcasts, and his love for them. Peter was right. Christ did go and preach to the spirits in prison. What else might we expect him to do?

He then refers to Paul's description in Romans 1:28–32 of the absolute decadence of that time and says that is how it is in this prison: "[It] is an exact picture of my surroundings and the nature of man so openly fallen." So much of what he then goes

on to say about the fallen state of all men, even those not condemned under the law, is so appropriate. He is quoting, and in-
terlarding with his own comments.

> "There is none righteous, no not one; there is none that under-
> standeth . . ." And the operation of the law is so that "all the world
> may become guilty before God." And that is the crux of my prob-
> lem—righteousness and relief from guilt cannot come from my
> punishment or the functioning of the law: "by the deeds of the law
> there shall no flesh be justified in his sight." But "while we were
> yet sinners, Christ died for us." [Do not misunderstand those last
> words; they are a testimony of the highest quality of the truthful-
> ness of what we have been taught in these days through the
> prophets of God. They need to be carefully considered.] When I
> understood that, when I really understood it, then I experienced
> grace, a great sense of forgiveness.
>
> So much remains to be done, so much restitution that I hope I
> will be allowed to make, but I won't have to buy into any more
> guilt trips. There will always be sorrow for my mistakes, and there
> may never be forgiveness by others I have hurt. But I don't have to
> beat myself into mental illness: "Where sin abounded, grace did
> much more abound." And I am humbled by the grace which he
> has given me. I, who was so full of insecurities and false pride, who
> felt superior to others, now know my true worth and am no longer
> afraid. I have lost my life, but found it.

Through the love of a friend who has helped him to accept
the mercy of God and to forgive himself, he has truly "come
unto Christ" and His goodness. He loves God, he loves his
neighbor, and he is coming at last to love himself.

God bless you, as I earnestly pray He will bless me and
mine, that we may have a sense of the mission and the meaning,
the measure of the gift, the beauty of the love of the Lord; and
that we may translate it into a fulfillment of those expectations
which He has clearly put before us, to love God with everything
we have and to love our neighbor as ourselves. We can do that
only by obeying His law and learning to be confident in Him, to
repent of our sins, to obey His commandments, to walk by the
Spirit, and to endure the injustices and the inequities of this
world with forbearance and with faith. In the name of Jesus
Christ. Amen.

CHAPTER 24

A Friend of Christ

For my part this morning I would like to talk about a wonderful blessing we can have and about one principle that every one of us must learn if we are to receive that blessing. The blessing is to be worthy to be a friend of Christ. The principle is forgiveness.

After a meeting attended by a group of students, one young man waited to ask me a question. "Elder Hanks," he said, "what are your goals? What would you like to accomplish?" I observed his seriousness of purpose and answered in the same spirit that my desire was to qualify to be a friend of Christ.

I had not responded to just such a question just that way before, but as I have since thought of that answer I gave, I am glad I gave it. I would not change it.

In ancient times the prophet Abraham was called the "Friend of God" (James 2:23). Shortly before His crucifixion, Jesus said to His disciples, "Ye are my friends, if ye do whatsoever I command you. Henceforth I call you not servants . . . but I have called you friends." (John 15:14–15.)

In 1832, to a group of elders returning from missionary service He repeated the same message: "From henceforth I shall call you friends" (D&C 84:77).

Address given at Tonga area conference February 1976.

Forgiveness

One of the principles Jesus taught us and that you and I must learn if we are to be His friends is forgiveness.

Christ's love is so pure that He gave His life for us. "Greater love hath no man than this, that a man lay down his life for his friends" (John 15:13). But there was another gift He gave while He was on the cross, a gift that further measured the magnitude of His great love: He forgave those who crucified Him, and asked His Father to forgive them also.

Was this act of forgiveness less difficult than sacrificing His mortal life? Was it less a test of His love? I do not know the answer. But I personally believe that the highest form of love, for God and man, is forgiveness.

Christ met the test of forgiving those who took His life. What of us? Perhaps we shall not be called upon to give our lives for our friends or our faith (though perhaps some shall), but it is certain that every one of us has and will have occasion to confront that other challenge. We will have to decide whether we will forgive someone who has harmed us. What will we do? What are we doing, because probably all of us have some reason to resent or be angry at others.

Someone has written that if we withhold our love from others because they have done some wrong to us, we show that we do not really know Christ or understand what He tried to teach us. For us it is as if He had not lived at all, that we do not think of Him or follow Him, that He means nothing in our lives. It means that we are not inspired by Him or touched by His spirit of compassion for the world.

Christ's example and instructions to His friends are clear. He forgave, and He told us: "Love your enemies, bless them that curse you, do good to them that hate you, and pray for them which despitefully use you and persecute you" (Matthew 5:44). What is our response when we are offended, misunderstood, unfairly or unkindly treated, sinned against, not appreciated, falsely accused, passed over, hurt by those we love, when our offerings are rejected? Do we resent, become bitter, hold a grudge, even hate? Or do we resolve the problem if we can, forgive, and rid ourselves of this burden of resentment? If we hate another we do not hurt him, but we carry a very heavy load on our minds and backs which does hurt us. How we act in such situations may well determine the nature and quality of our lives, here and eternally. A courageous friend of mine who has suffered many afflictions said to me recently: "Humiliation must come before exaltation."

The Lord requires that we forgive. We cannot be His friends if we do not. Our salvation depends upon it. In a revelation He said: "My disciples, in days of old, sought occasion against one another and forgave not one another in their hearts; and for this evil they were afflicted and sorely chastened. Wherefore, I say unto you, that ye ought to forgive one another: for he that forgiveth not his brother his trespasses standeth condemned before the Lord; for there remaineth in him the greater sin. I, the Lord, will forgive whom I will forgive, but of you it is required to forgive all men." (D&C 64:8–10.)

Now, Jesus taught us that we must not only *say* we forgive but must forgive in our hearts. We must really forgive and forget the wrong that was done us. If we do not, we are guilty of a greater sin than was done to us, and we stand condemned before the Lord. The person who is guilty of the original offense must still answer to the Lord, who will forgive him if he truly repents, but we are required to forgive all those who sin against us.

Therefore, Jesus taught us to pray, "And forgive us our trespasses, as we forgive those who trespass against us."

Does it not seem a supreme impudence to ask and expect God to forgive us when we do not forgive—both openly and "in our hearts"?

It is not only our eternal salvation that depends upon our willingness and capacity to forgive wrongs committed against us. Our joy and satisfaction in this life, and our true freedom, also depend upon our doing so. When Christ told us to turn the other cheek if someone strikes us, to choose to walk the second mile when we have been forced to walk the first mile, to give our cloak to the one who takes our coat, was it to be chiefly out of consideration for the bully, or the brute, or the thief? Or was it to relieve us of the destructive burden that resentment and anger lay upon us?

Failure to Forgive

The Apostle Paul wrote to the Romans that nothing "shall be able to separate us from the love of God, which is in Christ Jesus our Lord" (Romans 8:39). I am sure this is true. I bear testimony that this is true. But it is also true that *we can* separate ourselves from His Spirit. In the book of Isaiah it is written, "Your iniquities have separated between you and your God" (Isaiah 59:2). Again, it is written, "They have rewarded evil unto themselves" (Isaiah 3:9). Through Samuel the Lamanite we learn that "whosoever doeth iniquity, doeth it unto himself" (Helaman 14:30), and from the prophet Benjamin, "Ye do withdraw yourselves from the Spirit of the Lord" (Mosiah 2:36).

In every case of sin this is true. Such sins as envy, arrogance, unrighteous dominion, pride—these canker the soul of one who is guilty of them. This is true also if we fail to forgive. Even if it appears that another may deserve our resentment or hatred, none of us can afford to pay the price of resenting or hating, because of what it does to us. If we have experienced the bad feeling of these emotions, we know the harm they make us suffer. We are the ones who pay the penalty for our failure to forgive.

So the Apostle Paul taught the Thessalonians that they must "see that none render evil for evil unto any man" (1 Thessalonians 5:15).

It is reported that President Brigham Young once said that he who takes offense when no offense was intended is a fool, and he who takes offense when offense was intended is usually a fool. It was then explained that there are two courses of action to follow when one is bitten by a rattlesnake or some other poisonous creature. One may in anger, fear, or the spirit of revenge pursue the creature and kill it, or he may hurry to get the poison out of his system. If he removes the poison, he will likely survive, but if he attempts in anger to punish the creature he may not live long enough to finish it.

Years ago on Temple Square in Salt Lake City I heard a boy pour out his anguish, the anguish of his troubled heart, and make a commitment to God. He had been living in a spirit of hatred toward a man who had killed his father, who was a policeman. Nearly out of his mind with grief, he had been overcome with bitterness. On that Sabbath morning when others and I heard him he was touched by the Spirit of the Lord, and in that hour the Spirit flooded out the hostility that had filled his heart. He tearfully declared his intention to leave vengeance to the Lord and justice to the law. He would no longer hate the one who had caused the grievous loss. He would forgive, and he would not for another hour permit the spirit of revenge to fill his heart.

"Even as Christ forgave you, so also do ye" (Colossians 3:13).

I bear testimony, my brothers and sisters, that we must learn to forgive, even if we have been hurt by others, even if there is justice in our bad feelings. We must learn to forgive in our hearts; then we may expect God to forgive us. I bear this testimony in the name of Jesus Christ. Amen.

CHAPTER 25

"Behold the Man"

This Christmas story occurred in the middle of the summer some years ago.

The man opposite me in the room had the many stripes on his uniform that signified long and distinguished service; I was an apprentice seaman in boot camp. Nonetheless, Commander Hamilton as he had greeted me at the door had been most gracious—he called me "Mr. Hanks" and seated me with cordiality, and we talked as equals.

The commander, senior chaplain at the great training center, had invited me into his office to discuss the possibility of my becoming a chaplain. I was quick to explain that because I had interrupted my university training to serve as a missionary I had not finished an academic degree and didn't qualify for the chaplaincy under the navy's standards. He replied that he felt he might be able to do something about getting a waiver of that requirement, all others things being favorable.

Commander Hamilton was a rangy, strong-looking man for whom I had immediately formed a feeling of respect and admiration. I had learned that he was one of the survivors of the aircraft carrier *Yorktown* when she was sunk by enemy action in the war and that he had been in the water for many hours before

New Era article December 1975.

rescue. I was complimented and humbled that such a man would be considering his proposed action after having visited our group of LDS servicemen at the base.

"Before I recommend you to the Chief of Chaplains, Mr. Hanks, please talk to me about your experience in your Church, about what you think may help me in my recommendation of you as qualified to represent the Lord in the military chaplaincy."

I began to explain to him the lifelong experience of a young man in the Church that had helped me prepare for such a significant opportunity. We went back to the beginning—the early participation, the two-and-a-half-minute talks, the service as deacon, teacher, priest, elder, seventy; Scouting, seminary, institute, Sunday School teaching, leadership opportunities, missionary service.

As I talked, he who had been so courteous and kind and interested began to fidget, to lose interest, and I realized, as we sometimes do when we are seeking to communicate person-to-person, that I was not connecting, that I was losing the battle, and I became more anxious. Earnestly I tried to tell him what there is in the stage-by-stage opportunity in the Church for a young person to develop the qualities to be a servant of God.

After a time his demeanor completely changed, and he interrupted me, saying very brusquely, "Say, Hanks, do you believe in Jesus Christ?"

"Yes, sir!" I said. "Everything I believe relates to Jesus Christ. My faith, my life, center in Him as my Savior. The Church I belong to is founded on Him and follows Him as its living head. It is named in His name."

He said, looking at his watch, "Well, you have been talking for seven minutes, and you haven't said so."

I think I have not made that mistake again.

"Behold the Man"

When Pilate presented the Savior to the howling mob, he said, "Behold the man!" (John 19:5.) Would you be willing to try to do that for just a few minutes? What do you see? What do you hear? How do you feel? What do you know? Well, there are these things true about Him: His story is a redemptive story. He was in the beginning with God. He was a member of God's family, himself a god. "And there stood one among them that was like unto God, and he said unto those who were with him: We will go down, for there is space there, and we will take of these materials, and we will make an earth whereon these may dwell; and we will prove them herewith, to see if they will do all things whatsoever the Lord their God shall command them" (Abraham 3:24–25).

He was a god, an authority in the presence of His Father, a member of that divine group of godly persons. He was the creator of this world and all that in it is. Familiar to most of you is the testimony frequently referred to in Doctrine and Covenants section 76, and I read not for the ordinary connotation but to emphasize this great role He played, the responsibility He filled as Creator: "And now, after the many testimonies which have been given of him, this is the testimony, last of all, which we give of him: That he lives! For we saw him, even on the right hand of God; and we heard the voice bearing record that he is the Only Begotten of the Father—that by him, and through him, and of him, the worlds are and were created, and the inhabitants thereof are begotten sons and daughters unto God." (D&C 76:22–24.)

Elsewhere also in the record the message is clearly delivered. God through His holy Son created the world we live in. That Son was the *firstborn in the spirit*. Of all the spirit children of God, He was the firstborn, our elder brother, in fact; much else also, but in the spirit the firstborn. His mission was prophesied long before He came to earth. To some of us who have taught the Book of Mormon story and its great prophetic vision of Christ written long before He came, and have observed the response of people who seem to feel there is something suspect about the book because those who wrote in it knew of Him long before His coming, it has been reassuring and sweet to be able to read in the Bible such interesting thoughts as this, written at least seven hundred years before He came: "Behold, a virgin shall conceive, and bear a son, and shall call his name Immanuel." (Isaiah 7:14).

Two chapters later we find this: "For unto us a child is born, unto us a son is given: and the government shall be upon his shoulder: and his name shall be called Wonderful, Counsellor, The mighty God, The everlasting Father, The Prince of Peace" (Isaiah 9:6).

And all through this marvelous record is the promise of His coming.

He Was the Only Begotten

He was, we are taught, the Only Begotten in the flesh. That is, only He, in the manner and under the circumstances of His birth, came into this world begotten of the Father in physical form.

He Was Without Blemish

He alone was without blemish. He was perfect. And yet we are taught in the record that "though he were a Son, yet learned he obedience by the things which he suffered" (Hebrews 5:8). This statement is amplified in the Doctrine and Covenants: "And I, John, saw that he received not of the fulness at the first, but received grace for grace; and he received not of the fulness at first, but continued from grace to grace, until he received a fulness" (D&C 93:12–13).

Though He was without blemish, He learned and grew.

He Was the Servant of All

He was the servant of all. Sometimes when the ego prompts us to arrogance in our minds and our little prideful thoughts, the spirit and the power and the picture of a Savior kneeling and washing the feet of His disciples may come into view.

He Suffered

He suffered in both body and spirit. Three times Pilate declared that he found no fault in Him; he washed his hands of the Savior and turned Him over to the demands of the mob. Christ went to the cross and did willingly and alone what He did and had to do. Even though He had said, "Don't you know that I could call more than twelve legions of angels?" He did what He did willingly and alone.

Behold the man.

He suffered in body and spirit in a way we cannot really imagine. Have you read these words of His recently?

> Therefore I command you to repent—repent, lest I smite you by the rod of my mouth, and by my wrath, and by my anger, and your sufferings be sore—how sore you know not, how exquisite you know not, yea, how hard to bear you know not.
>
> For behold, I, God, have suffered these things for all, that they might not suffer if they would repent;
>
> But if they would not repent they must suffer even as I;
>
> Which suffering caused myself, even God, the greatest of all, to tremble because of pain, and to bleed at every pore, and to suffer both body and spirit—and would that I might not drink the bitter cup, and shrink—
>
> Nevertheless, glory be to the Father, and I partook and finished my preparations unto the children of men. (D&C 19:15–19.)

What He Asks of Us

What does He ask of us? In 3 Nephi is a magnificent statement He made as to what He did for us, what He will do for us, and what He asks of us. I refer to only an extract, but will you read it as if you had not read it before?

> Behold I have given unto you my gospel, and this is the gospel which I have given unto you—that I came into the world to do the will of my Father, because my Father sent me.
>
> And my Father sent me that I might be lifted up upon the

cross; and after that I had been lifted up upon the cross, that I might draw all men unto me, that as I have been lifted up by men even so should men be lifted up by the Father . . .

And for this cause have I been lifted up; therefore, according to the power of the Father I will draw all men unto me, that they may be judged according to their works. (3 Nephi 27:13–15.)

And then, after teaching what we know as the first principles, He said to them: "Therefore, what manner of men ought ye to be? Verily I say unto you, even as I am." (3 Nephi 27:27.)

Was He Relevant?

Well, how was He? Was He relevant? That is a great word in our time. Was His religion relevant?

We are talking only in headlines today, but I would like to make a few for you. In this season when we are repeatedly assured that there is great meaning in celebrating because our celebrations relate to Him and revolve around Him, will you ask yourselves, was He relevant?

Have you been tempted lately? Think again, as if you had never heard it, of the story of one who went into a wilderness and there was subjected to temptations of such great and difficult a nature that by contrast our own temptations, pressing and strong and emotionally involved as they are, might not seem quite so tough to bear. What were His temptations? Rehearse them again, not only for detail but also for application, for relevancy.

He was invited to use His miraculous powers for His own benefit and to abuse them, and He refused. It occurred to me the other day as I thought of this that I don't know of a single instance in which He used His powers for His own advantage. Not once. He had a great chance in one temptation to prove His Messianic claims—a short and easy road to recognition: "You are on this high prominence: cast yourself down and God will save you: the crowd will respond." And His answer was no. He wasn't after this quick and easy recognition. He had something else to do. The other temptation is more usual with us, perhaps. Of wealth and power and the things of this world He was offered much—just to capitulate, just to give in.

"For in that he himself hath suffered being tempted, he is able to succour them that are tempted" (Hebrews 2:18).

He met the test of proffered popularity like a man, like a godly man, like a Son of God. Following His great sermon on the Bread of Life "many of his disciples went back and walked no more with him" (John 6:66). They couldn't take it; the pressures were too great.

What Is Really Important?

Do you dislike hypocrisy? Do you appreciate integrity? Do you rejoice in somebody who has the backbone, in spite of pressure, to stand up and say it as it is? Do you like somebody who responds to pressure with vitality and honor?

Think just a moment about the kind of religion He taught and practiced. You may recall a time when someone asked Him what was really important, and He answered that it was to love God with everything you have, and to love your neighbor as yourself. And the man to whom He spoke said, "Master, thou hast said the truth," and repeated the words. He knew about loving God and loving his brother. Since the first time I read those words I have been deeply moved by the Savior's response: "Thou art not far from the kingdom of God." (See Mark 12:32–34.)

Jesus had the capacity to give attention to those things that matter most. I often think of what He said to the Pharisees, whom He called hypocrites: "For ye pay tithe of mint and anise and cummin, and have omitted the weightier matters of the law, judgment, mercy, and faith: these ought ye to have done, and not to leave the other undone" (Matthew 23:23).

He had breadth and scope; He had integrity and honesty. He had a great vision of the really weightier things—to treat each other with mercy, and to have this "faith unfeigned" of which Paul spoke (1 Timothy 1:5). But these were not to be done at the expense of obedience, for in this He believed.

I love and have long loved His respect for honesty. Do you

remember the occasion when an honest man, who didn't know all the answers, came to the Savior to seek directly from this great and godly one the succor that he needed? He had a little boy who was sick. Do you know how that feels? This good man wanted desperately to get some for help for his little boy, and he had tried with the Apostles, who had been unable to help him. I am interested in his response to that. He didn't "curse God" or them and die, or go some other way. He somehow had a basic responsiveness and intuitive faith that made him seek the Savior and ask for help. You remember that conversation, I hope. Christ told him all things were possible for him who believed, and immediately the man responded, "Lord, I believe; help thou mine unbelief." (See Mark 9:14–27.)

Have you ever really thought how it would be to face the Savior and confess that there were lots of problems you didn't really understand, many questions you couldn't answer? The life and well-being of this man's son were at stake, and he had the integrity to ask the Savior for help, professing and acknowledging that he did believe in His divinity, in His power, but asking, "Help thou my unbelief." In the spirit of this incident, it has never seemed to me necessary to pretend to know everything.

His Concern for His Fellowman

What about His concern for mercy and for His fellowman? We live in a time when it is appropriately fashionable to care about somebody else—even if we are only joining in the periphery of the clamoring crowd. We are going to start thinking about somebody else now who is different from us. If you want a real experience for Christmas, begin reading at Luke 10 and continue through ten chapters or so. May I recall highlights?

The Good Samaritan

There was a man injured and left at the roadside, needing help, said Christ. Along came a Levite, one of the temple workers, on his way to assist in important ordinances, no doubt—so busy, though, that he had no time for the wounded man. Then along came a priest, an officiator at the temple altar, who was so pressed that he had no time to spend with the man at the road-side. And then came the unloved Samaritan, who stopped and gave the wounded man aid. Then the Savior's question to the hearers of the parable as to which of the three was neighbor to the man. And, of course, the answer was obvious, that it was he who stopped and helped him. Have you heard anybody teach anything that improves on the lesson of that story?

The Prodigal Son

A little later in the book we read about a son who obtained his father's substance and wasted it; and the book is pretty explicit about his riotous living, about his sinking to the depths of an animal—that is how he felt about himself. That is how Christ pictured him. He actually was living with the swine, feeding them, and so hungry that he desired to eat their food; and then somehow he had the sense to look homeward, the deep response to who he really was. He thought it over again. The servants in his father's house were better off than he. We don't read about the big battle, but I am positive there was one, the big battle within him that caused him, I think—hesitantly, and I believe not selfishly but humbly—to take a faltering step toward home. I love the story's next simple truth that teaches us that his father, seeing him afar off, ran to meet him, kissed him, wept with him, and took him home. Oh, to be sure there was in the story that element we spend too much time worrying about—the son who had been doing well and who now was critical of this kindness shown to his faltering brother. The father's answer was sufficient. "You have lost nothing, son. Everything I have is yours. But your brother, who was dead, is alive again. He was lost, and he has come home."

Do you really think we'll discover anything more important than that? If you haven't yet needed to know that, you will. And I promise you that if you know it, you will be able to meet the tests of life with much more strength and faith and responsiveness to the Lord.

The Pharisee and the Publican

I mention another of these marvelous stories. There were two men, one of whom, the hundred-percent type, in prayer to God congratulated himself on his great record: "The Pharisee stood and prayed thus with himself, God, I thank thee, that I am not as other men are, extortioners, unjust, adulterers, or even as this publican. I fast twice in the week. I give tithes of all that I possess."

The other man, a publican, would not so much as lift up his eyes to heaven, but smote himself on the breast and said, "God be merciful to me a sinner." And of him Jesus Christ said: "I tell you, this man went down to his house justified rather than the other: for every one that exalteth himself shall be abased; and he that humbleth himself shall be exalted." (See Luke 18:11–14.)

The Woman Who Touched Him

Do you love sensitivity? I read again last night with great joy the story of the woman who couldn't reach Him. She needed help—if she could only touch His garments as He passed by! When she had done this and been immediately healed, He, knowing that something important had happened, turned to her in all that multitude and knew of her need. (See Luke 8:43–48.)

The Christmas Windows

The last question—how does all this relate to us and Christmas? Last night a dear friend repeated a story he had told me a long time ago. It may be enough of illustration. The windows of a great department store in New York City are used to express a special idea each year at Christmastime. In these windows there are pictured the affluent, the happy homes at Christmas, and the bridge abutment under which the hobos are gathered to cook a meal in a tin can. There are pictured the joyous, happy children, and there is the sick person in bed, and the woman with a baby, her face pressed to the window. And there is one message: "If Christ came tonight, to whom would he come?"

"Unto the Least of These"

Will you read the two scriptures that means as much to me at Christmas as Luke chapter 2, and will you read them as if for the first time, as if you had no real acquaintance with them? I am asking you to meet, face on, someone who is all of the things we said He was, and who, at the summation of His instruction about relationships with fellowman, self, and God, taught this story:

There will be a time when there will be a gathering together of people of all nations, some on one hand of the King, some on the other. "Then shall the King say unto them on his right hand, Come, ye blessed of my Father, inherit the kingdom prepared for you from the foundation of the world: for I was an hungred, and ye gave me meat: I was thirsty, and ye gave me drink: I was a stranger, and ye took me in: naked, and ye clothed me: I was sick, and ye visited me: I was in prison, and ye came unto me."

Then the righteous will respond. Could I interpolate? What would they say, these honest souls who want, who desperately want, to be worthy of Him? "Lord, when saw we thee an hungred, and fed thee? or thirsty, and gave thee drink?" ["Lord, we'd do anything for you. Honestly, that's how we feel in our hearts. But we don't remember ever seeing you sick or in prison and visiting you."] "And the King shall answer and say unto them, Verily I say unto you, Inasmuch as ye have done it unto one of the least of these my brethren, ye have done it unto me."

I love that affirmation, but I think the opposite as He told it is even more incisive: "For I was an hungred, and ye gave me no meat: I was thirsty, and ye gave me no drink: I was a stranger, and ye took me not in: naked, and ye clothed me not: sick, and in prison, and ye visited me not."

And what shall be the answer then? Indignation. ["Lord, this is not fair. When saw we thee hungry and fed thee not, etc.?"] And then shall the King answer saying: "Verily I say unto you,

Inasmuch as ye did it not to one of the least of these, ye did it not to me." (See Matthew 25:31–45.)

What is important about Him? What does He ask of us? Is He relevant? Does it really mean something to me?

Lifted Up

Consider these sweet, beautiful words: Peter and John were at the gates of the temple, where the lame man was begging them for alms. Peter said, "Look on us." And he, expecting some generous gift, heard Peter say: "Silver and gold have I none; but such as I have give I thee: In the name of Jesus Christ of Nazareth rise up and walk."

But the story doesn't end there. "And he took him by the right hand, and lifted him up." (Acts 3:6–7.)

I bear witness to you that this Church and gospel is the work of the Lord. This and every other season ought to involve us in a kind of special celebration, for He is the Savior. Through His divine love and power He lifts us, and will lift us. His religion is relevant. It means us. I bear witness of that.

CHAPTER 26

The Worth of Souls

One lesson to be derived from life is that we see things pretty much in the perspective of our own experience. We tune in on music of a particular kind to the extent that we have been exposed to it. We may be responsive to good things or other kinds of things in the degree to which we have prepared ourselves to be. That is true for everybody of every age, so I am very prayerful today that while we have much going on elsewhere and you have had a fine experience already and no doubt have other plans for the day, we can sequester just a few minutes to think together. I am going to pay you the tribute, and I say it in all sincerity, of trying an idea or two on you that I think will be helpful if you are in tune. I will try to be. I have prayed to be.

Darkness and Light

I had a kind of revelation today when the choir sang that marvelous hymn relating the first vision of Joseph Smith, whose picture is on the program today. I have sung it, as you have, lots of times and I have heard it many, many times. Yet today it struck me that in this song we get in capsule form a pretty good

Address given in the Salt Lake Tabernacle on Seminary S-Day 26 January 1974.

picture of what life is really all about day by day, week by week—
in your house and mine, wherever we are. This moving song has
verses that start out with a lovely morning, things seeming good,
bees humming, birds singing, music ringing through a grove;
and with a boy undertaking to talk to God, shyly, without any
experience but with great need. I was particularly struck by this
thought when the lines were sung that you know very well, but I
wonder if you have heard them lately: "When the powers of sin
assailing filled his soul with deep despair."

It is as real as those hard benches you are sitting on that in
our seeking—at the high times, the high moments, the pleasant,
satisfying, sweet, personally happy times—we are yet aware that
there can be introduced, if we are willing, powers that assail us;
and in effect, whether we like it or not, or whether we are ready
or not, they are going to be making the effort. I am not sure how
I would have reacted to that along the way, but I know how I
react to it now. There are powers that assail us, and when they
do they fill our souls with deep despair. All of us have felt that,
haven't we? Do you remember the words of the line following
the one I quoted? "But undaunted still he trusted in his Heavenly Father's care." It didn't say that because we are nice people
or we want to do the right thing either Joseph Smith or we
would be immune from the powers that assail. The promise for
us and for him is confirmed in his account—that because he
continued to trust even when his soul was filled with deep despair something happened and the something was a brilliant
light which descended and dispersed the darkness that had
gathered around him.

Last Tuesday morning I boarded an airplane at the Salt Lake
Airport and rode for just a short hour up, over, and down to Las
Vegas, where I was met by a stake president and a bishop who
were very sober in aspect. We talked about the experience we
were about to have, something of its background and roots. I
was there, you see, to speak representing the First Presidency at
the funeral of a missionary who had died four months after he
left home for the mission field. His parents and family were of
course desolated by that, sickened and heartbroken. My experience there was like that in the song. It was a lovely morning outside, and everything looked all right, but the problems of this
world were pretty heavy. And the temptation was to ask a lot of

questions that couldn't be answered, and to be discouraged and depressed by this terrible occurrence—a fine nineteen-year-old boy with everything going for him, serving a good mission, was suddenly struck down. His parents, who had sent him with hearts filled with joy and anticipation and expectation and who had received and sent all the letters bulwarking their satisfaction in his happy time, his great experience—these parents now sat there on the front row, and I had to stand and seek to explain to them the promises of God: what they really are, how they affect us, what life means, what the gospel means to life.

I would like to testify to you that for a few minutes I felt like an instrument in the hands of God, and that is the sweetest feeling I know. Some light was introduced, not because I was doing the talking but because it was true. We read the scriptures. We talked of this young man, his involvements, the effort he was making, the work he had done, the response of good people who had already come into the Church through his teaching. There came a light of gratitude to God, of comfort, of sensitivity, of tenderness, of closeness to the Lord. That light was sweet and warm, and it brought the gracious assurance that God lives, that His plan is in effect, that this world and our being in it are part of that plan; yet it is only a part. And I told my listeners of an experience I have seldom related, something that happened in England while I was blessed to be a mission president.

One night a fine young missionary came to the mission home with anxiety written all over his face. I knew there was trouble, and I stood to meet it. He could hardly speak through his excitement and his sorrow. He said, "Elder Christensen has been hit on his bicycle—hit by a car—and he is in the hospital in the emergency ward." We rushed to the hospital. A rather flippant little nurse was at the desk. I said: "I am President Hanks. I am the legal guardian of James Christensen, who was hit by an automobile. Can you tell me where he is?"

She said, "In the morgue!" From the look on my face she became a bit ashamed, recoiled, and said, "Oh, I'm sorry, didn't you know?"

I said, "No. I did not know."

"He was dead on arrival," she responded.

I leave out many of the details to speak with you of one

scene that I shared last Tuesday in Las Vegas with the broken-hearted family.

The day came in England when we were to prepare our companion to send him home to his good mother, who lives here in Salt Lake. She had no husband. This was her only son, and she had a younger daughter.

My heart was filled with sorrow as I went to the mortuary to dress our companion in his temple clothing. I took with me three missionaries. One, a choice young man, was a counselor to the mission president. The second had been riding alongside Elder Christensen on his bicycle when the latter was hit by the car that came through a stop light. He hadn't had time even to warn his companion—he just hit his brake and yelled, but Elder Christensen didn't ever see what hit him. This young man, who had been so upset, so sickened over it all, came with me to the mortuary.

A third missionary came too. This one, a little older, was staying with us in the mission home. He had experienced much of life already and made many mistakes, and out there where he was trying to preach the gospel and teach the principles of purity and virtue and repentance and forgiveness he had become so emotionally disturbed that he felt he couldn't finish his mission. He wanted to go home. I took a chance that day and invited him, too.

When the four of us reached the funeral home I went inside with the mortician. He and I did some preliminary things, and then I went back outside and said to my three young companions: "I would like to invite you to come in and help me put the temple clothing on Elder Christensen, if you would like to come. If you feel at all uncomfortable or uneasy, if you don't want to come, that is perfectly all right; I understand fully. In that case, just wait for me here. But if you would like to come in with me I think it will be a great experience for you." All three of them came in.

The funeral director was a giant of a man who was nationally known. He had performed funeral services for the king of England, who had died some years before. He had served at many, many funerals. His business, and he was tender at it, was taking care of those who had passed on. He stood by while these three missionaries and I tenderly, lovingly put on our companion the special clothing worn in a temple and by those being buried who have received the endowment. If you have been to a funeral or at a viewing where someone who is to be buried can be seen, you will have seen the beautiful white clothing.

I watched these three missionaries with as much tenderness of feeling as I have ever watched anything in my life. I felt so full of it myself. There was no horror-type feeling, no discomfort, nothing queasy or scary or objectionable. There was a spirit in that room such as I had never felt before, a particular spirit for that particular setting. I watched these strong, rugged young men, who loved this missionary, walk around him, adjust his clothing; then they would reach out and pat him just a little, just a touch. You see, we all knew something very, very well. We *knew* it. Jim Christensen wasn't really there, not in that form we could see. We were doing for him and his mom and sister the last sweet, brotherly thing we could do in England; but we knew—and our hearts were swelled with joy at this knowledge—that the "real" Jim Christensen wasn't lying before us. We thought he was with us, all right, and this was no spectacular thing—there was no vision, no voice. Just the strongest kind of assurance I have ever felt in all my life.

When we had finished our preparations I said to the funeral director: "We would like to kneel in prayer here. Would you like to join us?" He said, "I would be honored." And so we knelt, and I talked to the Lord. When we stood up the room was filled with the sweetest peace I have ever known.

When we had left the room the director said to me: "President Hanks, I have never known Mormons before. This is the first Mormon funeral I have had anything to do with, the first death of any Mormon I have attended. I have misunderstood. I have heard a lot of things about you people and I have misunderstood. Just let me tell you, please, that for the rest of my life I'll not forget what I felt in that room today, and you can count on it. I will do everything I can do to correct the misapprehensions that are bandied about in this land about you folks."

I suppose it really needn't be said, but I will just say it because it is so: he didn't charge for his services in that case. He wrote me a little note in which he said: "The gain and the joy are all mine."

I am saying to you today that in our lives, with their share of imperfections and bad memories and mistakes made and situations at home or elsewhere that aren't all we would like them to be, there will come these assailing powers. The song calls them "the powers of sin." And sin is darkness. Sin is action against knowledge. Sin is the breaking of the law. We are all guilty of that and we all know a little bit about the powers of sin. Do we not also know how they assail us and cause us deep despair? I do, and I think you do. Joseph Smith's blessing came because he refused to give in to that power, that threatening strength—that bad conscience, in our case, that sense of imperfection, those memories. He cried to the Lord with confidence in His care, and the light came. I would like to tell you there is real darkness and there is real light. It is important to know that while not being frightened of the darkness or preoccupied with it. But we must be aware that whenever we tread into the territory of sin we are subjecting ourselves to the powers that assail and depress and discourage us, and will destroy us if we let them. But if we have sense enough to trust in God our Father and to continue to cry to Him, to seek the light, it will come. In the darkest, most serious times it will come. I promise you.

The Great Worth of Souls

There are two ideas I would like to express on the basis of that foundation; two things of witness. One is that the worth of souls is very great in the sight of God.

About a block from here one day my wife and I sat with a lady who has been in a wheelchair for twenty-seven or twenty-eight years. It was Christmastime, our boy was with us, and Louise was telling us of an experience she had never shared with me before, though I have known her very well for a long time and loved her very much as a great Saint. She said that when she was back in New York working in the rehabilitation hospital helping other people, she one day had a conversation with a little boy she had known about and whom she had seen walking down the halls. He was born in a hovel, in a real ghetto-type setting. Because he had been blind from birth and because the setting was what it was, he was pretty much ignored. When he was just a child, a very little child, before school age, some people who were socially involved came into the home, tried to test him somehow, and announced that he was uneducable, he could never learn anything. "You can't teach him anything. He's a little animal; settle for it."

So he grew up crawling around the room, totally blind. He said later that when something had happened to him—for instance, when he would come across a penny on the floor on occasion—though he couldn't speak he would ask in his own way for pennies, because in his mind, which they said was uneducable, pennies meant going to school. You see, he had heard his brothers and sisters asking for pennies for their milk money, so pennies meant something outside of all this drab and dark life at home, and he tried to collect pennies thinking that maybe a miracle would occur and he could suddenly be like his brothers and sisters. When he was twelve years old he was taken to this rehabilitation institute by someone who came to his home, took a look with some sense of the worth of the human soul, fought for this little boy, and arranged that he have a chance. In the rehabilitation center they began to poke through this miasma of darkness that surrounded him. Out of it came what they said was one of the finest minds they had come across. He could learn, all right; he was brilliant. At age twelve this brilliant boy, having learned in a few months what it takes most of us twelve years to learn, and then some, was feeling his way down the hall to classes every day, by himself. He came to Sister Lake one day, having found in her a kindred spirit of great sympathy and love, and told her this interesting thing.

He said, "You know, Mrs. Lake, I used to think that being blind was the worst thing that could ever happen to anybody in this world, until I met Campy."

Campy was Roy Campanella, negro catcher for the Brooklyn Dodgers, a great baseball player, maybe as great a catcher as ever lived. In an automobile accident on a slick road one day Roy Campanella had run into a bridge abutment. This had severed his spine, and he had become a quadriplegic. He couldn't move. He could not take care of himself at all; he was totally helpless. Somehow Roy Campanella, Campy—who used to go out and try to help people, even in that condition—had become available to this little boy, who had understood the nature of Roy Campanella's problems. He now said to Mrs. Lake: "I used to think blindness was the worst thing that could happen to you in this world until I met Campy, and then I knew his problem was worse. But, Mrs. Lake, there is something even worse than that."

He explained what that even worse thing was. He said: "Every day I walk down these halls feeling my way to class, and people pass me by. I know they are passing me by because I can hear them talk and I can hear their feet on the hallway. Sometimes I smile and I look at them and I say, 'Good morning,' but nobody ever talks to me. I guess they think because I am blind I can't hear either or think either. I guess they think I don't feel anything, that I am not anybody. That's worse than being blind or helpless, Mrs. Lake."

I have thought about that often ever since I heard it. The scriptures say the worth of souls is very great in the sight of God. We look around us and it is relatively simple for us to feel compassion for someone who can't see or can't hear or is crippled in some way. What I am talking about today, though, and not minimizing the very great importance of our compassion and concern for such wonderful folks, is the multitude among us who really don't know each other, who don't understand their own worth.

"Just One Kid"

As I leave idea number one, let me tell you what I learned about fifty yards from here, out by the Joseph Smith monument; Hyrum and Joseph stand there in monument. It was my privilege to be a guide on Temple Square for many years, and one day I was sitting in the office talking with a person who had come to ask questions about the Church. As we sat conversing, the door, which had the word *Private* marked on it, was suddenly thrust open without a knock or an apology and an elderly man pushed into the room, came over to the desk where I sat, and said quite rudely: "How do I get in there?" He was pointing out of the window at the Salt Lake Temple. I thought he was a tourist who had become upset because the guide hadn't taken him in the temple, so with what I thought was admirable patience I began to explain to him what you have to do to get in there, what goes on in a temple, that members go for special reasons and not for meetings or for casual purposes.

I was in the middle of explaining all that when he rejected it, waved it away with a hand, and said: "You don't need to tell me all that stuff; I know that. I'm a Mormon."

This surprised me a little, because he was not an attractive person. He reeked of accumulations, years of accumulations, of alcohol and tobacco. As he spoke he was not completely possessed of himself. He was dirty, bearded, and—I'll just say it—he didn't smell good. I said, "Then if you are a member of the Church and you understand all this, what is it you wanted of me?"

He said: "Nothing. The old woman insisted that I come in here."

I said, "Oh."

"You don't have anything I want," he said, and he turned around and slammed the door and went away. The fragrance remained.

I tried to pick up the pieces and finish the interrupted conversation. When it was over I looked out of that window, right out here at those monuments, ruminating a little on the interesting experiences of life, and saw coming into view the same man with a much younger woman on his arm animatedly talking. She was trying to say something and he was answering. Well, it was interesting. I didn't want to intrude, but I left the office, went back to them, apologized for having been busy, and said, "Is there anything I could do to be helpful to you?" He quickly rejected me; she quickly reached out. In the conversation that followed I learned a couple of things you would be interested in knowing.

At age nineteen this man was thrown out of a Sunday School by a bishop's counselor who had been summoned by the superintendent who had been summoned by the teacher whose class this boy had disrupted. They had tried to reason with him on the way, but at nineteen he was pretty stubborn and pretty rugged and pretty tough and they couldn't budge him. He was going to sit right there. The bishop's counselor, however, was a farmer who knew how to wrestle mavericks and knew how to handle him, and he did. It had to be with two rugged hands. He picked the lad up, by the nape of the neck and the seat of the britches, escorted him to the front door, and threw him out.

Somebody in this scene, as I heard the story a long time later, objected and said he shouldn't do that, to which the bishop's counselor answered, interestingly, "Aw, let him go. He's just one kid." Well, he went, all right, and never came back. Nor did anybody go out to find what had happened to him. They had had enough of him. He was disruptive, an oddball; he was unreachable; they might even have used in terms of the Church the word used on the twelve-year-old—uneducable; he was not going to amount to anything. It was better that he should perish than that the whole class be constantly disrupted; all that kind of reasoning, maybe. Whatever happened, nobody went after him.

So he grew up as some others do around here, angry at the Church, an enemy to the Church, with his mind made up to do all he could to harm the Church. Have you read the scripture or heard it recently that when we reprove with sharpness we should immediately thereafter reach forth in love, with an increase of love toward him whom we have reproved, lest he esteem us to be his enemy? (See D&C 121:43.) Well, this young man became an enemy. He married, he moved to another state, he became a miner. His wife died after having brought him a family. He had married a second time, and that wife also had tragically died. He was now married to his third wife. He was seventy-nine years old. She had brought him to Salt Lake City. In one of those strange little quirks of fate she had become converted to the Church, but he wouldn't let her join. He, the member (nominally, all these years), refused to have anything to do with her becoming a member of the Church. So as a last desperate measure—and this explained what had happened to me in the office—she had brought him to Temple Square and into the office hoping that somehow he could be inspired to want to go to the temple. That to her was the dream.

Well, that's the whole story except for two simple questions that were asked. I said to him, "How many living descendants do you have?" With her help he counted them up: fifty-four living descendants. My other question to him was, "How many of them are members of the Church?" And I can quote to you as if he were speaking today on this great ten acres, because I can still hear it in my ear: "Ha! Ain't any o' them in the Church. They're a pretty hard lot."

If there were one other question to ask I suppose it might be: "Bishop's counselor, who was it you threw out of the door of the Sunday School that morning? Was it just one refractory kid?"

In that one person's lifetime he had become fifty-four other living, breathing, thinking, functioning, some-kind-or-other, human beings. Now, that's point one.

I couldn't be more earnest than to ask you today, humbly— not for my sake, not for the sake of those who love you, but for your sake—do you appreciate the worth of souls, yourself and others? When you make a decision that you may be making out of stubbornness or ego or emotion or appetite, out of the pressure of the moment, do you sense that you are not making a decision just for you, that in a very real sense you are deciding many other things also: things like who you will marry, what kind of home you're going to have, and what kind of children? Now, I am not suggesting that when we make a mistake we're through. I started out saying that's all wrong. We have made enough mistakes, though, you and I, to be able to face up to this. There are powers of sin that assail, and they are no joy. They depress and demean and discourage. They speak to us and say, What's the use? They sometimes cause us to settle for a level of life that is not good enough. So if, *if* you are on a road leading to some place you do not want to be, turn around. The simplest kind of sense tells you that if you stay on a road leading to some place you don't want to be you are going to arrive there. If you don't want to arrive where you're headed, turn around.

Our Influence on Others

The other point, quickly. Not only are we important, not only are other people important, but also each of us is important for the influence we can have on another life, in other lives. Oh, we don't want to look at ourselves with egotism, you and I. We may act a little cocky, we may pretend we have it made, but we know better. We are aware of our failings, and sometimes we feel empty. We don't think we're all that perfect, and yet we are faced with the recognition that what we do matters, that it matters to many. Let me give you the simplest kind of an example.

The other day I got a telephone call from a mother who said through her tears: "We just received a call from our son in California. They've been to the doctor this morning and Christine's tumor is gone." I said, "Gone? Are they sure?" She said: "Yes. All the medical tests indicate the tumor is gone."

Behind that is a long story I needn't tell you, a story of a beautiful young mother with beautiful little children who got more and more sick, more and more weak. Apparently the physicians she had didn't give her a full examination because she seemed to just have a case of the flu; they had not done anything about her condition until one got one look at her, took an X-ray, and said, "You are in real trouble." She had come to Salt Lake to be with her parents, hospitalized. A tumor was found that so engulfed her that when a fine surgeon started to operate on her at the hospital he just had to shake his head sorrowfully and close the wound. The only chance then was chemotherapy and radiation. They started it yet gave her no hope. They returned to California so they would have all the time they could together.

The telephone call said, "It's gone." Out of that comes a memory. I remember a day when that same young man, a fraternity member at the university, was in a meeting where they were planning their big forthcoming party. A lot of the men on the committee wanted a different kind of party, and of course he and the few Mormons who were part of the group were uneasy about that. What do you do about that kind of situation? One of the boys on the committee put down his dollar and said, "That's for the liquor." And the lad next to him said, "Here's mine." They went around the circle until they got to this fine Mormon boy who was a leader in school; very bright, but like all the rest of us wanted to be accepted. What do you do in such circumstances? Do you say "I am not putting any money in that foul stuff," or withdraw?

What this bright, sensitive, wise man did, with a big smile on his face, was put his dollar down a short distance from the pile

and say, "My dollar goes down for the soft drinks." Then somebody else added his, and "Me too," and "Me too," until that pile
was the bigger one. It is a simple thing, but I wonder how much
it meant to him that night and then ten years later, with his degree from the university and MIT, and a fine job and a beautiful
wife, and three little children, and the doctor's prognosis—She
hasn't got a chance. I wonder how much it meant to him then to
believe in something, to stand up for it, whether it was a little
thing or a big thing; not make a big fuss, not preach a big sermon, but just quietly in his own effective way follow his own
course.

Out of that committee room that night, to my personal
knowledge, there came other young men, strengthened, who
but for him would have put their dollar on the other pile as sure
as we are visiting here today.

Well, people are worth everything. That is what life is all
about. That is what the world is for. That is what the gospel
means. Look around you. The worth of souls is very great in the
sight of God. If you will accept my invitation, have the courage
and the sense to do what your conscience tells you is right rather
than what pressure tells you is expedient.

In World War II a lot of terrible things happened overseas. I
would like to leave you with a thought out of all of that that may
be worth remembering. I have been in the concentration camps
where the dirty, filthy stuff went on—the murder, the genocide,
the burning. I have seen those ovens. I have felt the feeling of
darkness in Dachau and some other places. Out of that I choose
to remember a sentence. A pamphlet is sold at Dachau for ten
cents. In it is quoted the words of one man who survived while
hundreds of thousands didn't. He said, "Man cannot trust himself in the hands of man." He meant that if men don't have God,
they are animals.

If you can put this all together, I pray God to help you do it.
There are problems in the world that depress us. There is a light
that can give us the strength, the faith, the courage, the inspiration to move on, to face our imperfect world and do what has to
be done. The basis for all of that is to believe in God. That is, to
believe that we are His children, and not alone I but also you
and every other child of God, and to accept the responsibility
that goes with the recognition that what we do matters.

Church Led by a Rock

I bear my testimony to you that I know that God lives. I know that Jesus is the Christ. I know that the Church is more important in the world today than it has ever been, not as an institution to get bigger but as God's kingdom to give us that circumstance in which we can best live His law. I know that Spencer W. Kimball has been prepared by God to do a certain work. Two years ago I wheeled him into the Salt Lake Airport in a wheelchair. If you know President Kimball you know that that is the last thing in the world he would want. If he could have put one foot in front of the other he would have walked, but he couldn't walk. We were going to a mission presidents seminar, and I had tried to talk him out of it: "President Kimball, how can you go?" I pushed him in a wheelchair. When we got to San Francisco I pushed him again to a car, and when we got to the motel I helped him inside. I really wondered if I would see him the next morning. We had two full days of meetings to hold. He had marks on his throat from radiation treatment for the cancer. His heart was so weak that he confided to me quietly that the doctor had told him his life was breath to breath, that it might be ended in a rather dramatic way—at the pulpit or anywhere else, he said.

He slept through that night. In the morning at eight o'clock he walked into the room. He talked to those mission presidents to start the program and he bore his testimony, and I would like you to hear one thing he said: "I knew President Grant when he was old and ill. I knew President George Albert Smith when he was elderly and ill. President McKay was elderly and ill. Joseph Fielding Smith [who was then President of the Church] is elderly. Now, I would like you to know one thing I know. God doesn't need a quarterback or a long-distance runner or a famous man to lead His Church. He needs a rock, and Joseph Fielding Smith is a rock." And then he bore his testimony.

Since then open-heart surgery has made President Kimball better in health than I have seen him in twenty years. The cancer was apparently brought under control. Standing here at Harold B. Lee's funeral service, he said he had never expected to be President of the Church. He was not ambitious. Believe him. He was not. He said, "Nobody has prayed more for President Lee than my Camilla and I," and he was telling the truth. Now he is President of the Church, and I testify to you before God that the Church is led by a *rock*, a rock of faith and love and inspiration; as good a man as I believe ever lived on the earth.

Now, you leave in the hands of the Lord the judgments that must be made for the Church. You make judgments for you, as I am obliged to for me, judgments that will express compassion and consideration for others, that will make me feel not superior to anyone but brother to everyone, that will make me know that however imperfect I am my influence can be useful and helpful, if I really love and if I really care.

I still find it hard to say words that as a little kid I somehow grew up not saying very much. I said them to my mother. I am a little uneasy in telling you that the girl I married is the only girl who ever heard me say them except my mother and sisters. But once in a while I feel like saying them, and although I feel a little shy about it I'll say them today: I love you. And the Brethren love you. And we would do anything we could do—anything—to try to help you understand how important you are to the Lord, to His work, to generations yet to come, to the world you live in. God bless you. In the name of Jesus Christ. Amen.

VI

Answers

CHAPTER 27

The Weightier Matters

In the Church we are all teachers in principle, and most of us, perhaps all of us in one way or the other, are teachers in fact. Some are professional, and many of the rest of us find our way into a formal classroom setting at some time in our lives. We are home teachers, or ought to be, or visiting teachers. By assignment we are all missionary teachers. In a home we are surely teachers, or in a neighborhood, or as counselors or comforters or friends.

I sat on an airplane recently with a young friend, a medical person, who said that for years he had been singing in the Tabernacle Choir and thus had not been able to attend priesthood quorum meeting. Anticipating the new meeting schedule, he had been earnestly looking forward to priesthood meeting attendance. The week before the first consolidated meetings were held he was invited by the bishop to teach Primary. You will discover that that means he cannot go to priesthood meeting again for a while. This little story reemphasizes what I am saying—that soon or late most of us end up doing some formal teaching. And if we do not, we are yet teachers in other ways along the route.

As a youngster I had mixed experience with teachers, some very good experience and some not quite so good that bothered

Address given at Brigham Young University devotional 25 March 1980.

me and caused me to be less faithful in attendance than I should have been and now wish I had been. But I didn't really enjoy the experience, because I was not comfortable with the teachers or the kind of teaching. I know now that they were very good men and that part of the problem was mine. But I also think that my youthful reactions were somewhat justified. Later when I had some outstanding teachers I became the more sure that anybody who undertakes to teach anybody anything ought to do some very serious thinking. At that age I began to formulate, and in a measure formalized by writing down, some feelings about teaching. I didn't know then that I would spend a major portion of my life in that endeavor, but I did have some very strong responses to and experiences with and feelings about being a teacher. A few of those I want to share, basically in terms of outline. But perhaps the outline will be sufficient to communicate the viewpoint. I label it *my* viewpoint. Much of this is my opinion, and I take responsibility for that but hope it will motivate you to do your own thinking.

Know the Scriptures

The first of these suggestions is that we teach from a strong foundation in the scriptures and with consistent attendance to the study of those scriptures. Christ answered the cynical question of the Sadducees concerning marriage in the resurrection, a resurrection in which they acknowledged no belief: "Ye do err, not knowing the scriptures" (Matthew 22:29). And so do we err if we do not know them. The scriptures center in the Lord Jesus Christ because it is He who is the center point in God's plan for all of us, for all of God's children. As we read the scriptures it is with Jesus Christ and His mission in mind, His life, His love, His teachings, His atoning sacrifice. These are the unifying heart of the holy books.

I have been thinking about what the scriptures themselves teach us about reading the scriptures. They contain so many significant and strong affirmations about *searching* and *seeking* and *asking* and *knocking*. One of them is the report about Paul, who, having been forced to leave Thessalonica, went to Berea. The record says that they in Berea were "nobler" than those in Thessalonica in that they "received the word with all readiness of mind, and searched the scriptures daily [to know] whether those things were so" (Acts 17:11).

The book of Deuteronomy contains a verse of special significance, one that perhaps is a little less known than many to which we might refer: "The secret things belong unto the Lord our God: but those things which are revealed belong unto us and to our children for ever, that we may do all the words of this law" (Deuteronomy 29:29).

That is beautiful and significant, every word and every concept. There are things still secret, as it were, with God. But there is much that He has revealed which belongs to us and to our children forever in order that we may do that which He wants us to do.

I repeat, we should be reading regularly in the scriptures to form a foundation for any kind of competence in understanding and teaching the fundamental principles of life, the *revealed* principles of life and salvation which God himself has given us. We read to know, to understand, to apply, to gain faith. There is much more in the scriptures that should be mentioned—the beauty, the comfort, the inspiration, the motivation, the encouragement, the enhancement of humility, that go with these fundamentals when we read for purpose and those purposes lead us to a basis on which to live and share.

So, get a foundation. And this cannot be done with an occasional attendance at class, though that of course should obviously be helpful. It requires personal effort and search.

Teach in a Positive Context

When we teach it must be done in a context of faith, not doubt. May we seek, search, knock, ask? Yes. Question? Yes. But always in a spirit of inquiry and discovery. Doubting, if it motivates us to move in the right direction and begin to search, can be constructive. But doubting can also immobilize and enervate and destroy. We need to search and teach in the context of faith.

I could illustrate this in many ways, and with some sorrow,

because I have known some whose faith I did not question but who undertook—I think with proper purpose in the beginning— to question, to challenge, in a manner that became doubt-inspiring, in a way which those who were influenced couldn't quite handle. We must not hesitate to say, "I know," when we do know. I read again this morning in Alma that he "stood upon [his] feet" and manifested to the people that he had been born of God (see Alma 36:23). Many times it is recorded that the prophets, the teachers, the leaders were moved to stand and testify, and did so. I believe in reading widely, in searching other sources that are good, but the voice that is listened to, the voice that means something, is the voice that says: "This I know. I have the conviction. The Spirit has borne witness to me that this is true."

The Teacher Cannot Know Everything

As we testify of what we do know we must learn how to say also, "I do not know," because as we have just been reminded there are matters that have not been revealed, much that is yet to be revealed. Teach principles that have consequence in salvation and not those details that may be questionable because there has been no clear revelation that would tie them in with our salvation.

I for one have no unease when there is concern and questioning and when viewpoints are adopted that are different from my own. But I have great concern when people who have such viewpoints—and when in all honesty I do not think those matters essential to my salvation or theirs or yours—set those viewpoints up as the measuring rod of everyone else's faith, and find those lacking or wanting who do not agree with them.

Wise Teaching

In the scriptures there are so many refreshing examples of wise teaching, of honest acknowledgment of limitation, of unwillingness to seek to force acquiescence in matters of detail that have no consequence in salvation or the faith and good life that lead to it. In 1 Nephi, for instance, is a statement about the "more part of all the tribes" that had been led away and scattered to the isles of the sea. Then come these instructive comments: "Whither they are *none of us knoweth*, save that *we know* that they have been led away" (1 Nephi 22:4, italics added).

Nephi teaches with power the great principle that God reveals his truths by the Spirit to the prophets, and he explains the teachings on the brass plates relating to the future of the family of Israel. He *does not know* the details of their places of dispersion but he *does know* that there will come a time when God "gathereth his children from the four quarters of the earth; and he numbereth his sheep, and they know him; and there shall be one fold and one shepherd; and he shall feed his sheep, and in him they shall find pasture" (1 Nephi 22:25).

He testifies that the writings of the prophets are true, and that "they testify that a man must be obedient to the commandments of God. . . . Wherefore, if ye shall be obedient to the commandments, and endure to the end, ye shall be saved at the last day." (1 Nephi 22:30–31.) In 1 Nephi 11 there is recorded the sobering inquiry from an angel to Nephi as to whether he knows "the condescension of God." In effect the Lord seems to be asking if Nephi understands how close to man God is willing to come, how far He is willing to go to help us, how much He loves us, how much He does and is willing to do for us. Read again Nephi's humble answer: "I know that he loveth his children; nevertheless, I do not know the meaning of all things" (1 Nephi 11:17). What a wonderful thing to know, and what an honest attitude of humble limitation!

Alma 7 records Alma's choice instructions revealing his attitude toward teaching and testimony. The prophet *knows* that God has power to do all things. He knows the vital truth that Christ is coming. He does not know exactly when. He does know that he is called to cry repentance, looking to that coming.

> For behold, I say unto you there be many things to come; and behold, there is one thing which is of more importance than they all—for behold, the time is not far distant that the Redeemer liveth and cometh among his people.

Behold, I *do not say* that he will come among us at the time of his dwelling in his mortal tabernacle; for behold, the Spirit hath not said unto me that this should be the case. Now as to this thing I *do not know;* but this much *I do know,* that the Lord God hath power to do all things which are according to his word.

But behold, the Spirit hath said this much unto me, saying: Cry unto this people, saying—Repent ye, and prepare the way of the Lord, and walk in his paths, which are straight; for behold, the kingdom of heaven is at hand, and the Son of God cometh upon the face of the earth. (Alma 7:7–9, italics added.)

In Alma 40 is another great example of teaching wisdom, a classic example of great faith in principle and perhaps a little impatience with too much emphasis on detail. Alma knows there will be a resurrection—"a time appointed that all shall come forth from the dead." He does not know exactly when, or in what stages, and is satisfied to know that God knows these things. He announces that there is a space between death and the resurrection and inquires of the Lord what becomes of men during this time. He receives an answer.

Behold, there is a time appointed that all shall come forth from the dead. Now when this time cometh *no one knows;* but *God knoweth* the time which is appointed.

Now, whether there shall be one time, or a second time, or a third time, that men shall come forth from the dead, it *mattereth not;* for *God knoweth* all these things; and it *sufficeth me to know* that this is the case—that there is a time appointed that all shall rise from the dead.

Now there must needs be a space betwixt the time of death and the time of the resurrection.

And now I would inquire what becometh of the souls of men from this time of death to the time appointed for the resurrection?

Now whether there is more than one time appointed for men to rise it *mattereth not;* for all do not die at once, and this *mattereth not;* all is as one day with God, and time only is measured unto men.

Therefore, there is a time appointed unto men that they shall rise from the dead; and there is a space between the time of death and the resurrection. And now, concerning this space of time, what becometh of the souls of men is the thing which I have inquired diligently of the Lord to know; and this is the thing of which I *do know.*

And when the time cometh when all shall rise, then shall they know that God knoweth all the times which are appointed unto man.

. . . Behold, it has been made known unto me by an angel, that the spirits of all men, as soon as they are departed from this mortal body, yea, the spirits of all men, whether they be good or evil, are taken home to that God who gave them life. (Alma 40:4–11, italics added.)

Alma testifies fervently and firmly and unequivocally of great principles but, I repeat, seems even a trifle impatient when people want to know details. Of many matters, it is written, he would "not say," though he was willing on occasion to offer his personal opinion (see Alma 40:20). So was Paul, as recorded in the great fifteenth chapter of 1 Corinthians (see especially verses 34–36). Don't be unwilling to say, "I don't know," because in truth there is much we do not know. Teach principles that have consequence in salvation. Avoid judging the faith of others on the basis of strong personal opinions in matters that may not in fact really relate significantly to salvation.

For instance, it is of great consequence for us to know that God created man and that He created the earth. Is it of equal importance to know the method or methods and the time involved? I do not think so. I know that God created the earth and I know why. "Behold, the Lord hath created the earth that it should be inhabited; and he hath created his children that they should possess it" (1 Nephi 17:36). I know that man is co-eternal with God, and that He clothed us, our eternal individuality, in spirit form and then made it possible for us to have earth life, through His gift, through His love. I know that He is our Creator and that His children are His special and crowning creation. But I take great comfort in the memory of personal conversations I had with President David O. McKay some years ago when I was concerned with these matters. His answer was about as I have expressed it. Then he said, "It would do no violence to my faith to learn that God had formed man in one way or another." Many times I was touched as he taught of God's love, of

His marvelous fatherhood, of His power, of the holiness of our Heavenly Father. He testified that God created this earth and us. But the methods and time seemed not so significant to him, nor do they to me.

In my youth I memorized from a great novel two sentences which I still remember that reflect a strong sense of wisdom and of appreciation for true faith. A young minister whose mentor was an older, self-sacrificing priest was about to leave his vocation because the older man was being unfairly treated by his administrative superiors. The older priest dissuaded him from resigning with these words: "You've got inquisitiveness and tenderness. You're sensible of the distinction between thinking and doubting. . . . And quite the nicest thing about you, my dear boy, is this—you haven't got that bumptious security which springs from dogma rather than from faith." (A. J. Cronin, *The Keys of the Kingdom* [Boston: Little, Brown and Company, 1941], p. 144.)

I seek faith. I am uncomfortable in the presence of "bumptious security which springs from dogma," and I express my own strong feeling that it is of utmost importance that we value love, faith, repentance, obedience, morality, integrity, and walking in the Spirit, and that we never undervalue these principles at the expense of less essential matters which may preoccupy some.

I believe, and I testify, that the principles God has revealed concerning our salvation are indispensably important to us and mark the path to His presence, and that the only evil any of us can ultimately experience is to be separated from Him, from Christ, and from our dear ones.

The Weightier Matters

It is my conviction that in our lives and teaching we ought to emphasize the weightier matters of the law, as Christ himself taught them. You will remember that as He castigated certain ones for their hypocrisy, He said, "Ye pay tithe of mint and anise and cummin [tithe in kind in their day], and have omitted the weightier matters of the law, judgment, mercy, and faith: these

ought ye to have done, and not to leave the other undone"
(Matthew 23:23).

I love the story of the man who, face to face with the Savior,
pleaded for help for his tragically afflicted son. He had gone to
others seeking assistance and they could not help him. Now he
came directly to the Lord. Christ asked him if he believed: "If
thou canst believe, all things are possible to him that believeth."
Do you remember what followed? "And straightway the father
of the child cried out, and said with tears, Lord, I believe; help
thou mine unbelief." (Mark 9:23–24.)

The child was healed. This honest, humble father knew some
things very well, though he apparently had problems with some
other matters. He knew who it was he faced. He knew that Jesus
was the Christ, and he had full confidence that He could heal
his son.

The Great Commandments

Teach the great commandments: To love God; to love one's
neighbor as oneself; to have faith in the Lord Jesus Christ; to repent and qualify for God's beautiful promises that He will forgive, forget, and never mention the sins of the truly penitent; to
receive and honor the ordinances of the gospel; and to walk in
the light of the Spirit, enduring the tribulations which come to
all of God's children in this mortal experience.

Link Arms with Good People

I testify earnestly that we ought to join forces with good
people who are seeking the same objectives we are, and that we
should walk with them as brothers toward those wholesome
goals as far as we can go.

I sat in a meeting at a university seminar where Elder John
A. Widtsoe, of the Quorum of the Twelve, in his older years was
one of several panelists speaking to the subject of alcoholism.
One stood representing a great Christian denomination and jus-

tified the use of alcohol in moderation, declaring that there is nothing wrong with such use. Another stood representing another part of the Christian world, a young man of considerable conviction, who announced that he differed with the viewpoint of the preceding speaker. He said, "I look upon alcohol, used even as it is used by men who think they are moderate, as a tool of the devil." He talked about the terrible destruction visited upon humankind through alcohol. Dr. Widtsoe was the last speaker. He was an internationally famous chemist and a man of celebrated intellectual accomplishment. He stood and said: "I think there is little need for me to add much today. I link arms with my young brother in what he has just said, and walk with him." And then he added, "Because I am a chemist and know something of the nature and effects of alcohol, perhaps I could talk a little about that." And he did, and let it go at that.

I have never forgotten the imagery and I have enjoyed the blessing frequently of trying to practice it. So let's link arms with good people who have similar or common objectives, and walk with them as long and as far as we can.

Be a Good Example

Learn and understand Alma 39:11. It is the declaration of a sorrowing father who, himself not always perfect, has some memories that are unpleasant for him to live with but who has sorely repented and is God's agent. He finds it necessary to speak the sad message to his own son, who has consorted with a professionally immoral person. The words are sobering to me in contemplation of my one day meeting my missionary father who died when I was a baby. Said Alma to his son Corianton concerning the Zoramites, "When they saw your conduct they would not believe in my words."

As teachers we need to ensure that our behavior is consistent with our teaching of gospel principles. Then when others observe our conduct they will be more inclined to believe our words.

Exercise Spiritually Each Day

Gather the manna daily. Do you remember the great lesson the Lord taught the children of Israel in providing manna for them which they had to gather daily? They had been slaves in Egypt and had forgotten their relationship with the Lord. To teach them and prove them the Lord required that they gather the manna every day except over the Sabbath. They could not collect it or store it. It had to be gathered every day. (See Exodus 16.)

Spirituality, that condition of closeness with the Lord through His Spirit, is like manna to us. We cannot live well without it, and it must be gathered every day. It isn't enough to have known, to have read, to have given, to have prayed, to have obeyed. That great series of verses in Alma 5 that move me so much begin with "If ye have felt to sing the song of redeeming love, I would ask, can ye feel so now?" (See Alma 5:26–31.)

Center on Christ

Finally, teach and testify of Christ. I repeat that it is my conviction that the only evil that can ultimately happen to us is to be separated from Him, from the Father, and from our loved ones.

I was trying to teach a lovely lady once who had terrible problems. The major difficulty was that she has concluded there was no hope for her. She had cut herself off, shut the door. She would not listen to, really didn't want to hear, promises which she felt applied to everybody else but not to her. She was making the most critical mistake that can be made, and that is to negate for her the gift God had given in the life of His beloved Son, who himself gave that life willingly for all of us. She was sure it couldn't apply to someone who had made the sad mistakes she had.

We read through the verses you might have chosen, some of you perhaps with greater wisdom than I did—portions of Isaiah 1 and section 58 and Ezekiel 18 and 33—the promise that God will forgive and that the sin is wiped out in His heart and mind when we truly repent, for He will never mention it; it is gone; that truly repentant, penitent children of God are forgiven. She seemed not to comprehend, nor to believe.

I turned then to two other verses that have become so precious to me and read them. I share them with you: "And now, my beloved brethren, seeing that our merciful God has given us so great knowledge concerning these things, let us *remember him, and lay aside our sins, and not hang down our heads, for we are not cast off*" (2 Nephi 10:20, italics added).

I watched the warmth and beauty of the Spirit of the Lord penetrate the hard curtain which had shut her off—her own doing. I saw a tear come. Then we were able to turn to this wonderful ninth chapter of the book of Moroni to read a line that I would wish all of us truly understood and had mastery of. Mormon is finishing his last recorded letter to his son. He has reminded him of some of the terrible problems of the time. He has been candid in this, laying out for Moroni his own sad view of things as they were. In summation he has declared the most unpleasant thing people could hear from a prophet, that he could not recommend them to God. But then he says to his own son, "I recommend thee unto God," and bears his witness and delivers his valedictory to Moroni in these marvelous words:

"My son, be faithful in Christ [that is where it starts and that is the heart of it all]; and may not the things which I have written grieve thee, to weigh thee down unto death; but may Christ lift thee up, and may his sufferings and death, and the showing his body unto our fathers [that is, his resurrection], and his mercy and long-suffering, and the hope of his glory and of eternal life, rest in your mind forever" (Moroni 9:25).

Don't let infamy, don't let sin, don't let what is happening in the world weigh you down. That is not what Christ is all about; don't let it grieve you. Let Him lift you up. And let all that He represents for us rest in your minds forever.

At the end of Enos's record we read: "And I soon go to the place of my rest, which is with my Redeemer; for I know that in him I shall rest. And I rejoice in the day when my mortal shall put on immortality, and shall stand before him; then shall I see his face with pleasure, and he will say unto me: Come unto me, ye blessed, there is a place prepared for you in the mansions of my Father." (Enos 1:27.)

I desire the faith of Enos. I believe it is my privilege to have that faith in the way Enos received it. I believe it is my responsibility to share that faith in humility with anyone I may, in my own household and neighborhood and beyond it. I will declare, I do know some things very well. And I will be willing to announce that there are some other things I do not know. What I know is that God lives and Jesus is the Christ, that there is a plan for man centering in Christ, our advocate with our Father, the Mediator, He who came not in the form of an angel but in the seed of Abraham in order that He might understand our infirmities, for we do not have a high priest who is unfamiliar with our problems. He is very familiar with them. The purpose of His program is to give us immortality and to open the door to creative life for us eternally; to help us to find joy and to share happiness, to build, to strengthen, to exude the warm and beautiful spirit that comes when we truly know God and Christ and love each other and undertake to share what is good.

In the name of Jesus Christ. Amen.

CHAPTER 28

There Are Some Answers

The music this morning was magnificent. I watched the shyness with which the young lady approached the podium, and I watched with interest when the A was struck on the piano. She tuned her A string tastefully but sturdily. Then I knew she was a good violinist. She was not going to be bothered by people who say, "Why didn't she tune it before she came?" One thing is certain about people who might say that—they don't know anything about a violin; they don't know that a bump, a change in the atmosphere in the room, just the number of people arriving, or a warm hand on the strings for a moment, can change ever so slightly the nuance, the atunement, the consonance. If you have ever heard a violin played that is out of tune, you know real dissonance.

The violinist made sure her violin was in tune with the accompanying instrument. And she didn't tune her D string to the piano, but with the A string, because there has to be consonance there, and then tuned each string with its neighboring string. So the violin was ready and so was the violinist; and because the accompanist also was prepared and ready, together they gave an impressive rendition.

Address given at the Salt Lake Institute of Religion 12 May 1978.

Answers Through the Spirit

As with all other important principles that I know anything about, the Lord has spoken on this matter. It is noted in the last verse of 2 Nephi chapter 32 that before we do anything in the name of the Lord we need to pray to the Father and get in tune. Before you do anything in the Lord's cause, be sure you are in tune. And you do that in part through prayer. The most important principle I know as regards spiritual things is the scriptural statement that only through the Spirit of God can we know the things of God (see 1 Corinthians 2:11).

I was at the University [of Utah] the other night on the griddle, as it were, responding to questions about conflicts between the city and the university, from which I graduated and for which I have great affection. I stood in this very spot for many years teaching at this institute, and in the west institute a little while before that. I think you are entitled to know that I have defended and spoken in favor of this university for years when it has sometimes come under attack. I believe you are the equal, at least, of any other student group in any other place, and that this is a great school.

As I spent a little time over there the other night these thoughts occurred to me again, and there was no condescension in this or any sense of superiority—far from it. I was modest and humble enough, with plenty of reason to be. I have been away from here a long time, and from strictly academic climes. I have been anxious to keep up, have read a bit and thought a bit, and stayed in touch with the newspapers and some periodicals, and so forth. But young, sharp minds, or older ones, involved with academic pursuits can ask hard questions. I didn't come fearing and trembling. I came whimsically and left whimsically. But I thought along the way in that rather pleasant encounter that there is a principle involved I should speak about tonight.

That principle is the one I have just stated: The things of God can only be known to us through the Spirit of God. It doesn't matter how good, ethical, moral, decent, or brilliant the individual is, unless the Spirit of God carries the message, that person will never understand the truth.

That message is evident throughout the scriptures. Paul was

writing about it two thousand years ago, trying to help the Corinthians understand that just being very bright in the mind was not enough. Just being extremely well educated is not enough. Just being good and decent and even noble and lofty in life and concept—these are not enough. What we have to have in order to understand the things of the Spirit is the Spirit. That is what Paul meant in the first book of Corinthians in the second chapter when, after talking about things greater than eye has seen or ear heard or that have entered into the heart of man, he said that we can know them through the Spirit.

If there could be a better witness on earth than this, I am not aware of whom he may be. If you want an evidence of Paul's brilliance, his marvelous education, his learning, and his skill and capacity to communicate, just take half a day or maybe less and bless yourself by reading over and over these epistles he wrote. They were not written as books but as letters to his friends, and they are full of light and knowledge.

Who is this Paul who thus wrote? He is none other than Saul, enemy to Christ, enemy to Christians, enemy to anybody he thought was dangerous or charlatan or eating at the vitals of the state. He was not only a very bright man but also a very determined one. He was willing to stand by and hold the cloaks of people who were stoning a Saint to death—an accessory to murder—because he was so sure Stephen was wrong, as well as these other followers of the Christ. He is the one who got turned around by a light and a voice, and was not the same for the rest of his life, despite the kind of torments that we can only dimly imagine (see 2 Corinthians 11:23–27).

What did he say? Forty stripes, save one, five times? That's 39 blows with the whip five different times; shipwrecked, imprisoned, all the rest. Finally he gave his life—and never wavered. This was the same man who originally did all that damage to the Church, all that mischief. When he saw the light and heard the voice he could not be turned aside from his course—and was not, either by enemy or by friend. (He was willing to take on Peter over the issue of Jews retaining their rituals when they became Christians.)

What happened to Paul? What happened is that he got turned around and he received the Spirit. He was very compassionate. He understood that to the Greek Christ's teachings were foolishness and to the Jew a stumbling block (see 1 Corinthians 1:23). But he said, "He that soweth to the Spirit shall of the Spirit reap life everlasting" (Galatians 6:8). In the second chapter of 1 Corinthians he explained that the natural man—that means the man without God, without the Spirit in this world—just cannot understand these things. "Neither can he know them, because they are spiritually discerned."

In that little line is a very great lot of sense. I plead with you to know it. It may save your life, because if you are alert and awake you will find questions of magnitude that can only be answered through the Spirit. You will find minds that are admirable and characters that are lofty, people of decency and integrity, who do not believe. I am talking about the kind of person you really admire and maybe want to emulate but who doesn't know what the humblest here can know through that Spirit. And furthermore, this person I have described can never know that you don't know. He may say, talking about the various ways of knowing, that he doesn't think you know, but he can never know whether you know or not. The only way to know is through that Spirit.

When the Light Comes

In Joseph Smith's story (see Joseph Smith—History) are two lines I call to your attention and invite you to consider. You know the First Vision story—the search, the darkness that almost overcame the boy, and then a line that says, "When the light rested upon me I saw. . . ." We customarily do not stop where I have just stopped. What he says is, *"When the light rested upon me I saw. . . ."* and then tells what he saw and what the two Personages did. Think of the first words, *"When the light rested upon me."* When the light came, when he had the light, he could see. A few lines later he says, "When the light had departed, I had no strength."

Perhaps you haven't read it that way. Maybe you will from now on if you haven't, because the message is the same as that in section 50 of the Doctrine and Covenants. What are you called to? What are you ordained to? Why do you preach the gospel? And how? *"Through my Spirit."* If you do it through my Spirit it is of me. If you don't, if you try to do in it some other way, however well educated and bright you are, then it isn't of me. And if you try to learn my word in any other way than through that Spirit, then that isn't of me, either.

That may be the most sobering single lesson I now know in connection with what I know about the Lord and the love I have for Him. I hope that when you find questions that are tough you will put them up on the shelf for a while with the understanding that with the growing light we don't suddenly come into the brilliance of the sun. The scripture says that too, that the light "groweth brighter and brighter until the perfect day" (D&C 50:24). We grow, step by step.

Ideal of the Free Society

William Rees-Mogg, editor of that great newspaper the *Times,* came from England to Salt Lake City to honor President N. Eldon Tanner, who was being saluted as a giant in the community. In his talk Mr. Rees-Mogg spoke of an ideal, the most hopeful and important ideal in the world, which rested itself on the democratic organization of free men and depended upon something particular about the character of those men. He spoke of this ideal as that upon which the great British Commonwealth was founded, and then similarly about the United States. He spoke about freedom being something that doesn't just happen; it has to be merited, brought about, preserved, and retained. And he told how. Then he asked this question: "How stands this ideal of the free society with free men depending upon their own self-discipline to maintain the responsibility which the community requires if it is to survive?" Then he answered the question: "That, I believe, is the principle which gave your nation its greatness in the world and made it perhaps the most successful experiment in political society that the world has ever seen. When I am here [in this community] I know that that spirit is still strong. Long may it remain so, and long may its enemies be confounded."

Now, obviously I am not suggesting that such qualities as free men of character, self-disciplined, accepting a responsibility in their community, are the unique or exclusive possession of members of this Church. What I am saying is that Mr. Rees-Mogg found here that ideal, which he feels is moribund, on its deathbed, elsewhere on earth. Why is it here, if it is?

Within about one month after this event I heard about a dozen people give speeches in this community. The last was Joseph Rosenblatt at the Brigham Young University commencement exercises. Mr. Rosenblatt was born here of a Jewish father who came here at the age of fourteen from Lithuania, speaking no English. He started peddling in this community and became something special economically and otherwise. Joseph, paying tribute to his father, wept. (He is past seventy himself.) His father, every morning when he awakened, addressed God in the Old Testament way, much like a cantor of ancient times. This father, the peddler who became a wealthy man through his own efforts, spoke all his life of "my Mormon valleys."

The question I am asking (and obviously it is too big to even get started with here) is a serious one to consider. Mr. Rosenblatt, who has been honored by many universities, including this one, meant no disrespect to any of the others when he said that his award at Brigham Young University was his greatest honor because of the sponsoring institution and the character of its people. Mr. Rosenblatt was speaking of an ideal planted here and still alive and reasonably strong. What are its elements?

I read in the *Saturday Review* a time ago this quotation from John Wharton. He is talking about a painting which Gauguin considered his greatest work, entitled, "Whence Come We, What Are We, Whither Go We?" Wharton says: "Both the painting and the title struck me as masterpieces. For you cannot answer those three questions without starting a whole train of other profound questions: Is life meaningless, or divinely purposeful, or something in between; is there a God; is there a soul; is the soul immortal; are we punished or rewarded in a hereafter for our acts on earth; is there a goal to which our actions should be directed?" And then he says that for six thousand years the same questions have been asked and "a series of priests, philosophers, and politicians have been on hand, ready, and willing—

but never fully able—to offer completely satisfying answers."
(*Saturday Review*, 3 December 1966.) Can you?

Maybe that is part of this ideal involving free men of character with a sense of responsibility and self-discipline assuming ac-
countability for the nature of the community, about which Rees-
Mogg spoke.

Revealed Answers

There are answers to those questions, not possessed in their
fulness by any one of us but revealed in sufficiency by God in
these books and to living prophets. These answers are basic and
beautiful and important, answers even about God himself. One
such answer says: "Thus saith the Lord, Let not the wise man
glory in his wisdom, neither let the mighty man glory in his
might, let not the rich man glory in his riches: but let him that
glorieth glory in this [if you have anything to congratulate yourself for or to be really happy about, let it not be wealth, worldly
wisdom, or might, but let it be this], that he understandeth and
knoweth me, that I am the Lord which exercise lovingkindness,
judgment, and righteousness, in the earth: for in these things I
delight, saith the Lord" (Jeremiah 9:23–24).

In the scriptures there are answers that are marvelous. And
there are some other interesting things that are being said outside of scripture. An article in the *Los Angeles Times* reported
something written on a graffiti wall at a Catholic university. You
are all well acquainted, I think, with a conversation between
Christ and His Apostles in which He said, "Whom do men say
that I am?" They gave Him some answers and then He said,
"But whom say ye that I am?" (Matthew 16:13, 15.) This is what
the students wrote:

> Jesus said unto them: "Who do you say that I am?"
> And they replied, "You are the eschatological manifestation of
> the ground of our being, the kerygma in which we find the ulti-
> mate meaning of our interpersonal relationships."
> And Jesus said, "What?" (*Los Angeles Times*, 19 January 1974.)

What kind of answers? Simple ones, basic ones, believable ones, humbling ones that do not bring God and Christ down to my level but exalt me with the notion that being Christ's and joint heirs with Him I may become like Him and His Father.

What does that mean in practice? It means a lovely girl sitting across a table in a mission interview answering a question from a visiting brother who had just said to her: "Sister, I wish I had an hour to talk with you, or half an hour, but I don't. I have about ten minutes, and then I must go to catch an airplane to keep faith with other people in other places. Knowing that you are finishing your mission, and having had a chance to just look in your eyes for a minute, I know there is something you could tell me that I ought to hear." She looked surprised, and she smiled to see if I was kidding. I wasn't. She thought for half a minute and then told me. In many ways it is the favorite thing I have heard in years and years. I give you only the headline:

Two brothers on missions, she a senior in college and earning her own way. A musician, a lovely person, she had decided she couldn't heed the promptings of the Spirit which were telling her that she was to go on a mission. She hadn't really ever contemplated it; her brothers were there. Her dad ran a little farm in Idaho which he had scratched over, sacrificed for, leased some of, and sold some of to keep her older brothers on missions. She just knew there wasn't anything left to sell or lease or anyplace else to get any money, and that her dad would insist on helping her if she went. So she just decided against it.

In her final year she went home for Christmas as usual, sat in the old front room in the old rocking chair looking at her father with that line across his forehead where his hat fit, noting the old suit and the gnarled hands, and her eyes welled with tears. She saw the threadbare carpet and thought of her mother in that old blue cloth coat, the one she'd had for years. And as they rocked they talked, until finally her father said, "Sweetheart, do you really want to go on a mission?"

"Daddy," she said, "we never talked about a mission."

"I know," he said. "Do you really want to go on a mission?"

"Daddy," she said, "I know that Bob and Bruce are on missions and that you don't have the money, and that you'd insist on helping me. And I know you can't sacrifice any more, and I don't intend to permit you to. I haven't any thought of going on a mission, Father."

After a pause he smiled and said, "Sweetheart, do you really want to go on a mission?"

She cried and said, "Yes, Daddy."

He said: "Then I'll tell you a story. When the Lord told me you wanted to go on a mission quite a while ago, I went out into the field, having fasted and prayed, and talked to Him. I said, 'Lord, my sweetheart wants to go on a mission and I have to have the privilege of helping her. How am I going to do it?' He said, 'Plant onions.' I said, 'How's that?' He said, 'Plant onions.' I said, 'I guess I'd better talk with you later, Lord."

He went home, worked the fields that day, fasted some more, and the next morning talked with the Lord again. " 'Lord, may I make myself perfectly clear. I've got to have a way to make some money to help my beautiful daughter. How am I going to do it?' And the Lord said, 'Plant onions.' I said, 'Yes, sir.' I went home, bought some seed [borrowed the money to do it], planted the seed, and began to pray and cultivate the crop. The Lord tempered the elements to the crop. It was a bountiful harvest. Others just don't grow onions around here. It's just too far north, too cold, usually. I sold the crop at a good price, paid my tithing, paid back what I'd borrowed, paid the taxes, and put the rest of it in the bank for you."

He went over to a drawer, got out a brand new bank book with one name on it—hers—and one entry for several thousand dollars, and said, "The Lord has provided for your mission."

She said, "Brother Hanks, I don't have any trouble believing in a God who loves us and understands our needs and in His wisdom will provide for them, because I have that kind of a father." I wept and said: "Thank you. I have never known a father at all, and you are very very fortunate in yours." She said, "I know."

There are some answers that have to do with purpose in life and the duration of it and the meaning of it and how it should be lived and the consequences of how we choose. Yes, there are some answers.

Strength of Home and Family

What else? I give you out of many very interesting current examples two wonderful ones. There is an article by Michael Novak. Some of you may know him as a professor of philosophy, a writer of consequence. The article is in *Harpers* and is entitled "The Family Out of Favor." It has a lot to say that is really fascinating. You will get the meaning of it if I read just these last lines. He is talking about those who loathe marriage and celebrate its demise. "Each sign of weakness in the institution exonerates them from personal failure," says Novak. And then he talks about the family and the home. "The work place is not designed with family needs in mind, neither our working hours. Yet clearly the family is the seedbed of *economic skills, money habits, attitudes toward work* and the art of financial independence. The family is a stronger agency of *educational success* than the school. The family is a stronger teacher of the *religious imagination* than the church. *Political and social planning* in a wise social order begin with the axiom, 'What strengthens the family strengthens society.' " (The italics are mine.)

Then Novak thinks of the Sunday paper, maybe, or other media where we read which highly paid movie star is living this month with which other one, and he says: "Highly paid, mobile and restless professionals may disdain the family (having been nurtured by its strengths). But those whom other agencies desert have only one institution in which to find a central nourishment." He then speaks of the role of father, mother, children, the absolutely critical center of social strength, and finishes: "One unforgettable law has been learned painfully through all the oppressions, disasters and injustices of the last thousand years. If things go well with the family, life is worth living. When the family falters, life falls apart." Novak, of course, is not a member of this Church.

Several of the marvelous examples I have referred to here come from without Church borders but they testify to and strengthen these principles in which we believe. The genius is not that we are unique in them but that we share them with wonderful people, that they are scattered like glimmering lights across the earth, and that they have been gathered together by one assigned to do so by God in the latter times.

Let me share with you this other tender thing. After the war in the Pacific, which we ended with some bombs, the United States tried and condemned and put to death a number of people. One of them was General Homma, a Japanese commander. After that happened one of our Associate United States Supreme Court justices said it was a terrible blotch on American justice; but it nonetheless happened. General Homma wrote to his wife while he was awaiting his execution:

> In the twenty years of our married life we've had many differences of opinion and even violent quarrels. Those quarrels have now become sweet memories. . . . Now as I am about to part from you, I particularly see your good qualities, and I have completely forgotten any defects. I have no worry about leaving the children in your hands because I know you will raise them to be right and strong. . . . Twenty years feel short but they are long. I am content that we have lived a happy life together. If there is what is called the other world, we'll be married again. I'll go first and wait for you there but you mustn't hurry. Live as long as you can for the children and do those things for me I haven't been able to do. You will see our grandchildren and even great-grandchildren and tell me all about them when we meet again in the other world. Thank you very much for everything.

And then he wrote his children:

> There are six men here who have been sentenced for life. It will be better to be shot to death—like dying an honorable death on the battlefield—than spending a disgraceful life in such a cage the rest of one's life. Don't lose courage, children! Don't give in to temptation! Walk straight on the road of justice. The spirit of your father will long watch over you. Your father will be pleased if you will make your way in the right direction rather than bring flowers to his grave. Do not miss the right course. (John Toland, *The Rising Sun* [New York: Random House, 1970], p. 400.)

General Homma shared some of the special truths we know.

To summarize: *There are some answers.* Please seek to learn them. *There is a way to live*—individually, in families, with our fellowmen—that is gracious and civil and committed and exemplary and repentant and forgiving; and *there is a Spirit* through which things which are from God can be understood.

I think of your youth and your strength and your capacity and the complexities of your lives and the pressures on you and pray God to bless you. Move only very slowly away from established paths, please. Move very slowly, if at all, away from what has been of such great moment to your own spiritual or actual forebears, which in their conglomerate form an ideal that people like Mr. Rees-Mogg and others recognize when they come here.

In the name of Jesus Christ. Amen.

CHAPTER 29

Coming Home to the Answers

I am very grateful for the privilege of being here. It is, of course, indispensably important that one who stands here have the accompaniment of the Spirit. What I have to say will not be new or extraordinary. The witness of the Spirit can make it important to you.

In London, when my family lived there, one morning I reached up and took down a book I had only recently placed high on a shelf to safeguard it from the curiosity of our little boy. As I took it down, dust fell in my face and on my white shirt and caused me to contemplate with some wonderment how quickly that which is precious can become dust covered unless we hold it at hand and keep it clean.

There is another thought, less exalted but I think equally interesting, and perhaps relevant in an indirect way. It is the story (no doubt apocryphal at best) of the man who achieved high prominence as a ship handler. In fact, after a time he became so proficient in piloting ships through dangerous offshore channels that he became famous. His life seemed quite ordinary except for his ascendancy to high prominence. It was noted, however,

Address given at Brigham Young University devotional 15 October 1974.

that he had one idiosyncrasy. Each morning as he began his day, he would go to a desk, unlock one of its drawers, take out a paper, read it, and then solemnly put it back, lock the drawer, lock the desk, and go about his pilot duties. When he died, those who had known him well and admired him took occasion to see what that very important ritual had involved. They unlocked the desk, unlocked the drawer, took out the paper, and read: "The left side of the ship is port. The right side of the ship is starboard."

If what I am now to say seems unusual, take a look and see if there is some dust. Maybe we can blow it away.

Preserving the Good We Have

G. K. Chesterton involved me in some very important thought a time ago, and then again recently when I read in his introduction to his great book *Orthodoxy* these words: "I have often had a fancy for writing a romance about an English yachtsman who slightly miscalculated his course and discovered England under the impression that it was a new island in the South Seas. . . . There will probably be a general impression that the man, who landed (armed to the teeth and talking by signs) to plant the British flag on that barbaric temple which turned out to be the Pavilion at Brighton, felt rather a fool. I am not here concerned to deny that he looked a fool."

Chesterton then explained that if we look upon the man and conceive him to feel like a fool, we are wrong. He may in fact look like a fool, discovering what he had recently left and finding there what he had gone away to look for. But in fact he did not feel like a fool. There is no joy so great as coming home and finding there what you have gone away to get. Chesterton listed some very interesting ideas when he explained that this man—after having left his home port, wandered lengthily, and then come back to his original moorings—had found that which he had in fact gone out looking for, not knowing he had had it at hand all the time.

Let me quickly and oversimply overstate some of Chesterton's ideas: The world does not offer its own explanation for its own being. There is magic and miracle in it, the magic and miracle have meaning, and because the magic and miracle of the world have meaning there must be someone who designed and created it. There is something in the world, he said, that is personal, as in a work of art. The purpose is beautiful in spite of the defects. We owe obedience to Him who purposed it, and we must have humility and restraint in the use of the blessing.

Chesterton's last idea, about what the man had gone away to find and actually came home to discover, was a little more esoteric and a bit more difficult to understand and explain. I suspect he means that there is in this world the obvious reality of a continuum. Man is husbanding; he has, in effect, retained the good which came from some cataclysm. There has been some ruinous thing before, he says, which makes it important that what we have here be enjoyed and appreciated and perpetuated.

To the extent that we have intellectually or spiritually or in our behavior left our old moorings because they have come to seem to us provincial or limited or embarrassing, how would it be to consider what we have left behind and what in fact—like the prodigal who finally came home—we must return home to really enjoy? I have in mind three simple answers and would pray to be able to share them with you under the guidance of the Spirit of the Lord.

Finding Answers in Gospel Teachings

We need to apply personally what has been said. I remember a good friend who said to me, out of respect for our lengthy association from childhood until our involvement in some graduate work, that he was about to write a thesis, the object of which was to explain what he had learned after he left home. He was going to tell about his emancipation from the "provincialism" of the Church. I listened respectfully and said that would be a very interesting thing. Then I said: "If you write it, I would like to be the first to read it, or one of the first. But in fact, my friend, you will never write it."

"What do you mean?" he said.

I replied: "You can't write it because you're too ignorant to write it, and I don't mean to be discourteous; I mean to be realistic. You couldn't write it because you have no real idea what it is you think you have outgrown. Tell me about the Book of Mormon, the Doctrine and Covenants, and the Pearl of Great Price. Tell me about the Bible, about the standard expositions of the doctrines of the Church. Have you read any of them?"

And he had to say no—he had not read one. Yet he was going to announce to the world what he had overcome and left behind in seeking a new island in the South Seas. "Well," he said, "we shall see."

I said: "If you really go to work and discover what it is you are leaving behind, you will never write it, either, because I know what is deep inside you. If you do that much, you'll stay home."

There came a day when he announced to me with a glint in his eye, a loving and I thought promising glint, that he had decided to change his thesis. And he never did the work to find out what it was he was leaving.

What is it? For one thing, if we have been wandering in some sort of odyssey like Chesterton's and then get back to home port, we find that the most important answers to the most important questions that mankind faces are here—answers that at some time in every life an examination must lead one to desire. We need answers about God, ourselves, Christ the Mediator; about life itself, its true nature. These questions and answers are central in our existence, in our living with some kind of dignity and integrity and making a contribution. What does our information give us about God and Christ and ourselves and life? I suspect you know the answers as well as I do. May I blow dust off one or two of them for a few moments.

God taught us of himself that which we can comprehend. He revealed, He said through Paul to the Romans, His eternal power and Godhead to the extent that people could understand it (see Romans 1:20). He left us, of course, with much to learn. He left us to revere and stand humbly before His holiness because our thoughts are not His thoughts and our ways are not His ways, and as the heavens are higher than the earth, so are

His thoughts higher than our thoughts (see Isaiah 55:8–9). We have never conceived that we understand everything there is to know about our Heavenly Father. I read a line or two from Elder Albert E. Bowen of the Council of the Twelve, whose mind, we will remember, was second perhaps to that of few and whose faith was very great: "God is not an abstraction but a celestialized being, a benignant Father of the spirits of men having a bodily form. But he [Joseph Smith] did not purport to tell all that God is, nor even himself to have comprehended God in his fullness. On the contrary, he declared that the majesty and power of the Almighty, his might and dominion in their fullness, are beyond the capacity of mortal men to conceive and outside all human power of description, a transcendence of glory such as eye hath not seen nor ear heard nor entered into the heart of man."

Our Father has taught us that men are destroyed through lack of knowledge, and the knowledge He had in mind was truth and mercy and a knowledge of Him as He taught us through Hosea (see Hosea 4, 6). In many ways and under many beautiful expressions He taught us what, in fact, He wants us to know. We have now to learn and to grow in our eternal journey from knowledge to knowledge until there comes a time when we see, not through a glass darkly but face to face, and then know as we are known.

No scripture I have recently come to love again is more meaningful to me than the last words of the last chapter of the book of Job. This great prophet, with all the problems he had, was invited by her whom he loved the most and who was closest to him to curse God and die: "Dost thou still retain thine integrity? curse God, and die" (Job 2:9) because you are in trouble. But Job would not. Later he testified that he would see God standing on this earth. His testimony is well known and beautiful and impressive—"Whom I shall see for myself" (Job 19:27). Having passed through that great, long experience he came at the end to talk to the Lord in such beautiful, simple, humble terms: "Therefore have I uttered that I understood not; things too wonderful for me, which I knew not. . . . I have heard of thee by the hearing of the ear: but now mine eye seeth thee. Wherefore I abhor myself, and repent in dust and ashes." (Job 42:3, 5–6.)

Having run the course, having come to know, really know—not through language or circumlocution or answer, but by the seeing of the humble spiritual eye—he saw just how much he had not known. He saw how much he had uttered that was far too wonderful for him to himself understand, and he looked upon himself with an appropriate sense of limitation and a reverence for God.

Concerning Christ, what do we find when we come home again? I bear testimony that the beautiful, wonderful instructions of the record are true, that "he himself hath suffered being tempted" (Hebrews 2:18), that He "was in all points tempted like as we are, yet without sin" (Hebrews 4:15). He gave His life for us, that unto all who look for Him He should appear the second time.

When we come home we find that He is what He said He is, the divine Son of the Living God, our advocate and mediator: "For behold, I, God, have suffered these things for all, that they might not suffer if they would repent; but if they would not repent they must suffer even as I; which suffering caused myself, even God, the greatest of all, to tremble because of pain, and to bleed at every pore, and to suffer both body and spirit—and would that I might not drink the bitter cup, and shrink" (D&C 19:16–18).

When we come home we find the records and the prophets who lived in the past speaking to us in consistent terms: "The Spirit itself beareth witness with our spirit, that we are the children of God: . . . heirs of God, and joint-heirs with Christ." (Romans 8:16–17.)

As to life itself, we find its everlastingness and meaning and beauty and purposefulness when we look around us at home. I think of examples with which I am personally familiar who, having wandered for a time, or having actually remained here, have come to the safe mooring and learned the truth about life's meaning and purpose and the hope and promise of an everlasting future.

Internalizing True Principles

I come now to a second idea, and that is that simply to know these truths is not enough. We must choose them and live them, personalize and internalize. It is not true in our time, as it was not in the time of Paul, that to have the name necessarily means that we have the blessing. He is not a Jew who is one outwardly; he is a Jew who is one inwardly (see Romans 2:28–29).

I have a wonderful young relative who suffered a terrible experience in the loss of her mother. She survived it through faith, although the rocky going caused her to leave port for a while. She spoke of this at a farewell testimonial:

"As a youngster I was taught many beautiful, wonderful things I loved and responded to. I was taught, for instance, about a man who came riding along on a camel and saw someone lying at the wayside who had been beaten by robbers. He saw others who should have known better than to do so pass by the wounded person, but he himself got off his camel and helped. I made up my mind as a little girl that if I were ever riding a camel and I came to somebody who had been beaten and left at the roadside and needed help, I would get off my camel and help him. That's about as close as I really came in my heart to the story of the Samaritan.

"I also heard the story after the war about the man in Dachau who, when he was freezing, took off his sweater to give to a person who was dying. I made up my mind: If I am ever in a concentration camp and I have a sweater and someone else is dying, I will take it off and give it to him. That is about as close as I came to understanding what the gospel is really all about. Now I have begun to understand."

Do you know the course she followed on her odyssey home? She went down into central city in Salt Lake City and became the "Cubmaster" for a group of little children who didn't enjoy the blessing of leadership or, many of them, of a family who cared. It wasn't a drop-in with punch and cookies at the children's hospital; it was one, two, three, or four days and nights a week. She gave and gave and gave until she came to understand that in giving was real joy, surcease from pain and grief, expiation of sorts. She found her happiness and, having come home, discovered that that which she had left behind was in fact what she had returned to.

Developing Personal Testimonies

The third idea has to do with testimony. We find some answers that are understandable, that make life meaningful. We find direction in how we live, and we find, if we look around us or start back home, that marvelous phenomenon we call testimony or witness.

Last week, faced with the responsibility of praying in general conference, which is a little different from speaking, I sat through a long morning before that ten o'clock meeting reading the scriptures, joyfully, happily, comfortingly reading the scriptures. I wish we could go over the ground together. May I share just two wonderful stopping places.

Our land is in trouble, and we know it, and so is the world, and we know it. May I read something my eyes fell on that morning: "If my people, which are called by my name, shall humble themselves, and pray, and seek my face, and turn from their wicked ways; then will I hear from heaven, and will forgive their sin, and will heal their land" (2 Chronicles 7:14).

So said the Lord.

Then, and even more comfortingly, I read again from the magnificent eighth chapter of the book of Romans what I am sure each of you has read and what I hope you will refer to again and again:

> The Spirit also helpeth our infirmities: for we know not what we should pray for as we ought: but the Spirit itself maketh intercession for us with groanings which cannot be uttered. . . .
>
> Who shall separate us from the love of Christ? shall tribulation, or distress, or persecution, or famine, or nakedness, or peril, or sword?
>
> Nay, in all these things we are more than conquerors through him that loved us.
>
> For I am persuaded, that neither death, nor life, nor angels, nor principalities, nor powers, nor things present, nor things to come,

Nor height, nor depth, nor any other creature, shall be able to separate us from the love of God, which is in Christ Jesus our Lord. (Romans 8:26, 35, 37–39.)

I would like to bear testimony to you that some of us, all of us to a measure, when we go away looking for something that may seem more satisfying, will find what we really want when we head back home and land on the shores of England, as it were. This is the Lord's work, and I know it and rejoice and thank God for that knowledge. In the name of Jesus Christ. Amen.

CHAPTER 30

The Answers Are True

Long ago, Isaac sent his son Jacob to find a wife. The Bible says: "And Jacob went out from Beer-sheba, and went toward Haran. And he lighted upon a certain place, and tarried there all night, because the sun was set; and he took of the stones of that place, and put them for his pillows. . . . And he dreamed, and behold a ladder set up on the earth, and the top of it reached to heaven: and behold the angels of God ascending and descending on it." (Genesis 28:10–12.) The Lord spoke to him.

Then Jacob said something I thought of yesterday as we sat in this somewhat different worship hall, a hall not dedicated to worship but made worshipful, for me, by the spirit and witness of those who here have prayed and spoken and sung. "Jacob awaked out of his sleep, and he said, Surely the Lord is in this place; and I knew it not. . . . This is none other but the house of God, and this is the gate of heaven." (Genesis 28:16–17.) This place has been made into the house of God while the Saints of God are worshiping. For us it has been, in a real sense, the gate to heaven as witness has been given here, in utter sincerity, of the purposes for which we meet and the convictions upon which we base our adherence and allegiance to The Church of Jesus Christ of Latter-day Saints.

Address given at Melbourne area conference February 1976.

The testimonies that have been borne have been sure and, to me, sweet, and my heart has been responsive to them. The President of the Church spoke to us, and all of us pulling for him and praying for him and responding to him were uplifted. Others have spoken. We have been taught. We have heard again and again the declaration that this is the gospel and this is the Church of Jesus Christ, that we know it to be true, that we all ought to be sharing it.

My question for a few moments is: What is it of which we testify? What is it we love so much that we would gladly share it, at any cost, if that cost were required? What is our position in this great city and this great country and in a world where there are so many different and sometimes contending voices: Our position is not one of arrogance and self-congratulation; that would mean that we misunderstand or fail to understand the nature of the message. It is, instead, one of great appreciation, of gratitude to God, and a desire to share with others that which He in His goodness has given to us.

What is that?

Definition of Religion

I read once a definition of religion which has seemed to me since (and it is nearly a lifetime away) both all-encompassing and very helpful when we assess what it is we would share. Elder John A. Widtsoe the Apostle fashioned it, he who had come as a convert from other points of view and had become so marvelously successful an advocate of that which God had revealed to his heart. He said that religion should be three things. It should offer us the answers to the most significant and serious questions that ever we ask, questions which we may succeed in avoiding for periods, but to which all sincere human beings ultimately come—questions about God and Christ and life and man and sin and affliction and resurrection—basic questions. So true religion should offer us answers that our minds can deal with and our hearts respond to. It should, secondly, give us a way to live, bring us a guide to living, to conduct, that will help us to find happiness here and now as well as look for it in the great eternal worlds. And thirdly, religion, giving us *answers* of the revelation of truth and a *guide to living* in order that we might profit from that truth, must also give us that confirming witness which testifies this is true and which motivates and encourages us to live this way.

Elder Widtsoe concluded with this, his own conviction that "religion at its highest and best is the devotion of one's whole soul through search and service and reverence to the highest cause in the universe, that of cooperating with God in bringing to pass the immortality and eternal life of man."

When we seek to explain to ourselves, to our children, to others what motivates a worldwide missionary effort, what motivates you to do what has been done in your coming here today, and what impelled some of us to come from half a world away so as to be with you, we may well accept that simple outline, so very thoughtful and to me so very valid.

Significant Questions and Answers

What answers are there? Obviously, in these few moments we can only hint, and can maybe do that better by example than by preaching. I confess I would love to do the preaching, because in these books and in the declared word of His living oracles are the answers God has revealed, which give men the truth they need to find the way; answers to the very basic questions about our Heavenly Father and our relationship with Him and Christ the Mediator and Advocate, of whom we have just heard movingly in song and prayer; answers to our own origins and purposes and possibilities; answers as to life's meaning. Are these answers significant? I just looked again in the book of Hosea and read the words written long ago by that prophet under the inspiration of God, as he said, speaking for God, "My people are destroyed for lack of knowledge" (Hosea 4:6). He made very clear what kind of knowledge they lacked, and whose lack brought them destruction. He said, "There is no truth, nor mercy, nor knowledge of God in the land" (Hosea 4:1).

When the Lord Jesus Christ himself taught us in marvelous prayer to the Father what is the most important of all knowledge, of all truths, He said, "This is life eternal, that they might know thee the only true God, and Jesus Christ, whom thou hast sent" (John 17:3). This truth, then, is central and paramount. Christ spent much of His wondrous ministry teaching us to know our Father and giving us a realization that as we knew Him, the Christ, so would we know the Father. Can you think, without my saying more than just a hint of it all, what He taught people about His Father—that He had seen His Father and heard from His Father and had come here to express the intents of His Father, to do the will of His Father? You remember, surely, the lessons of the bread and the stone. Will a loving father give you a stone when you ask for bread, and so forth (see Matthew 7:7–11). Remember the lesson of the prodigal, who, when he had done everything wrong, finally humbled himself enough, came to his senses, and started home, believing, wanting to be a doorkeeper, a servant in his father's house, rather than be the way he was.

Do you remember that beautiful expression the Lord Jesus Christ used in introducing us to His Father? The father in this story is the father of the prodigal, but Christ is teaching us about our Father. Seeing his son afar off, heading home, the father ran to meet him, took him in his arms and wept, and kissed him, took him home and had him cleaned up and clothed, and had a great party held for him. When there was some objection by the brother who had stayed on the job, and who did not really comprehend, the father said, "This my son was dead, and is alive again; he was lost, and is found" (Luke 15:24). This is the Father who, through the prophet Jeremiah, taught us that we should not glory in wisdom or wealth or power, but that if we are to glory about anything it should be this: "That he understandeth and knoweth me, that I am the Lord which exercise lovingkindness, judgment, and righteousness, in the earth: for in these things I delight, saith the Lord" (Jeremiah 9:24). The God whom Isaiah said waits to be gracious is lovingly waiting to be gracious and merciful, if we will come to our senses and head home (see Isaiah 30:18).

The scriptures are full, and I love to preach the truth. The truth is that God lives and is our Father; that Christ, His holy Son, lives and is our Savior; that life is eternal, purposeful, and fruitful; that we, children of God, came from Him, are here for a reason, and may, if we choose—because we're going to live everlastingly, whether we choose or not—live with God our Father and our loved ones forever, in a progressive, growing, creative, working, learning, living, loving world. Well, these truths are real. They are the most important answers men can find to the most important questions that can be asked.

I was in the southernmost province of Korea a few years ago when a young district president, new in the Church, rose and began his beautiful testimony with these words: "One year ago I was very far from the knowledge of God and Christ." He meant that he had known nothing of them, had no feeling for them, had had no real influence in his life from them, and then had come, through the instructions of young, humble servants of God, to a knowledge of that truth which had changed everything. Now he was not only a member but an elder and a district president in an area where he had been pressed into service quickly. He said, "One year ago I was very far from the knowledge of God and Christ," and he bore his beautiful testimony.

Baptism by Immersion

I thought of a day when a man who had spent more than half a century in the ministry came to Salt Lake, after having met two of our missionaries in California, to find out if all the members of the Church had what he had felt in these two humble young men. (He had come to the headquarters of the Church thinking he could get the question answered best there.) They had not been able to reach him with scripture or reason. He had the degrees, the experience, half a century in the pulpit. But they had reached him through a spirit he could not fail to feel and could not explain.

We had a long talk which I cannot share with you, but the heart of which came when I said to him: "Doctor, there is just one question I need to ask you. Have you been baptized by an authorized administrator for the remission of your sins?" He got a hurt look in his eye. He said, "Elder Hanks, after this wonderful experience of brotherhood and the feeling we've had together, are you telling me that you think I have to go down in a pond of water like a little child to make some kind of a covenant with God?"

I opened this book and began to read from Matthew chapter three, words with which you are very familiar: "And Jesus answering said unto him, Suffer it to be so now: for thus it becometh us to fulfill all righteousness. Then he suffered him." (Matthew 3:15.) That is, Jesus was baptized by John.

Now this courteous, gracious, wonderful man almost struck the book from my hand. He said: "I know very well what that says, but nowhere is it explained what it means. Christ was sinless. What does it mean to fulfill all righteousness? Nowhere is it written." And I said, "In this, my beloved friend, you are wrong, because it is, in fact, written." Then I opened, as you missionaries would do, to this wonderful Book of Mormon passage, the thirty-first chapter of the second book of Nephi, and read almost verbatim for him the conversation he and I had just had. "Now, if the Lamb of God, he being holy, should have need to be baptized by water, to fulfil all righteousness, O then, how much more need have we, being unholy, to be baptized, yea, even by water!" And then notice:

> And now, I would ask of you, my beloved brethren, wherein the Lamb of God did fulfil all righteousness in being baptized by water?
>
> Know ye not that he was holy? But notwithstanding he being holy, he showeth unto the children of men that, according to the flesh he humbleth himself before the Father, and witnesseth unto the Father that he would be obedient unto him in keeping his commandments. . . .
>
> And again, it showeth unto the children of men the straitness of the path, and the narrowness of the gate, by which they should enter, he having set the example before them.
>
> And he said unto the children of men: Follow thou me. Wherefore, my beloved brethren, can we follow Jesus save we shall be willing to keep the commandments of the Father?
>
> And the Father said: Repent ye, repent ye, and be baptized in the name of my Beloved Son. (2 Nephi 31:5-7, 9-11.)

I watched a great, white, wonderful head bow, and a tear hit the carpet. And then I heard the voice, through the tears, say,

"Elder Hanks, it appears there are some things we should talk about. Do you have some time?" We sat in an office on Temple Square in Salt Lake City, and I taught him some answers he himself had been seeking for more than fifty years in the pulpit. And after a period of readjustment of his thoughts through the Spirit, he found those two young missionaries in California and went down like a child into the water and was baptized by immersion for the remission of his sins. Then he had hands laid upon his head to receive the gift of the Holy Ghost, received the priesthood, and, at the age of eighty-one, became a noble, reliable, courageous teacher of the gospel.

Live Christ's Teachings

The answers are marvelous, and I testify that they are true. I testify that these answers are true. What else, then, according to Elder Widtsoe's beautiful outline? If we teach the answers—and we must, of course, find them through our own search and our own service and our own prayer—then we must also be living the life to which the answers lead us. Can we think today, without the message in any detail, of what the Church says to me as an individual about my life, to me as a husband, to me as a father, to me as a neighbor, a citizen, a human being, what it says about my mind, my body, my eternal soul, which is a combination of my body and my spirit? When I think that guidance comes to me, and has come all the days of my life, through His appointed servants, through His scriptures, through the witness of His Spirit, I rejoice and thank God.

When Christ, teaching the truth about His Father, reached out with His example and His love, He taught us that there is a way to live which is abundant, rewarding, fulfilling, full. There are so many marvelous ways to exemplify it. When He and His prophets taught us the truth there was the intention that we be wise enough, honest enough, to give those truths application in the way we live every day.

In that context I will never forget the nineteen-year-old American boy who stood to bear his testimony in the northernmost part of South Vietnam. We had two hundred fifty Latterday Saint men there, all that way from home and all in the thick of the action. It was a place called China Beach near Da Nang, and the air was filled with the sounds of warfare: airplanes, mortars, and artillery, and even small arms fire. One by one these strong men came to the pulpit, shed their tears, thanked God for their families at home, for their country and this chance to represent her, and particularly for the gospel and the love it brought into their lives. Even under these terrible conditions there was not any whining or complaining.

The nineteen-year-old took a few minutes; I take only a moment to tell you what he said. He had gone out on a search-and-destroy mission with a deep feeling in his heart that he was never going to come back. He had been through the worst of the war, he thought, had not suffered any wounds, but now had come to feel that he was never going to get back. He even wrote a letter of farewell to his parents. This feeling just filled him. They were out one day, two days, three days, four days; there were some skirmishes, and some mines erupted, but nothing happened to him. They came back to base camp; he was uninjured, not touched. He could not understand it. He was sure that feeling was the correct feeling. He was sure he had had a premonition. He sat on a log, filthy and hungry, bewildered by what was going on in his head and heart, while other men rushed in to the showers.

As he sat there, the sergeant in charge of his outfit came near. He said: "Smith, get on your feet; get in that shower; get yourself cleaned up; we're going into town, and *this* time, you're going with us. We're going to show you what a big man does when he gets away from his mommy, and you're not with your mommy anymore, Smith. We're going to show you how a big man behaves when he can make up his own mind."

The young man who stood behind that pulpit, pale, tears coursing down his cheeks, said: "I knew then what the premonition was all about. It wasn't a bullet or a mine; it was something worse. I looked him eye to eye, even though I was scared to death to the point where I could hardly keep my knees straight, and I said to him: 'Sergeant, oh no, I'm not. I'm not going this time, either. You're right, Sergeant. A big man can make up his own mind, and I've made up mine. I'm not going with you.' " He said, "We looked eyeball to eyeball for seconds, and then he turned around with curses in his throat about my manhood and my courage and went his way. I sank on that log, and when they were all gone I found a place and got on my knees and thanked God. I knew the war wasn't over, but I won that battle, and if God will bless me, I'll win the rest."

True Answers

I would like to bear testimony that a big man or a lovely lady can make up his or her own mind and that making up our minds now, *ahead of the crisis*, is the wise thing to do. There are a hundred other things to say, but I close with an example of that other element in real religion that Elder Widtsoe said was so important. "The answers that come are true. They are here. One who has the will to search and the humility to bend a knee will find out. This way to live is the good and wholesome and happy way. There is no better way."

What then of this convincing, converting witness, this testimony that gives sense to all the answers and gives us the courage to live the right way? I was with President Kimball and others less than three weeks ago in Cleveland, Ohio, at a great meeting. We had a lot of wonderful Latter-day Saints bearing testimony to great crowds of choice people who had come as friends to hear what they had to say.

Among those whom I had the privilege of interviewing in front of a microphone before eighteen or nineteen thousand people was Miss Teen Canada of two years ago. She joined the Church. At eighteen, she is headed for Brigham Young University. She had been interviewed by others—newspeople who pressed her on the kind of home she came from—and she gave them wonderful answers. Her mother, not a member of the Church, a beautiful person, sat there and listened to her lovely daughter extol the home in which she had grown, extol her mother and father and family.

Finally, one of the newspeople asked her what I later asked her in front of that huge group. "If you had such a lovely home, if you already lived a life of honor and cleanliness and integrity, why did you join the Mormon church? What did they have to give you that you didn't already have?"

She smiled, this beautiful girl who gave such mature, impressive answers. She said: "I was very privileged to grow up in that kind of home, and I do have that kind of parents. I didn't really have to change the way I was living at all. But it seems to me that it's been years that I've been looking for others who live that way, for a young man I could be seriously interested in who lives that way, for the kind of person I could have as my close friend who lives that way. In the Church I found them. Then, I found out that this is the way God wants people to live, and the Spirit of God authenticated in my heart that this is His Church and His way." And then she looked at her mother and said, "My brother joined the Church, and we have something going for us, don't we, Mom?"

I would like to bear testimony to you out of the very serious, deep convictions of my own heart that the answers are here to be learned, and there is no arrogance in that because the knowledge we have of those answers imposes upon us the greater responsibility. "Every member a missionary," yes; but first, every member a true Christian, every member learning the answers and living the life and bearing in his and her heart that confirming witness we call among us a testimony of the gospel. I know God lives. I know Jesus is the Christ. I know this is His church and that there will be in us, to the measure that we learn and live His law, that sense of deep conviction that will cause us to know the truth and live the truth. I pray for that for me and mine and for all of you in the name of Jesus Christ. Amen.

Index